Rookie Real Estate Agent

Rookie Real Estate Agent

LAUNCH A
LIMITLESS CAREER
THAT LASTS

JAY PAPASAN

Keller
🏠INK

Published by KellerINK, an imprint of Bard Press, Austin, Texas.

ISBN: 978-1959472162

Cover design and interior layout by Cindy Curtis-Rivera
Taco illustration by Rose Smith

For Allison Tsakiris, who left us too soon
but will never be forgotten.

Contents

The Tao of Taco

What do tacos have to do with launching your real estate career? While tacos are a delicious, happiness-inducing form of nourishment, we're not talking about our favorite Mexican dish. Taco is our family dog. Surprisingly, he has a few things to teach us. So let's taco 'bout success in real estate.

My wife Wendy and I adopted Taco from a neighbor's litter ten years ago and promptly fell in love. Taco is a Brittany and lives a very certain way. He is predictably energetic and friendly with guests. Outdoors, he is always alert, scanning and searching for squirrels or birds that might stray into his path or our yard. His mannerisms come from both training and bloodlines. Brittanys were bred for bird hunting in the French countryside. They are known for their work ethic and versatility. They have white and orange patterned coats, wiggly bob tails, and high-set ears that the American Kennel Club says "convey the breed's essential eagerness."

A *tao* is a way of life, a code, or a doctrine. Whenever the Mandalorian says, "This is the way," you can imagine he is referencing their code of conduct or tao for living. If we were to craft the "Tao of Taco," it would go something like this.

1 Always Greet Strangers

Some dogs bark when the doorbell chimes, ready to defend the den and fend off interloping postal workers. Not Taco. His ears shoot up. His tail becomes a metronome at ten-times speed. He crowds the doorway, eager to meet whoever is there. Every stranger is an opportunity to make a new friend and score a belly rub.

2 Presentation Matters

I've known junkyard dogs that simply don't care about their cleanliness. Taco has an almost feline obsession with grooming. Afternoons will find him lounging on the sofa, licking his paws clean. After a day in the woods, he'll comb out burrs with his teeth. I don't think this a common trait in Brittanys. Taco spent his early years trying to befriend our late cat, Midnight. Maybe she taught him a thing or two.

3 Be Vigilant for Opportunity

Once we're out and about, every bush, every tree, and many things we just can't see must be thoroughly investigated. He taps into an olfactory database of dogs, stray cats, neighbors, and wild critters. I'm sure he logs every new entry, "Wowzers, an armadillo moved into the 'hood!" And, of course, he marks his territory as well.

4 Focus for Success

Once Taco detects prey, the whole world falls away. Bred for pointing, he freezes in place, snout aimed at his quarry, with his right paw raised. He is locked on his prize. This will not end until the bird flies away or he is called off. Focus like this is rare. It is truly a superpower.

5 Follow Your Passion

Taco is always happiest in the field. While he's only been proper hunting a few times, he always *thinks* he's hunting. And there is nothing he loves more. We have a property outside of town. As we walk through the fields, Taco runs zig-zag patterns in front of us. He porpoises through the tall grasses. You just see his head and shoulders breach while he scans ahead. His joy is self-evident in every bound. We have to limit how long he runs free to save him from exhaustion. Taco was made for this very thing, and he loves doing it more than anything.

6 Find Your Pack

Dogs' affinity for their packs is one of the main reasons they were domesticated to begin with. Whatever room we are in, you will find Taco. Most often, his chin will rest on my lap or a paw across my foot. If he needs space, he curls up where he can see us. He snuggles on our bed at night until we close our books and turn off the light. He then descends to sleep on a cushion by the bed. We hear his doggie dreams at night.

I've had the good fortune to work with, interview, and write about the most successful real estate sales professionals in the world since Gary Keller, Dave Jenks, and I wrote *The Millionaire Real Estate Agent* twenty-two years ago. Every year, Gary and I work with a research team and we interview hundreds of the best of the best to keep our models current. This book was actually born when we started asking millionaire agents, "What did you do in your first year that other agents don't?"

Here's the surprising truth. Change a few words and "Tao of Taco" could easily be the "Tao of the Millionaire Real Estate Agent."

1 Always Greet Strangers

Top agents are world-class connectors. They don't simply meet strangers, they connect. They stay in touch and build relationships.

2 Presentation Matters

This is a relative idea depending on where you live and who you serve. My hometown of Austin tends to be laid-back and you're as likely to see jeans and flip-flops at an open house as designer labels and Italian leather shoes. Rural areas might trend casual and urban areas more formal. Whatever the case, top agents show up as professionals in every way.

3 Be Vigilant for Opportunity

Top agents are always lead generating. They launch their days prospecting and marketing for clients. When they are out and about, their ears are tuned to detect real estate conversations. Like Taco, they have a nose for opportunity.

4 Focus for Success

Once they have a prospect, they know what it takes to win the client. Occasionally, everything comes together quickly. An acquaintance needs help, and they know you are the solution to their problem. Many other times, patience and follow-up are required. One top agent knocked on the same door for eleven years until the owner was finally ready to sell.

5   Follow Your Passion

Real estate can be challenging. It's absolutely competitive. The agents who rise to the top tend to love what they do. Maybe they didn't enjoy the work in the beginning, but over time, as their skills and impact grow, they uncover a passion for their work.

6   Find Your Pack

You won't do this alone. No one does. Even solo agents surround themselves with professionals. Vendors, coaches, mentors, colleagues, friends, and family all provide support along the way. Top agents invariably will point out the key relationships that propelled them to the top.

Contracts, regulatory statutes, zoning laws, and mortgage lending requirements. If you search for "complicated" in real estate, you won't have to look far. However, the principles that drive success in this industry are actually quite simple.

The Tao of Taco works for Taco, and I promise it can work for you.

Make an Impact!

Jay P.

Instead of wondering whether you can succeed in real estate, ask, **"Why not me?"**

CHAPTER 1

Why Real Estate?

I didn't really choose real estate. I started working at a real estate company as a newsletter writer. I was looking for work as a writer and found it. Then, like Pam and Jim in *The Office*, my real estate friendship drifted into romance. I got bit by the real estate bug.

I coauthored my first book, *The Millionaire Real Estate Agent*, with Gary Keller and Dave Jenks. A career guide, we published it in 2003 and it has gone on to sell over 1.6 million copies. Many just call it the "Red Book." Over the next couple of years, I helped interview more than 120 millionaire real estate investors for our follow-up title, *The Millionaire Real Estate Investor*. That's when love struck. My wife, Wendy, and I started investing. We flipped a home with Dave. We turned our first home into a rental and moved up when we had our first child.

By 2009, both kids were in school, and Wendy was ready for the next chapter. We talked about her options. While she'd had a successful career in marketing and PR, we'd learned a lot about entrepreneurship and investing in the past few years. We decided to form what would become the Papasan Properties Group. There was a lot to juggle. We had two young kids with drop-offs, pick-ups, and field trips. I took an executive role running education for Keller Williams Realty while also writing and promoting our real estate books. After the kids were in bed, Wendy would often work late to prepare for her days running the business. She practiced her conversations, did her lead generation, and followed up on every lead. In her first full year, she sold eighteen houses. As soon as she could afford it, she brought on an assistant. Not long after, we added more admin staff, showing agents, and buyers' agents. Over the first ten years, the Papasan Properties Group sold over 1,200 homes. Today, they have sold over 2,300 and counting. Woah, I co-wrote *The Millionaire Real Estate Agent* with no real estate experience and now I was married to one.

Real estate has completely transformed our lives. When Wendy and I met, I was an editor at a New York publisher, and she was a marketing professional. We were (and are) nerdy bookish types. Neither of us studied business. We have English and journalism degrees. Owning real estate and businesses wasn't something we even dreamed about. Today, we own a portfolio of investment properties and a thriving real estate sales business. And those pursuits have led to other opportunities to own, invest, and run other businesses.

All of this opportunity started with choosing real estate! We are no different than you. The good news for you is you don't have to accidentally fall into a career in real estate. You can choose it today.

Five Reasons Why Real Estate Is a Great Career Opportunity

You've picked up this book, so you must be aware of some of the many opportunities a career in real estate presents. Maybe you're already working on your license and eager to start. Perhaps you're still trying to figure out the transition from your current work to this new career. Or, possibly, you're still on the fence about taking the plunge into the deep end of full-time real estate. Whatever the case may be, this path can unlock unimaginable opportunities.

To write this book, our team and I interviewed hundreds of successful agents who started their real estate careers from every conceivable walk of life. We talked to former teachers, law enforcement officers, bankers, investors, bartenders, retail salespeople, marketers, designers, soldiers, waiters, accountants . . . you name it. Even quite a few who have never done anything but real estate. What they all have in common is that they made the leap, put in the work, and quickly or eventually came to love what they do. We bet that you'll fall in love, too.

While there are many reasons, here are five things about a career in real estate we love.

1. Freedom and Flexibility

The idea of working for yourself and setting your own hours draws a lot of people to real estate. You have the freedom to choose when you work, what you work on, and how long you'll work. When life happens, good or bad, you can be flexible.

Agent Aubrey Martin moved to Hillsboro, Oregon, in 2017 and began her career in real estate. From the start, she built her business to maximize her time. "I don't want to choose business over my children, ever," Aubrey says. She and her husband had sadly lost their first child fifteen years prior, and she really wanted to be able to able to be the best parent she could be for her two later sons and daughter.

Each year, she determines how many clients she needs to serve and then only works until she hits that goal. If she says that she's helping forty families and then taking her kids to the beach, then that's what happens. The number of transactions may change each year but what doesn't change is her commitment to sticking to it. That's the freedom that real estate can give you.

What many people fail to realize is that freedom and flexibility can cut both ways. The work is the work. If you lean into your newfound freedom and flexibility, you'll need to be more focused in the time you commit.

2. You Get to Help People with Their Greatest Asset Purchase

As an agent, you are not just selling people houses. You are helping them purchase or sell what is often their most valuable asset. It impacts their lifestyle, shelter, security, and retirement. You will guide people toward the biggest purchase of their lives, a place to settle into, and a place to call home. An agent is the person who makes this all possible. You get to make people's dreams come true.

Jason Abrams, an agent from West Bloomfield, Michigan, says, "When I got licensed my hope was that selling real estate would take me across town. Twenty-five years later it has taken me all over the world. I discovered early on that people don't curl up at night with their stock and bond portfolios, but they do curl up in the warmth of their homes. The kitchens where we celebrate are the same as where we cry. The bedrooms where we sleep are the same as where we lay awake. The reasons people move are equally joyful as they can be sorrowful. Homes become the backdrop for the theater of our lives and for brief moments I get to be part of the play. That's the gift. Receiving it has been more rewarding than I ever could have imagined."

This impact gets bigger the more you do what you do.

Tiffany Fykes, an agent from Nashville, Tennessee, explains, "Real estate is a business that allows you to build up the communities in which you live. Our team has transformed the culture of our neighborhood through hosting events and being an integral part of that neighborhood. It's hard to find a more symbiotic relationship between a community and a business. Being involved in the community is part of the job and that kind of impact is so rewarding."

3. Low Cost of Entry

If you're looking for one of the least expensive self-employment opportunities on the planet, you've found it. Will Van Wickler, from Falmouth, Maine, decided that real estate was his future before he even graduated high school. He says, "I was in a humanities class and the guidance counselors came around talking about getting ready for SATs and college. I remember sitting there and thinking to myself, 'There's no way I'm going to go to four years of college and spend $50,000 a year and for what?' I wanted to build a business."

Will started an IT consulting company and asked one of his clients how to get started investing in real estate. The client told him to the best way was to get his license and learn. So, at nineteen years old, Will got training, took his test, and $500 later had his license and became an agent. During the first year that followed, he worked part-time and made over six figures. By the time he was twenty-three years old, he was grossing over $1 million in his real estate business.

Now, the cost to become an agent varies by state, but it is typically around $1,500 for classes, exam fees, and license fees. Compare this to CPAs, who are usually required to hold a bachelor's degree as well as take the CPA exam, which can cost up to $5,000; attorneys, who enter their field having easily paid more than $100,000 on education, exams, and licensing; or even franchise owners of the world's largest coffee chain, who can spend more than $300,000 to start. Beyond the $1,500, you'll need a car, phone, and a laptop. Most agents recoup their investment with their first closing.

Because you'll be self-employed—a business owner as well as the business's sole employee—you want to have some savings to get you through the first few months while you build your business.

4. No Financial Ceiling

No matter if you're salaried or hourly, working a J-O-B job will limit you to a fixed income. Except for bonuses and overtime, what you'll earn each paycheck will be determined in advance. Raises will always be outside of your control—a full-time job working for someone else always has financial limitations.

In real estate, there is no financial ceiling. You are rewarded by how well you do the work. If you do the right things at the right time often enough, you will be rewarded financially. The better you perform, the better your pay. Phoenix, Arizona, agent Brett Tanner says the opportunities for high-performing agents can be limitless. "Real estate agents sit in the best possible seat imaginable to live big lives and create massive wealth," he says. "The skills top real estate agents learn allow them to take advantage of all the opportunities that come their way." In other words, no one can limit your earning potential except you.

5. Inside Opportunity to Invest

As an agent, you have the inside track to the best real estate finds. You know everything about a property before anyone else does. You understand how value is created in an asset class that has created wealth for countless millionaires. Many of the best investment opportunities first passed through an agent's hands. This puts you in a perfect spot to invest.

There is a difference between being in the real estate investing business and being in the listing and selling business. Savvy agents understand that every property listing is also an opportunity to invest.

Jenni MacLean, an agent from Bozeman, Montana, got her license with investing in mind. She'd had a condo and duplex in her portfolio, and even though she loved her agent and thought of her as a mentor, she wanted to get the inside scoop. Now that she's licensed, Jenni gets to see what's hitting the market first. Plus, she has a professional community to help her spot good opportunities.

Why Not You?

Many agents come to the profession with stars in their eyes. They think that they're going to sell a few houses here and there and earn giant commission checks right off the bat. Some see it as an opportunity for supplemental income, a part-time gig, a side hustle. And while it's true that no other career offers the flexibility and earning potential of real estate, newcomers often get caught up in the myth of the reality TV real estate mogul. They miss the fundamental truth in this business that happens when the cameras aren't rolling. You get out of it what you put into it.

And what you put into it is up to you and you alone. Instead of wondering whether you can succeed in real estate, ask, "Why not me?"

CHAPTER 2

Own Your Mindset, Own Your Future

In an experiment on learning, psychologist Carol Dweck gave a group of four-year-olds jigsaw puzzles to solve. She started with an easy one. When they finished the easy puzzle, she gave them a choice: redo the easy one or try one that was a little bit harder. The kids paused at this question, not because they didn't know which puzzle to choose, but because they were confused as to why someone would want to keep solving the same easy puzzle. Even when they started to furrow their small brows and mutter "hmms" as they stewed over the pieces to the harder puzzles, they wanted to move forward no matter how difficult the challenges became.

If Dweck did the experiment with adults, the choices would have probably looked different. According to Dweck, there are two distinct categories of mindsets: fixed and growth. People who have a fixed mindset believe that abilities are set in stone, that levels of intelligence, personality, and character are innate and therefore "fixed."

On the other hand, people with a growth mindset believe that the cards life deals them do not define the entire scope of their capabilities. Instead, they provide a starting point. Meaning our basic qualities—talents, aptitudes, temperaments—are not innate and can grow and change from experience.

Throughout our lives, we become socialized to believe that failure is one thing: bad. But failure leads to growth. Infants learning to walk fall constantly but get back up. They don't decide to never try again. Instead, they are determined to get where they want to go—as wobbly as the journey may be.

While success is simple, it's rarely easy. For those of us embarking on a real estate career, we will likely experience a lot of failure and rejection on our way to success. The mindset you have will help you overcome these setbacks and keep moving toward your dreams.

Set Your Mind Right (and the Right Action Will Follow)

The way that we think frames the way that we interact with the world. How we "set" our mind determines how we will experience what happens in our lives. Our **mindset** is our way of thinking or feeling that shapes how we make sense of the world and ourselves. Our mindset is reflected in our behavior.

Mindset Before Behavior

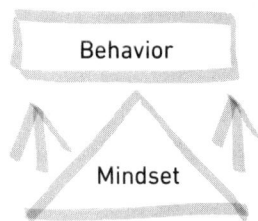

Figure 1

Because *how* we think determines what we do, it's important to understand *why* we think what we do. To ensure that our actions get us to where we want to go, we need to examine our beliefs.

The truth of the matter is not everything we believe is true. Things that we've witnessed, gone through, or been told shape the way we see things, and therefore shape our mindset and behavior. These falsehoods that we've been taught are truths are what we call **MythUnderstandings**. And, getting to the bottom of them is the first step in examining our mindset and actions.

The Six MythUnderstandings Between You and Success

Every real estate agent starts with many MythUnderstandings running through their heads. The key to achieving success is to first acknowledge these thoughts for what they are: lies and limitations. When we do this, we can build motivation and habits around what is actually true. To help you get to success more quickly, we're going to dispel some of the most common myths that real estate agents face when getting started.

Changing our outlook takes conscious effort over the course of our entire lives, and sometimes we even revert to old ways after experiencing significant evolution. By continuously striving to embrace a mindset that allows us to learn and challenge ourselves, we can improve along the way.

The Six MythUnderstandings Between You and Success

Myth #1: Before I take action, I feel like I have to know everything.

Truth: You'll never know everything so delaying is pointless.

Myth #2: I'm not a salesperson—I don't know what to say or do.

Truth: Sales is a skill—you can learn what to say and do.

Myth #3: I don't have a local network.

Truth: No one does until they build one.

Myth #4: If I ask people for business, I will annoy them.

Truth: If you help people solve problems, they will be grateful.

Myth #5: I won't get hired because everyone already has an agent.

Truth: You won't know until you ask.

Myth #6: I'll figure the business stuff out later.

Truth: If you figure it out sooner, you'll thank yourself later.

We've all fallen prey to a MythUnderstanding. But focusing on the next step allows us to go farther down the path toward our goals.

Myth #1: Before I take action, I feel like I have to know everything.
Truth: You will never know everything, so delaying is pointless.

When we asked hundreds of successful agents what they think is the most common mistake agents make, almost all of them gave the same answer: new or nervous agents think they have to be an expert at everything to do anything. These successful agents refuted this "belief" universally. Here's the truth: You will never know everything, so delaying your start is pointless.

New York agent Jenn Baniak-Hollands says she saw this firsthand when taking a training course at the beginning of her career. "The people who failed were the people who were scared of getting it wrong," she says. "Those folks had trouble growing their business. It's impossible to know everything before you do something." The people who fail are not those who get it wrong, but the ones who never start.

Too much time prepping means not enough time doing. Springfield, Missouri, agent Jen Davis puts it best when she says, "In anxious times, productive activity lowers anxiety." Being productive will help you reach your goals faster than worrying about what to do first. Agonizing over the font on our business cards before we know anyone to give them to is not a recipe for success.

To become an expert at anything you have to start from nothing. This doesn't mean going into the field with zero knowledge of the industry. But if you've gotten your license, joined a brokerage, and have a method of transportation, you're probably ready to start lead generating. California agent Deb Jolly says too many agents spend hours and hours developing their website, editing photos for social media, and taking classes instead of diving into what is actually going to propel their business. "One of the biggest mistakes is when a new agent comes in and thinks they've got to learn everything before they talk to people," she says.

With a slew of classes and trainings available, it's easy to get bogged down in trying to perfect every aspect of our business before we go out into the world. But this is not what breeds success. What will get you to your goals is practicing conversations so you can connect with your sphere and door knock in your neighborhood. Learn as you go and learn from your mistakes. Getting ahead of the game soon is what will propel you to reach your big goals.

Myth #2: I'm not a salesperson—I don't know what to say or do.
Truth: Sales is a skill—you can learn what to say and do.

Being successful at sales means understanding what the needs of others are and being able to meet those needs. Not everyone was born with the gift of gab or the art of persuasion. In fact, the best entrepreneurs differentiate themselves by finding a compelling way to meet the needs of their potential clients better than their competitors. As Mike Weinberg writes in *New Sales. Simplified:* "In sales, our incredibly important, incredibly straightforward job is to connect with [...] customers and prospective customers to determine if our solutions will meet their needs. The more and better we do that simple job, the more successful we will be." And most great salespeople get this way through practice.

Researcher and author Susan Cain points out that modern Western culture tends to favor extroverts when it comes to perceived talent and capabilities. This is common for people in sales and service industries. Sometimes introverts are viewed as plain inferior. But we know that isn't true. About half the world identifies as introverted. Bill Gates, Lady Gaga, Oprah, and Albert Einstein have counted themselves among their ranks. Heard of them?

The truth is you don't have to be an extrovert to be good at sales. You don't even have to be experienced. When you open your mind to learning new tools and practice using them, nothing can get in your way of becoming successful.

What is truly fundamental in building a business where people choose to work with you is having the ability to listen and help solve problems. However you identify on the personality scale—extrovert, introvert, or ambivert (that's somewhere in the middle)—you have to be someone that people can come to know, like, and trust. Building skills around these fundamentals will look different for everyone, but they are available to anyone who is determined to master them.

Myth #3: I don't have a local network.
Truth: No one does until they build one.

People start out fresh all the time. They move to new cities, enroll in new schools, relocate to a different floor in their office's building. Not knowing people isn't the end, it's actually the beginning. There are always ways to network and build your database, no matter how foreign a situation you find yourself in.

Take what you know and go from there. If you have kids, the PTA at their school is a great place to start. If you're an avid Chicago Cubs fan, so are about 3 million other people—join a group that appreciates the team's stats like you do. There is always a launch pad for networking.

Agents David and Toni Zarghami ran a successful real estate business in North Carolina. Eventually they had children and moved to Sarasota, Florida, to be closer to family. They uprooted their lives and their business. They started from scratch. As David remembers, they knew two people in Florida—Toni's parents. They had no sphere to work from whatsoever.

"It was really painful that first year," David says. "Toni was a top five agent in North Carolina; she was on billboards and had this amazing relationship with a builder. We had to roll the dice and just bet on ourselves that we could do it again. We put our noses down and went to building our business."

They did what they had to do. They went knocking on doors and generated leads online. They networked wherever possible and got their names out into the community. They enrolled in courses and hired a coach. They didn't get a listing for six months after they moved. Nine years later, they have sold 225 units and grossed almost $4 million in commissions in one year. Remember, even millionaire teams start from nothing.

Myth #4: If I ask people for business, I will annoy them.
Truth: If you help people solve problems, they will be grateful.

Most people tend to wait until the end of a conversation to tell someone they're looking for business. Their MythUnderstandings keep them from being upfront in their communication. They're afraid people will think of them as rude or off-putting if they come out of the gate asking for a lead. But imagine the scenario from the other perspective: a friend you haven't spoken to in a while reaches out to you. They ask how your family is and if you ever got that raise. You talk for twenty minutes or so, catching up on passed time. And then, at the end, they ask you if you're thinking of selling your house. Wouldn't you feel caught off guard? Like all that chatting was just a means to a sales end?

Here's an uncomfortable truth: it's not rude to be straightforward about the purpose you're reaching out for. Turns out most people appreciate honesty. While it may be harder for us initially to get straight to the point, chances are the people who know us will want to help us if they can. Business conversations don't have to avoid personal touches, but the order in which we present our reasons for getting in touch matters.

Being genuine and leading with the reason why you are reaching out sets the tone for an honest conversation. This is true for both people you know and people you don't know that well or at all. The reality is you are providing a service as a real estate agent.

Mimi Bond, an agent in Austin, Texas, struggled with this MythUnderstanding at the start of her career. She was unsure about how people would react to her asking for business. "It was a mental challenge that I had to overcome," she says. "I had to think, 'Well, this is my main source of business, and if I really want to succeed in the following years I need to double down on my database and hone in on it.'"

Arlington, Virginia, agent Pam O'Bryant agrees that the road to success starts with yourself. She says, "First you teach yourself that you're a huge asset to your network, then you teach your network."

Helping people find a home is not annoying. Guiding people through the paperwork of homeownership is not irritating. Assisting someone with the biggest purchase of their lives is the opposite of those things. You're an asset. A huge one. Fulfilling dreams is part of being an agent, and we can't fulfill those dreams if we don't know who needs our help. Every transaction should be a win-win.

Myth #5: I won't get hired because everyone already has an agent.
Truth: You won't know until you ask.

Agents who have closed hundreds of transactions hadn't closed any at one point. It may feel like everyone already has a real estate agent—but you won't know if they do until you ask. And, even if they have a real estate agent, that agent may not be staying in touch with them. If that's the case, they're not asking, and *you* are. And, at the end of the day, there's a job to be done and you're there to do it.

There are even some advantages to being the new kid on the block (literally). As a new agent, you'll bring a fresh perspective, energy, and an abundance of time to someone in the market to buy or sell.

To make up for a lack of experience, you'll have to set yourself apart in a different way. Do this by starting small. Become an expert for a hyperlocal area—maybe near where you already live. As a new, licensed agent, you will have access to every house on the market. Study neighborhood trends, keep up with new listings on the multiple listing service (MLS), and become an expert. Then, when you're introducing yourself to potential clients, you can share your expert knowledge. Agents who have multiple clients won't have the time or organization to preview all the homes in the area the way you do.

One agent we interviewed leveraged her abundance of time in this way. "I attended 300 open houses between the time I finished classes and received my license—about three weeks. By the time I had access to our MLS, I knew the inventory. Once I saw what information the MLS provided, I was ready to start as a knowledgeable agent, not a new agent."

Myth #6: I'll figure the business stuff out later.
Truth: If you figure it out sooner, you'll thank yourself later.

When you're just starting out, it's easy to focus on learning the ins and outs of real estate. You can forget you are also building a business. You'll be thinking about what you can do each day to help you get closer to finding your next client, or helping your current buyers and sellers get to closing day. As important as these activities are, they are not *all* that you are doing.

The second most common piece of advice we got while talking with successful agents was that they all wished that they had taken themselves seriously as a business, sooner. Not only would having a business-owner mindset have helped them think bigger-picture, it also would have helped them build better habits and systems to support those big goals. In Chapters 3 and 9, we'll introduce you to the fundamentals.

"Stop thinking about real estate. Start thinking about owning a business," says Gene Rivers, an agent from Tallahassee, Florida. "Go to Wendy's, a Chevrolet dealership, or a law firm and you will see them all using systems, tools, and people in generating business, servicing the consumer, making the sale, and following up. If your small business is to succeed, you must get clear on your mission and vision, then build a plan using systems, tools, and people based on the wants and needs of real estate consumers."

Don't sell yourself short or waste future-you's time: you're a real estate business, just as much as you are an agent, from day one.

Finding Your BIG Why

There are a lot of MythUnderstandings and hard times you'll have to overcome in your career. When you have a growth mindset, this will be easier to do. And there's a secret to building this foundation. It's the ultimate fuel for your actions. It's your **Big Why**.

A Big Why is your core motivator for doing what you do. Finding your drive and motivation requires unlocking your Big Why. It will remind you of your personal purpose and the purpose of your business. And it must be a BIG Why if you want to become highly successful. *Why* are you starting a brand-new career that makes you feel a little scared and unsure? *Why* do you spend hours a day knocking on strangers' doors? *Why* are you hosting open houses every weekend? To answer these questions, you'll need to know your Big Why.

Say you want to become a real estate agent that makes more than $100,000 a year. Okay. That's fine. Why? If you don't know, what happens if you don't hit your income goal? If your answer is, "Oh, I would just keep saving or spend a little less and try again next year," then your Why for doing it is not big enough. There's no real reason to keep knocking on doors.

When we were writing *The Millionaire Real Estate Agent*, we interviewed an agent from Los Angeles, California. She has been an elite agent for decades, but that's not how it started. She was working in fashion when her marriage ended. Suddenly, she had to support herself and her daughters by herself. Failure simply wasn't an option. That's a Big Why. When people tell me their Big Why I will often ask, "What will happen if you fail?" The responses don't fall on a bell curve. It's actually just the opposite. Those with aspirational ones might shrug and say they will do something else. The idea of failing at an authentic one is the opposite. I've seen people tear up and become emotional. They have something deep within them driving them forward. Those agents tend to succeed against the unlikeliest of odds.

If you're not sure of your Big Why yet, that's okay. You can start with a small why and do the work to get to a Big one. It's important to remember that when the work gets tough—which it will—and when the day-to-day activities of lead generation and cultivation become tedious and stressful—which they do—your Big Why is what will pull you through. It will give you purpose.

Embrace Being a Fiduciary

A salesperson can become good at making sales by simply practicing skills that are required for the job: prospecting for clients, having constructive conversations, knowing their market, and the like. They can do the work and collect their check. They can repeat these motions again and again and be a good salesperson. This is a limited approach. A great salesperson is great because of one thing: they don't think about sales. They focus on the value they deliver through the service they offer. They focus on helping people make the best possible decision, regardless of the sales outcome.

This is being a true **fiduciary**. A fiduciary educates and guides clients through the process of purchasing a home. They get to know the people they are working for and determine the solutions that suit their clients best. They answer questions, provide support, manage unpredictable situations, break bad news, and make people's dreams come true. If we are caught up in whether someone says yes or no, if our only concern is collecting a check, we're not going to get very far. That's the truth. When you discover what your passion is behind getting someone into a home of their own, you can provide the service needed to be a fiduciary and get on the right path to achieving success. When we go from transactional to thinking about our client's experience, from our perspective to theirs, the real estate industry is magical.

You've Got This!

So, we've established this will be hard, rewarding work. We hope you're feeling excited about the journey ahead. You can absolutely do this.

Maple Grove, Minnesota, agent Mckenzie Anderson says reminding yourself that you can achieve success when the going gets tough is the most important thing you can do.

"It's so important to just dig your heels in. Even when it's hard, even when it's messy, even in the roller coaster of the ups and downs that this industry presents, keep moving and focus on the good," she says. "That's what's going to close transactions, and that's what's going to make people be attracted to you. That is what matters."

Be kind to yourself and remember who you are. You'll face challenges and probably hear the word "no" from a lot of different people. Focus on your Big Why and remember that your dreams are within reach.

CHAPTER 3

Deliver Value and Get Paid in Real Estate

So, you've decided to conquer the real estate world. With some motivation, hard work, and this book to guide you, you're ready to charge onward into life as an agent. After all, you've replaced the MythUnderstandings that might have held you back with the truths. You've fired yourself up with your Big Why and embraced your fiduciary heart. You're ready for the housing market!

But wait. Before we get to the ins and outs of real estate sales, you need to understand how you provide value and make money, along with the costs of doing business. Understanding how money works in real estate will help you set clear goals and reach them. Being able to explain the value you provide will answer the question of why someone would hire you. "We are strategists," Tenafly, New Jersey, agent Stacy Esser says. "We educate instead of sell, and when we educate our prospective clients on why our strategies will work for them, we provide value and build a predictable business." The value you give determines the value you get.

To help us illustrate how income is earned and kept as an agent, we want to show you how to use the Budget and Economic Models by going over three different examples of what finances could look like in practice for a rookie. The three examples—an agent with a cap, an agent without a cap, and an agent on a team—were chosen because it's likely you will find yourself in a situation similar to one of them. They use varying commissions and fees, conversion rates, and costs of sale, but they have one thing in common: a net income goal of $100,000. By using this formula, an agent can easily determine how many appointments, agreements, and closed units they need each year to reach their income goal.

Before we walk you through these examples, let's talk a little about the value you provide to clients. Value is the heart of everything that you do as an agent. It's the foundation of all your skills and services. Understanding the value you provide will help you become invaluable.

Building Your Unique Value Proposition

As a real estate agent, you need to build a **value proposition** (also called a unique value proposition or UVP). It should offer services particular to you, solve specific problems, and communicate what you do better than anyone else. It's the benefit a customer gets from choosing to work with you instead of the other 4,000 agents in your market.

Your value proposition is also innately connected to the cost of your services. You want to make sure that you are providing your clients with value, so that they think of working with you as an investment rather than an expense. Having a clear value proposition helps you articulate what people get for their investment.

The challenge is that value is subjective. The old saw about one person's trash being another person's treasure isn't far off.

It's hard to believe, but at one point in time, ordering a lobster at a restaurant would turn heads. Not because of an ambiguous "market price," but because it was considered a "poverty food" that desperate people ate in desperate times. Everyone thought it was better to toss it in the trash than put it in your mouth. It wasn't until train travel took off that people began valuing lobster.

With trains becoming more and more popular, the need to feed passengers grew, and with it, so did the need for canned foods. At some point, someone realized that lobster was cheap and that it could be preserved. They also realized that if you didn't know what it was, you might think it tasted alright. It was a perfect fit for trains filled with hungry people who had never visited the Northeast. As a result, canning companies began selling lobster to hungry well-to-do passengers. And with its newfound popularity, the lobster started its journey from garbage cans to five-star restaurants.

Throughout that journey the way a lobster tastes never changed. What changed was that lobster was finally presented to diners in a way they would value. And value it they did. Pass the melted butter, please!

Agent and lawyer Laurel Starks of Rancho Cucamonga, California, spent years developing a unique value proposition that combines her expertise in real estate with her divorce law practice. While some people advised Laurel not to brand herself as a divorce specialist, Laurel knows it has grown her business. She is the expert in divorce real estate, making her a sought-after agent for the many people going through a separation in her area. "I recognized early on that there was a big disconnect between real estate and family law," she says. "I've built my business to serve the gap between the two. Having a focus has allowed me to not get distracted."

Chances are you're still building out your value proposition as you learn about yourself in the industry. As a new agent, your value proposition might simply be the time you have to give clients your undivided attention. It also might stem from previous experience like Laurel. You may not be an attorney, but maybe you're an investor and have flipped several homes. You know how to rehab a home! Maybe you grew up in Lake Placid and "There's nobody who knows Lake Placid like I do!" Sell what you've got. It will only get easier.

Agents start as real estate specialists like other skilled tradespeople and must be licensed to practice. You're also a fiduciary, which is much rarer. As you help more people, hone your talents, and identify the tasks you enjoy, your value proposition will evolve. You'll find what market you enjoy working in. Be thoughtful in learning where you shine and develop your value proposition based on the unique ways you can serve your customers.

The Path of Money in a Real Estate Transaction

Unlike a lot of jobs where you collect a bi-weekly paycheck, real estate is a little more complicated. We know we promised to show you three examples of the path your money might take as a real estate agent. But first, for the examples to hit home, we want to better explain where the various parts of your commission check go.

We've developed models you can use to help plan your business financials. Every business has a **Budget Model**. *The Millionaire Real Estate Agent* (also known as MREA) shares one for seasoned agents. We've adjusted it accordingly for rookie agents. Your business will have different incomes, costs, and expenses. Using the Rookie Budget Model, you can reliably figure out what your net income might be.

The Rookie Budget Model has four elements: GCI, COS, expenses, and net income (before taxes). Your **GCI**, or **Gross Commission Income**, is the total amount of revenue earned from the sale or lease of residential or commercial property. The emphasis is on the G for "gross." It is your top line for any transaction and for your overall financials. GCI represents your income from all sales activities including leasing, buyers, sellers, listings, and any referral fees earned. Then, there are other expenses and deductions that must be accounted for to arrive at your net income. To start, you will have to deduct **costs of sale (COS)** and **business expenses** to determine your **net income**, or profit, from the transaction. COS are any costs you incur *only* if the transaction closes. These include team and brokerage splits, referral fees paid out, etc. (We don't include taxes in COS because city, state, and federal income taxes vary so much from individual to individual and from region to region. Just remember, they will be taken out of your net income, at the end of the day.) Expenses include all other business costs that are paid when the service is rendered or the product is purchased. Some are recurring, like your telephone bill, and some are variable, like hiring a contractor to build your website. Finally, there is your net income—the pre-tax profit you earn from your business.

The difference between GCI and net income can be significant, so it's important to understand. Our research has shown that a rookie real estate agent can expect to pay COS of around 20 percent of their GCI. Likewise, they can expect their annual expenses to add up to roughly 20 percent of their GCI. This would leave a net income of 60 percent *before taxes*. You can think of it as the "20/20/60 Budget Model." Depending on your business approach, brokerage, expense management, and taxes, your actual take-home pay will vary. Both COS and expenses are taken from your GCI to get your net income, and taxes are taken out of that net income. While we aren't calculating taxes into our Budget Model, it's safe to assume if you're making the type of money you want to make, you should be saving anywhere around 25-35 percent to pay the government. So, you might need to adjust your GCI goal higher in order to meet your after-tax financial goals.

The Rookie Budget Model

Gross Commission Income (GCI)
COS (20%)
Expenses (20%)

Net Income

Figure 2

The Rookie and MREA Budget Models are usually displayed like the above, with your GCI at the top to mirror the more detailed profit and loss (or P&L) statement that you'd get from a bookkeeper. When you think of your finances this way, you're thinking like a professional.

A Budget Model is just that—a model. It won't replace the need to have an actual P&L as you're running your business. The Rookie Budget Model serves to give you a high-level idea of how much GCI you'll need to generate to hit your annual profit goal. Later, we'll also provide an Economic Model that outlines the activities you need to do to hit your income goals.

A Note on Referral Fees

There are numerous benefits to building a network of agents in your database. At the top is referrals. If you have a client who is relocating and you know a reputable agent in the area where they are moving, you can refer them to that agent and earn a referral fee in exchange. The same works in the opposite direction. If an agent has clients moving to your area, they can refer them to you for a piece of the commission (typically 25 percent) if the clients decide to work with you. Referral fees are COS, so no one gets paid until less the transaction closes.

Concord, New Hampshire, agent Ryan Hvizda built much of her early business on agent-to-agent referrals. "You never know who you might meet and who they might know that's coming into your market," Ryan says. "Getting a database plan in place with those agents and nurturing them just like you would with friends and family is key. We send them our holiday card and keep in touch. Then when we get a referral from them, we follow up with that agent and let them know we made a connection. When we're under contract and the transaction is solidified, we send a thank-you note. Our main goal is to show them that how we treat them is how we treat their referral as well." Ryan says that more so than your personal network, other agents understand the business. When you make connections with other agents, they might think of you when their friends and family are moving into your area, and when agents in their office are looking for a trusted agent to send a referral to in your market.

Remember, even when you refer friends, family, and clients to another agent, make sure they are as competent, as their service will reflect on you.

The Budget Model can be worked from top to bottom to estimate your net income based on projected GCI. Or it can be worked from bottom to top to identify the GCI you need to earn to hit your net income goals.

For example, if you expect to earn $125,000 in GCI next year, you'll have to account for 20 percent in both COS and expenses. Take that GCI and subtract COS ($125,000 x 20 percent = $25,000 in COS) and expenses ($125,000 x 20 percent = $25,000 in expenses) to project a cool $75,000 in net income before taxes.

Calculate GCI to Net Income

$125,000	GCI
− $25,000	COS
− $25,000	Expenses
$75,000	**Net Income**

Figure 3

When you work it backwards from a net income goal, the math changes.

Let's say you want to net $100,000 in your first year. That's a huge milestone for most agents. In this example, you start with your $100,000 net, and add in your expenses and COS. You calculate your COS and expenses ($166,666 x 20 percent = $33,333 each.)

Calculate Net Income to GCI

$100,000	Net Income
+ $33,333	Expenses
+ $33,333	COS
$166,666	**GCI**

Figure 4

While you're starting with our 20/20/60 Budget Model around COS, expenses, and net income, a more accurate picture of your budget will emerge. Maybe you are super thrifty, love holding opens, and tend to invest more time and elbow grease than money. You might find that your personal model has expenses that run lower, maybe 10-15 percent. You could also discover that you have a gift for agent-to-agent referrals and so your COS run higher than the standard model.

Amy Smith-Magur, an agent out of Latham, New York, knew she wanted to start tracking her expenses right away because she had experience tracking expenses while managing a commercial property. However, working as an agent and for herself was different than what she was used to. "It was a lot of trial and error and conversations with my accountant to figure out what qualified as an expense," Amy says. If you're feeling unsure about how to track your spending, consider hiring a professional. Use any tools at your disposal to ensure you're maximizing your profit and not overspending.

And in case you haven't heard this enough yet—save for your quarterly taxes. In fact, you may want to create a separate account to set aside estimated taxes as you go. Tax rates always depend on the amount of money you earn each year and may also depend on the state in which you practice real estate. While we can't give out tax advice, it is *crucial* that you plan for quarterly taxes. Working for yourself is very different than working for a company that pays taxes for you. It can be quite a shock for people who don't plan properly. We know it's an added expense, but hiring an accountant or bookkeeper may be in your best interest. Taxes are taken out of your net income, not your gross, so it's hard to estimate an exact amount to save. That's where the professionals come in.

Forgetting to account for taxes is one of the biggest mistakes new agents make. But don't just take our word for it. Here's what Atlanta, Georgia, agent Susan Lombardo has to say: "When I was a brand-new agent, I didn't know how fast [the business] would grow for me. And at the end of year two, my taxes were way more than I had put aside to save for them. There was more than six figures in taxes.

"I had never been self-employed, so I was not set up at all. When that bill came, I was completely sideswiped. I had no clue I would owe that much because I had no clue that my business would grow that fast.

"It was a very painful lesson. I got stuck having to pay a monthly tax bill, and I thought, 'Well, this is never going to happen again.'" After that, Susan made a very intentional decision. She says, "When you know you have the potential to earn the kind of income that we can in this business, you have to treat it like a business, and you have to set yourself up." So, she set herself up with a CPA. "I did not ever have a surprise tax bill again," Susan concludes.

If you're the agent we think you are, you may have your sights set on netting $100,000 in your first twelve months. Since we have to aim at a target, we might as well aim high, right? We're going to use this as your goal in our examples throughout this book.

And speaking of examples, it's finally time to take a look at what your earnings could be as a listing agent with a cap, a solo agent, and a buyer's agent on a team. You can also find the full Economic Models for each of these examples in the Appendix. Let's dig in!

Example A: Earning Your First Listing Commission as an Agent with a "Cap"

For this first example, we want you to imagine you're the perspective of an agent who helped their client sell their home. This means you've earned your first **commission**. Go you! A commission is a fee paid to a real estate agent for transacting a piece of business or performing a service. In this transaction, the seller of the house agreed to a commission rate that allowed you to earn $10,000 in GCI.

Like most agents, it's possible you've never gotten a check this big for a single professional project in your life. It's definitely worth celebrating. But remember, your net income, or take-home pay, from this sale is not actually $10,000.

The first step of breaking down your GCI versus your net income is your brokerage split, which falls under COS. For the purpose of this example, we will say you hang your license at a brokerage that does a commission split of 70/30. For this transaction, that means you get $7,000 (70 percent) and the broker gets $3,000 (30 percent). The brokerage you are licensed with may offer a **"capped" commission split** policy. Under this system, once an agent reaches their "cap" or their max annual payout to the company, they stop splitting their commissions with the brokerage. Brokerage splits and caps vary from office to office. In general, capped models tend to ask for a larger split than uncapped models. Just like agents, different brokerages have different value propositions and their fee structures reflect that and the local market. Since this is your first transaction, you are still operating under the regular split.

Explaining the Broker Split

The amount an agent splits their commission with their broker varies per brokerage. But the reason agents have to pay this fee is because the brokerage is the one who carries the risk and ensures the legal compliance for their real estate transactions. It is also the broker's responsibility to help the agent receive adequate education and training throughout their career. Different brokerages offer different levels of training and different split values. This is why choosing the right brokerage, and team if you opt to join one, is important.

After paying your broker split, (a COS), you need to consider your expenses. This includes things like marketing materials, signs, lockboxes, your cellphone, insurance, and gas. We estimate that, over the course of the year, this will be about 20 percent of your GCI or $2,000 for this transaction ($10,000 x 20 percent). Note, that's a conservative estimate for a full-time starting solo agent. So, after paying or setting aside money for expenses, your net income is $5,000. And this is *before* taxes (which could be anywhere from 25 to 35 percent, and you should plan to put it aside)! We hope you now see the importance of this discussion.

Now, this is still a large amount to receive at once. This is why we discussed treating yourself like a business in the previous chapter. Businesspeople manage their bottom line. They are thrifty on expenses and work with tax advisors to pay what the government is owed and not a penny more.

Hopefully you've done your due diligence and created a lead generation machine that has multiple closings coming up in your **sales pipeline**. A sales pipeline is the way contacts, leads, and clients move through different stages of doing business with you. After you get a few home sales under your belt, you will start to understand your average GCI per transaction and your average net income per transaction.

Example B: Earning Your First Commission as an Agent without a Cap

Again in this example, you've just earned your first commission. Except this time, you worked on the buyer side. During your buyer consultation, which we will talk about in Chapter 13, you secured a signed agreement. You laid out your value and the services you offer to your clients, and settled on a fee structure that amounts to $8,000 for the sale.

This $8,000 is your GCI. Just as before, you need to deduct your COS and expenses to get your net income. In this example, you do not work under a capped system and your broker offers a brokerage split of 95/5. That means you keep $7,600 (95 percent) of your commission and pay your brokerage $400 (5 percent) for this transaction.

For expenses, we again recommend setting aside 20 percent of the total commission, or $1,600 ($8,000 x 20 percent). Although your brokerage offers a generous split, they charge for other expenses. You pay a monthly fee to your office of $1,000 for training, technology, errors and omission insurance, and other services. In this case, you pay higher than our rule of thumb. If you paid out your monthly fee with this transaction, you have $2,600 in expenses. This conservatively leaves you with $5,000 in net income *before taxes*.

Example C: Earning the First Commission as an Agent on a Team

You see the pattern now, right? However, in this example, you're a part of a team. This means your COS is higher than in Examples A and B. Team splits may vary by role and region, but unlike brokerage splits, they are rarely capped. If you were working buyer leads on your team, a common team split would be 50/50. That's what we'll assume in this example. Agents agree to these splits because of the value teams offer, like hands-on training, a steady supply of leads, and lots of administrative support before and after the transaction. In many cases, the support gives agents a lot of time back, too.

In this example, you closed a buyer side that earned you $10,000 in GCI. Your primary part of your COS is with your team—that 50/50 split. So, both you and the team earn $5,000 in GCI from the sale. Then, set aside 10 percent of your GCI ($10,000 x 10 percent) or $1,000, for expenses. That's probably high since your team is likely taking care of a lot of the expenses, but better safe than sorry. You can always adjust your percentages if you need to. This makes your net income $4,000 on the transaction before taxes.

While the team example presents the lowest income per transaction on the surface, there is a good reason many rookies choose to join a team. Leads. The lead flow on a team tends to be higher. This means you can earn income faster and do more business than you might alone.

Now that you've seen what your net income could look like after one transaction in three different scenarios, let's look at how you can use this information to build out financial plans for your business. The first step is to calculate your conversion rates.

Calculate Your Conversion Rates

Your **conversion rates** represent your ability to move prospective clients from leads in your database to the consultation and all the way across the finish line to a closing. More simply, they're the percentage of clients you're able to retain across multiple steps in the transaction. The transition between each of these different activities is what we call a conversion. The percentage of clients you move from one step to the next determines your conversion rate.

Conversion rates allow you to accurately build your business plan. What percentage of the people you talk to are interested in an appointment or consultation? This can vary wildly based on how you generate leads. If you're talking to random people at the mall food court, the conversion rate is probably going to be as sad as the shellacked dishes behind the counter at the stir fry joint. If you're meeting people at open houses (read: people who are demonstrating an interest in real estate), conversion rates will be higher. Emails, online advertising, and postcards convert at low rates. Actual conversations on the phone or in person are more productive.

Things get more predictable once a potential client agrees to a buyer or seller consultation, or an **appointment**. Now it's a skills game. How good are your consultation skills? What percentage of your appointments will result in an **agreement** to list or sell with you? Likewise, skills will inform the percentage of agreements that result in an accepted contract by your seller or for your buyer. Finally, you'll look to your contract-to-close skills to get those contracts to an actual **closing**. The closing is the finish line for your client. Someone walks out with a set of new keys, and you get paid for your hard work!

Everyone who is in the business of sales—whether it's cowboy boots, speed boats, or homes—is in the conversion business. The ability to move sales from appointment to agreement to closing is a combination of the value you deliver and your skill in communicating it and delivering on it. Your value is your services, your expertise, the unique ways you deliver them, and the quality of the professionals with whom you surround yourself. Denver, Colorado, agent Tyler Shields advises, "Every step of the way, seek to add value. Know your client, audit their needs, and seek to match your value to their needs." He adds, "When the time is right and the value is right, the client will be ready to move to the next step of the process with you."

Understand Your Economic Model

Breaking down your activities and connecting them to your financials this way is your business's **Economic Model**. The Economic Model begins with the projections from your Budget Model and then guides you backward to how many appointments with buyers or sellers you'll need to hit your net income goal. It can be almost impossible to connect the dots between your daily activities and a weekly or monthly income goal. There are just too many variables in between. On the other hand, you can design your plans around the number of appointments you need each week or month to stay on track to hit your income goal. That's the point of the Economic Model. It helps you connect the dots between your daily tasks and your annual goals.

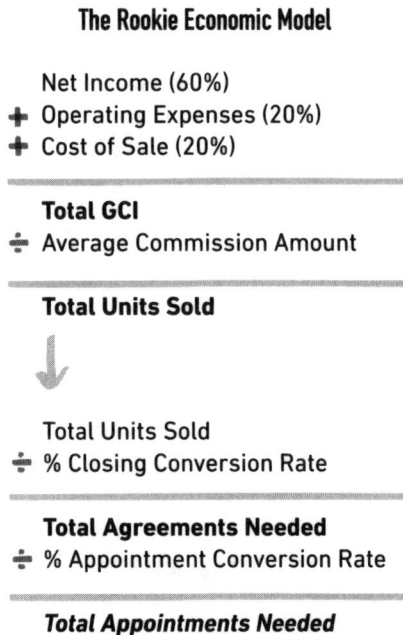

The Rookie Economic Model

Net Income (60%)
+ Operating Expenses (20%)
+ Cost of Sale (20%)

Total GCI
÷ Average Commission Amount

Total Units Sold

↓

Total Units Sold
÷ % Closing Conversion Rate

Total Agreements Needed
÷ % Appointment Conversion Rate

Total Appointments Needed

Figure 5

Using the preceding Economic Model, we'll focus on a solo agent with a goal of earning $100,000 in net income before taxes. Everything will be rounded *up* to a whole number. You can't take a third of an appointment or a quarter of an agreement. While rounding up may force us to do a little more in pursuit of our goals, that's not a bad thing. You'd rather overshoot the mark than fall short, right?

Step 1: Calculate Units Sold

The first step is to take the GCI from your Rookie Budget Model and determine how many transactions you will need to close to hit your net income goal. Next, divide your projected GCI by your average commission earned. For this example, we're plugging in an average expected commission of $10,000 per transaction, so we have

$166,666 / $10,000 = 16.6. This means you need seventeen closings to reach your net income goal. Yes, just like we said, we rounded up!

Calculate Units Sold

	$100,000	Net Income (60%)
+	**$33,333**	Operating Expenses (20%)
+	**$33,333**	Cost of Sale (20%)
	$166,666	**Total GCI**
÷	**$10,000**	Average Commission Amount
	17	*Total Units Sold*

Figure 6

Step 2: Calculate Agreements Needed

Once you know the number of closed transactions you need, you can continue working the Economic Model to discover how many agreements with buyers and sellers you'll need in order to close that many transactions.

Agreements are a big milestone. That's when a buyer or seller prospect becomes a client. With your buyer clients, you will help them identify properties that match their criteria, write offers, negotiate a contract for sale, and then navigate the closing process together. With your seller clients, you must market their property to prospective buyers well enough to attract an offer your seller accepts. Then guide them through the closing process.

For the Rookie Economic Model, we're using an assumed conversion rate of 75 percent to find the number of needed agreements. There is no hard science behind that assumption. We asked lots of real estate sales coaches with extensive experience working with rookie agents and that was their recommendation.

We've seen talented agents in strong markets convert at much higher rates. We've also seen those same agents convert fewer agreements to closings during a market shift. To get to seventeen closings with a 75 percent conversion rate, you need about twenty-three agreements (17 / 75 percent = 22.6, or, rounded up, twenty-three).

Calculate Agreements Needed

17	Total Units Sold
÷ **75%**	Closing Conversion Rate

23   *Total Agreements Needed*

Figure 7

Step 3: Calculate Appointments Needed

By continuing to track conversion rates and applying them to the Rookie Economic Model, you can find out the number of appointments you need to set with potential buyers and sellers to net to those twenty-three agreements. Again, after consulting with our coaching leaders, we will assume a 75 percent conversion rate (23 / 75 percent = 30.7 or, rounding up, thirty-one). So, you need to set thirty-one appointments this year to reach an annual net income goal of $100,000.

Calculate Appointments Needed

23	Total Agreements Needed
÷ **75%**	Appointment Conversion Rate

31   *Total Appointments Needed*

Figure 8

Let's recap, working from the bottom up. When you hold thirty-one appointments with potential buyers and sellers, you can expect twenty-three of them to contractually agree to work with you. Of those twenty-three clients, you can project that seventeen will close at an average of $10,000 in commissions/fees. Those closings should generate the $166,666 in GCI you'll need to cover $33,333 in COS, pay $33,333 in expenses, and net $100,000 in income, before taxes, for the year!

A Full Economic Model Calculation

	$100,000	Net Income (60%)
+	$33,333	Operating Expenses (20%)
+	$33,333	Cost of Sale (20%)

	$166,666	**Total GCI**
÷	$10,000	Average Commission Amount

	17	**Total Units Sold**

	17	Total Units Sold
÷	75%	Closing Conversion Rate

	23	**Total Agreements Needed**
÷	75%	Appointment Conversion Rate

	31	*Total Appointments Needed*

Figure 9

Also rounding up, when you break those thirty-one appointments across a twelve-month calendar, you end up with about three appointments a month. So, if you set three appointments a month and your conversion rate stays consistent, you'll meet your goals. Sounds totally doable, right?

Build Your Model Along the Way

When Gary Keller and I wrote *The Millionaire Real Estate Agent*, Gary shared a story from his college years. During class one day, when twenty-something Gary was being a bit of a know-it-all, his professor told him: "You know, Gary, people have lived before you, and you might be wise to go study their lives as you're building your own." Though it took some time for the message to sink in, Gary began to understand the foundational truth that success leaves clues. If you follow those clues, you can often find a blueprint to success of your own. Those blueprints are what we call models, which is what you just learned in this chapter.

Along your journey to real estate success, you'll want to create your own path, design your own future, and build your own empire. We say go for it. But there are some things that we know just *work*. The Budget and Economic Models are a couple of them. We also know that dialing in your conversion rates takes time. So does knowing your COS and your business expenses.

You will need to be doing business before you have actual data you can use to calculate these rates. After you have these numbers, it may take some time to figure out what kind of lead generation yields a high conversion to set appointments. Then maybe a bit more time to see how you can more effectively convert appointments to agreements. Finally, how you can fine-tune your systems so that more agreements result in closings. By tracking these numbers, you'll be able to focus on getting returns for your efforts. But starting on solid footing with a solid model to point you in the right direction is the best launch pad we can offer.

Really, you'll build your personal "Rookie Real Estate Agent Model" along the way. But start with this base model in mind as you learn. As Lubbock, Texas, agent Han Li says, "Real estate is good money, but it's not easy money." When you start out, you may feel like you don't have the right answers to everything. You'll be exercising muscles you may not have used before to grow stronger in your business. Every skill you build will help you successfully complete the activities you need to do to reach your net income goal. And although it's not easy, knowing what goals you need to hit along the way will make the process that much simpler.

CHAPTER 4

Become a Market Expert

Real estate attracts all kinds. You'll meet design devotees, architecture aficionados, people people, and nosy neighbor types who love nothing more than touring people's homes and seeing how they live. Maybe I'm in the last category. On a morning walk with my wife, we popped into a new listing in our neighborhood. I remember checking out a closet in the guest bedroom and finding fifty pairs of blue jeans. "Who has that many pairs of jeans?" I wondered. Turns out the home was owned by a retiring FBI agent. I don't know why this sort of thing delights me, but it does. Real estate also attracts (and creates) data nerds. So much of this industry is driven by economic and sales trends that either you love it going in or grow to love it over time. Market data is the language of sales.

Maybe numbers aren't your thing (yet). That's okay. You'll soon learn that the numbers involved in real estate really just represent people and the activities they can do. It isn't like that precalculus exam you took in high school. If you're someone who is curious about and likes people, then these numbers will come to you pretty easily.

This chapter serves as a playbook for how to understand the real estate market. We'll cover what you should be paying attention to on a national and regional level, as well as what you should know about the towns, neighborhoods, and local areas you serve. This expertise will not only help set your business up for success, but it will equip you with the knowledge you need to be of service to your future sellers and buyers.

As a new agent, understanding the real estate market is crucial. As agent Jen Davis explains, "Real estate is a relational business. The value we offer isn't friendship. The value is knowledge. And our knowledge is market knowledge and how we communicate it." Part of your value to any potential client will come from your market expertise—of course it does! Your clients aren't real estate professionals, and you are. That's why they need you.

Real estate knowledge is actually non-negotiable. It's a foundational customer expectation. As my friend and Washington, D.C.-area, agent Sarah Reynolds Oji likes to point out, "Meeting customer expectations isn't a value proposition, it's a service." When you learn to do it better than the competition or in a truly unique manner, add it to your value prop. For now, understand it is just part of doing your job. So, you might as well do it well. Gary Keller says, "When people want 'experienced' agents, they are wanting expertise and professionalism." The good news is you can quickly learn to explain the same data as a seasoned agent. Just because you weren't listing homes five years ago doesn't mean you can't interpret how home values have changed in the past five years. The numbers tell the tale.

"How's the Market?"

This question is by far the most frequent question you'll get once people learn that you're in real estate. So, let's explain how to answer it. The short version is that you can always pose a question in response. "Why do you ask?" Only when you know what a potential client needs can you offer informed advice.

The real estate industry, like any business, operates based on the relationship between supply and demand. In real estate, supply can be broken out into two categories: the number of existing and new homes for sale. Demand is the number of active buyers in your location. Your market will be defined by the balance of available supply at a given moment and the number of buyers willing to purchase from it. Supply in real estate is called **inventory**. As the inventory of available properties goes up and down, it creates a ripple effect. Inventory defines the state of the market. It will change how real estate is sold as well as how fast it will sell and for how much. In the US, we measure inventory in months of supply. Months of supply is calculated as the number of months it would take for all the inventory to be sold if no new properties are listed. For example, you would have four months of supply if there were forty properties available and ten buyers were buying each month. We'll cover that in more detail shortly.

The Three Kinds of Housing Markets

1 **Balanced market**

2 **Buyers' market**

3 **Sellers' market**

There are three core real estate markets: a balanced market, a buyers' market, and a sellers' market. These markets are constantly moving based on the current supply and demand. Depending on what kind of market you're working in, the way you answer, "How's the market?" will change.

1 Balanced Market

A **balanced market** is one where supply and demand are pretty equal. There are just about as many buyers as there are people who want to sell houses to them. The market has about four to six months of inventory.

"While historically we've viewed a balanced market as six months of inventory, when we examine more recent data, the relationship between months of supply and price implies balance is closer to five months," explains real estate economist Ruben Gonzalez.

Balanced markets are fleeting. They usually appear during transitions between sellers' and buyers' markets. They rarely last.

2 Buyers' Market

When seller supply exceeds demand, you're in a **buyers' market**. There are more houses available to purchase than there are people able to buy them.

Home prices tend to decrease in buyers' markets, as sellers are competing to move their homes quickly. This puts the buyer at an advantage where they may get the right home for a more affordable price. Buyers have more leverage to ask for other concessions like repairs and paid closing costs.

Buyers' vs. Sellers' Market

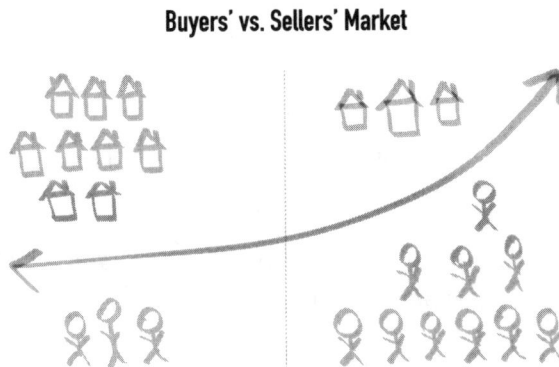

Figure 10

Historically, when there is more than six months of inventory, the market is considered a buyers' market.

3 Sellers' Market

When buyer demand exceeds seller supply, you're in a **sellers' market**. There are more people wanting to buy homes than there is available inventory. This swings negotiating power in favor of sellers. Listings can be priced higher and fewer concessions are offered. Sellers and listing agents can even hope for a bidding war that will edge up the final sales price.

A market is considered a sellers' market if there is less than four months of available inventory.

A Note on Seasonality

The real estate market has seasons where it seems like everyone is moving, and other times of the year when it seems like no one is ever going to move again. Generally, these peaks and valleys of activity follow the school year. No one wants to move midway through their kids learning decimals and fractions. Okay, that might be a bit of a . . . tangent.

Seasonal Sales Cycles

Source: SHIFT

Figure 11

As an entrepreneur, knowing that the real estate market acts seasonally means you should take these ebbs and flows into account when you're looking at your numbers. Has your conversion rate really gone down because you suddenly don't know how to talk to people, or is it just that it's March?

Keep seasonality in mind because it may affect your income.

Seasonal Income Cycle

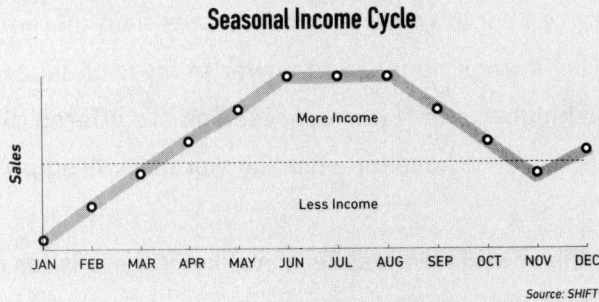

Figure 12

If there are times of the year when fewer real estate transactions occur in your market, you will need to plan ahead for how you can weather those slumps financially.

Market Shifts

Whenever the supply and demand in a market shifts, transitioning from a period of greater or lesser inventory and faster or slower pace of sales to its opposite, you're in a **market shift**. The times they are a-changing and you must change with them, padawan.

Shifts get a bad rap. Some people find them to be tough periods for their businesses. That's understandable! You'll have to adjust your approach and change can be tough. But we want to remind you that tough times make tough people.

Transitional Markets

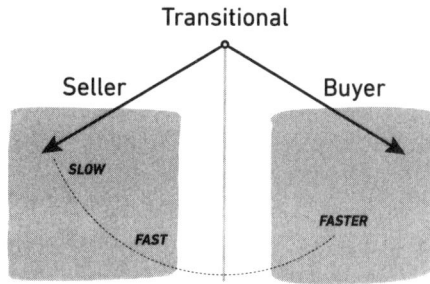

Figure 13

How long a shift takes depends on a host of factors like changing interest rates, inflation, and employment. Shifts tend to happen slowly at a national level and appear very quickly when they show up in local markets.

Shifts typically play out similarly, but they originate uniquely. No two shifts are caused by the same thing. In 2008, the banking industry collapsed and took the real estate market with it. In 2020, it was a world-wide pandemic that basically froze the market before unleashing a flurry of buying. Who knows what'll cause the next one—trying to predict them isn't worth your time or anxiety. Just know that good times create bad times and bad times create good times. It's a cycle. It's never a question of whether the market will shift. It's a matter of *when*.

Now, if you find yourself in a shifting market: Don't panic! There are always people who need to buy and sell real estate. Granby, Colorado, agent Sheila Bailey says that while the market will always affect your business, you can use it to your advantage no matter the situation. "I think stronger agents will actually thrive in worse or shifting markets," Sheila says. "They'll dig deeper and take more market share because of their ability to be an expert in that marketplace." There is opportunity in *every* market. You will be able to find people who need your services and help them, and if you are good at finding people to help, you will not only survive the market transition—you will come out stronger.

Depending on what kind of market you're working in, the way you show houses and work with clients will be different. Throughout the rest of this book, you can look for market-specific advice in text boxes marked with this symbol .

"How's the (Local) Market?"

When someone asks you about the market, they are invariably asking about the local market. While national trends impact local ones, the vast majority of your clients will buy and sell locally. When we talk about becoming a market expert, we're talking about becoming an expert on *your* market.

Your local market can mean your **MSA (Metropolitan Statistical Area)**, which is an urban area including adjacent counties or towns. For example, "greater Chicago" would include some 284 municipalities. You'd probably know or be able to find data on the whole MSA or any of those townships from Aurora to Naperville.

At the same time, you should be familiar with your market down to its neighborhoods. You may even specialize in one or more.

For example, if you live in Upstate New York near the French-Canadian border, knowing that there's a new bus station in the Bronx probably won't be very valuable to your clients. However, knowing that the Québécois Maple Syrup Cartel, whoops, I mean the Federation of Québec Maple Syrup Producers, doesn't have jurisdiction in the states can come in handy. That friend of yours who wants to tap their backyard trees and sell "artisan" syrup doesn't need to worry about the "Maple Leaf Police." Now that's something that might be valuable.

Generally, keeping the following data points in mind will help you master your local market trends and needs.

Six Local Market Data Points to Know

1 Inventory   *4* Interest rates

2 Days on market   *5* Local flavor and amenities

3 Prices   *6* Jobs

1 Inventory

The relationship between inventory and demand defines the real estate market. Conveniently, the real estate industry has a way to relate these together into one statistic called **Months' Supply of Inventory**, which is often shortened to "months' supply" or just "inventory." It is a mouthful. To find this number, use the following formula. The resulting number shows how fast, at the current level of demand, all of the available properties would sell if no others came on the market.

Calculating Months' Supply of Inventory

Homes available at the end of the month
$\div$ Total home sales from that month

─────────────────────────────

Months' Supply

400 homes available
$\div$ 30 sales that month

─────────────────────────────

13 Months' Supply

Figure 14

Most real estate agents call this the inventory level in a given market. It is the first and most important piece of data you need to know about your local market.

If supply and demand govern the value of real estate inventory, then it is a pretty good idea to know when there is going to be more supply—when new properties are being built.

These trends show up in national and local levels and they have big effects on the market. For example, there was a national shortage of available supply in single-family starter homes in the United States in the early 2010s. Part of this was a result of the **Great Recession**, an economic downturn that began in late 2007 and lasted until 2009. According to the National Association of Homebuilders, in the decade that followed the Great Recession, construction rates on new homes dropped by nearly half.

Home Construction Across the Decades

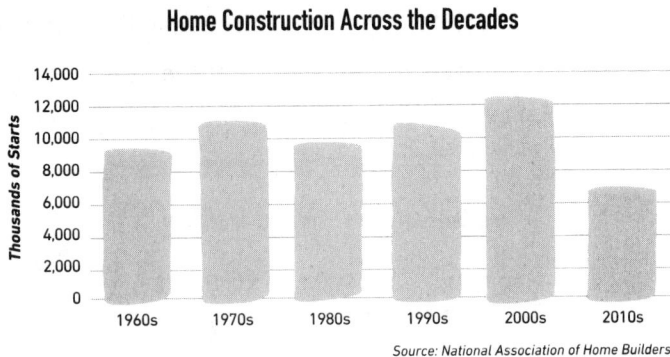

Source: National Association of Home Builders

Figure 15

This drop in construction combined with a lack of focus on building affordable housing meant that a decade later, in the 2020s, there was a much greater demand for housing than there was supply. As many as 2.5 million homes are considered "missing" from 2020s inventory because they simply were not built.

Because new construction affects supply, it is especially important to keep an eye on. In many urban areas, new construction happens on the outskirts of town where there is available land. These new builds tend to be more affordable than resale homes in a more cosmopolitan location and are excellent choices for first-time home buyers.

As a real estate agent, you'll want to build relationships with investors and builders in your area. Austin, Texas, agent Chris Hall estimates that 40 percent of his first-time buyers choose new construction.

2 Days on Market

As you watch inventory on the MLS or your local board, you should also track the average number of days a listing stays on the market. This important stat is called **Days on Market (DOM)**. Historically, it wouldn't be unusual for a home to take sixty to ninety days to sell. That's a great perspective, but your seller wants to know the current number and whether it's trending up or down for similar properties in the area. Unlike market inventory levels, DOM can be very specific to certain types of properties and neighborhoods.

Knowing DOM will not only give you a baseline for any seller clients you serve, but it can also help you navigate buyer expectations if you are helping buyers make offers. You'll be able to spot the "market of the moment," which is the kinds of properties that are selling the fastest.

Agent Tiffany Fykes says, "Every time I'm able to walk into an appointment and from memory talk about the market numbers, it tells my clients that they can trust me to advise them well." Many people are uncomfortable with numbers, so if you're able to confidently speak to them about the specific market numbers in their neighborhood, town, or city, then your expertise will help them make the best decision. For Tiffany, "Numbers build the client's confidence in me as a professional, and I make sure I'm telling them something about the market that they may never consider."

3 Prices

It should probably go without saying that if you are helping others buy and sell a product, you should know what the going market rate is for that product. Home price trends are perhaps the most-fixated-on statistics in our industry by both buyers and sellers. As people make the largest financial transactions in their lives, there is a huge amount of concern about both the value of their purchase as well as its potential value over time. It's important to not only be able to accurately price a home, but to also be able to put your market into historical context for your clients and describe the trend in home prices.

As a listing agent, sellers will expect you to advise them on pricing their homes competitively. When you're working with buyers, they will want reassurance that they are purchasing a home at a reasonable cost. Having your finger on the pulse of pricing in your area allows you to advise them appropriately. Fort Mill, South Carolina, agent Rebecca Cullen says that when sellers don't understand the market, they may risk undervaluing their assets or overpricing them. "In my experience, providing an accurate pricing strategy is 90 percent of the reason why a home will sell or sit on the market," she says. "While I don't have a crystal ball, I am able to help all of our sellers interpret the current market conditions using statistics and facts. When we are in agreement, this strategy ensures our properties sell quickly, attract the right buyers, and maximize their return on investment."

Aside from market knowledge, your goal is to be able to advise any potential clients about the fact that, historically, home prices tend to increase. This means that a house is an asset that appreciates—it increases in value over time.

Home Prices for the Past Thirty Years

9.9% Above Trend

21% Above Trend

96
222
166
222
297
351
390
408
422

Long-term Trend = 4%   Annual Median Home Price (in Thousands $USD)

Source: National Association of REALTORS®

Figure 16

When you average out the increase in home prices over the past thirty years, even with the peaks and valleys of buyers' and sellers' markets, homes show a long-term appreciation rate of about 4 percent. Part of this appreciation comes from the fact that a home is a collection of construction materials like insulation, wiring, and cement. These materials tend to increase in cost with inflation, as does the labor required to assemble them into a house. All in all, there are not many investments that have such reliable, long-term results.

Another win that comes from keeping up with price points is that it can help you identify areas of opportunity. Prices can vary vastly over even small geographies, and being familiar with the pricing landscape and price trends within neighborhoods will help you inform clients on how to best meet their budget and financial goals.

4   Interest Rates

Mortgage interest rates and lender regulations can greatly impact your market. Think of mortgage interest rates as "the cost of money." The higher interest rates are, the more expensive it is to take out mortgage loans. When interest rates rise, buying power starts to drop because it becomes difficult to afford the monthly payments on those loans.

Interest rates have a disproportionate impact on **affordability**. Affordability is calculated by looking at the cost of buying a median property (price) with the median salary (income) at the current mortgage interest rate. A 1 percent increase in mortgage interest rates will increase the monthly cost of owning a home on a thirty-year mortgage by about 10 percent. That ratio also applies to falling interest rates. It's rare for incomes or home prices to fall or rise by 10 percent in a single year. The same cannot be said of interest rates, which is why you need to know and understand them.

Mortgage Interest Rates for the Past Fifty Years

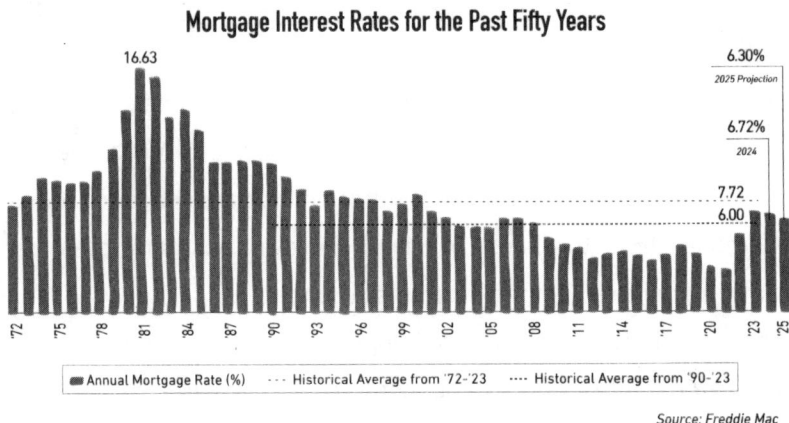

16.63

6.30%
2025 Projection

6.72%
2024

7.72
6.00

▬ Annual Mortgage Rate (%)   ···· Historical Average from '72-'23   ···· Historical Average from '90-'23

Source: Freddie Mac

Figure 17

When you're tracking mortgage rates, there are a few things to keep in mind so that you can advise appropriately. The first is that for most of the modern real estate market, the most relevant mortgage rate is for the thirty-year fixed-rate mortgage. This averaged 6 percent from 1990 to 2023. The recent period of "cheap money" following the Great Recession was largely unprecedented and may not return in the future. The second is that interest rates, for most loans, can be refinanced. For example, following the high mortgage interest rates in the 1980s (12 to 18 percent), there was a period of massive mortgage refinancing when rates dropped below 8 percent in the 1990s. You will want to ensure that when you connect clients with lenders you advise them to ask about different mortgage programs and the pros and cons of each.

For many potential clients sitting on the sidelines, the direction of interest rates can be a huge factor in their motivation to buy or sell. When rates fall, buyers may leap off the fence into the market trying to lock rates and save money. When rates trend up, buyers may lose interest, pardon the expression. In some cases, sellers also choose to wait if their current mortgage is at a favorably low rate. With your market expertise, you can advise potential clients on whether these beliefs are valid for their situation.

5 Local Flavors and Amenities

Part of being a local market expert is knowing your area like... well, a local. You should be excited about and share the things that make your area a great and unique place to live. Getting to know and love the area you serve will make you better at helping your clients than anybody else.

Troy Williams, an agent from York, Maine, pursued real estate because it gave him the opportunity to stay where he loved and serve his neighbors. He went to college for business and planned on going into finance. However, after meeting with potential employers, he realized that to go into finance, he would have to work and live in a city. "That is not anything I'm interested in at all," Troy says. "I grew up in a small town and didn't want to leave. So, I revisited my passions and real estate was like, 'Well, why don't I do that?'"

To get started, Troy decided to write a letter to about 400 people who were friends or that he had either worked with in the past or people he might want to work with in the future. He wrote, "I'm giving you an update. I'm graduating college and staying in town, and I've decided to go into real estate full time." After that, he began working at a local real estate office while he prepared to get his license. In Maine, licenses aren't required to work with rental clients. So, when a person who was relocating and looking for a rental called the office, they were passed to Troy. "I started talking to [a potential client], and the first thing I said to him was, 'Can I ask why you don't want to buy?' He told me that he'd lived in the area before and thought that prices had risen beyond his budget. I reassured him that he could probably find something, if he knew where to look. I ended up spending two days with him and finding him a house before I was officially licensed."

Agents at the home office helped Troy get the client referred to a licensed agent and get the paperwork across the finish line. "When I got that commission check, it was a defining moment for me," Troy remembers. "I just said to myself, 'This is going to work. I'll be just fine.'"

What does your market have that makes it unique? If you're on the coast or on a great lake, you've probably got miles of beaches to enjoy. Northwest or Northeast? Mountains, foliage, snowmobiles and skiing! Are you in the land of barbeque, bluegrass, and bourbon in the Southeast? How about some Southwest flare with rodeos, dance halls, and tacos?

What's exciting about real estate is that it's ultimately about where people live and play. You should know the perks and flavor of your market on a neighborhood level. Do you know which school districts have the best soccer teams? What areas of town are best for catching live music?

Where are the best restaurants? It may seem like this is a lot to discover, but chances are, you already know what makes the place you call home or do business in a winner.

6 Jobs

Remember how affordability is calculated? Income is one of the three factors used to determine the affordability of homes. And how do we get income? Jobs. While this is the last of the key market data points to know, it may be the most important. The health of your local job market is the foundation of the market itself.

When a new factory gets built or a company moves its headquarters to town, you get an influx of new jobs. Unemployed people find work. New workers move to the area. Employers may need to hand out raises to retain existing employees. All this adds up to incomes rising, which can create demand for homes. It can also spur building when the local supply lags behind demand. Demand tends to heat up markets. The same is true in reverse. When the local mill closes and a big employer moves away, the job market may cool and take the real estate market with it. Unemployed workers will be motivated to sell, but without demand, they may not get their asking price.

Tracking your local job market can be a little like having a forecast for the future of your real estate market.

Where Do I Find All This Data?

There are many places you can go to learn more about the six local data points to know, as well as national real estate market trends. Build a habit to keep on top of these developments so that you will be able to provide real-time advice for your clients.

1. Your Local Board or Listing Service

Statistics on your area should update monthly and yearly in your local board, listing service, or MLS. You can use this to track months of inventory and other sales trends.

2. Local Chamber of Commerce or Business Journal

If there are going to be any major developments, or if there is going to be a new company coming to your area, chances are your local chamber of commerce or business journal will have the scoop first. Being an active member of your chamber will also give you great networking opportunities with other businesses.

3. Mortgage Partners, Attorneys, and Title Offices

Other professionals who help people through life changes and real estate transactions have information that could be useful to you. Reach out to your mortgage brokers and ask if they have any recent insights they can share—or check in with legal professionals who might be helping potential clients settle estates.

4. Regional Federal Reserve Beige Books

The Beige Book is a report published by the Federal Reserve System that shares current economic conditions across the twelve Federal Reserve Districts. It characterizes regional economic conditions like inflation and prospects based on a variety of mostly qualitative information gathered directly from each district's sources. Reports are published eight times per year and are available for free download from the Federal Reserve website.

5. Your Own Data

The more transactions you have under your belt, the more real-life data you collect about your market. Pay attention to the trends that you see emerging—like an increase of people looking to move to a new neighborhood or a question that keeps coming up in your consultations. Being connected to your community and your clients will enable you to provide them fiduciary service at the highest level.

Your Knowledge Is a Core Service You Provide

Becoming an expert in real estate means becoming a master of your market—understanding how both local and national events combine to create your unique situation. Your greatest value to your clients is your ability to help them make an informed decision about their next real estate transaction. And that includes having a firm grasp on local market trends. Los Gatos, California, agent Andy Sweat says showcasing your worth as a market expert before, during, and after a transaction is what will make your clients stick with you. "It's a long-term commitment to being knowledgeable and keeping your people informed," Andy says. "You have to show people your worth." Keeping on top of developments and trends and understanding the context of your current market is how you deliver the best possible advice.

"Being the market expert differentiates us from the consumer," agrees Joe Delia, an agent from the Detroit, Michigan, area. "That's where we step in as fiduciary on their behalf as we're able to take that data, digest it, and put together a plan as a result."

Hartford, Connecticut, agent Jessica Starr keeps current so her clients know they can count on her. She says, "I'm always setting expectations and educating the entire time, even if they've done this before. I don't want to surprise anybody."

Be proud when people start asking, "How's the market?" because it shows they trust that you know something of value. As you learn the lead generation tactics that you can choose from in the next chapter, don't forget that this value is the foundation for most of the connections that you will form.

People do business with people they know, like, and trust.

CHAPTER 5

Start Lead Generating and Cultivate Your Database

At the beginning of my career, I was an editorial assistant to an executive editor at HarperCollins Publishers in New York City. As a part of my role, I handled his expense report. He'd meet literary agents for breakfast, lunch, happy hour, and dinner some days. A typical morning would involve him stopping by my cubicle to drop off a wad of receipts from the day before, while juggling a cup of coffee, a bagel, and several daily newspapers. At some point, I realized his expense account was substantially larger than my annual salary. At the time, I remember feeling resentful about the lavish perks he enjoyed. It wasn't until we were writing *The Millionaire Real Estate Agent* that I actually understood what was happening. My editor was a lead generating machine. He networked from dawn to dusk. It was no surprise that my cube was littered with dozens of manuscripts and proposals from the best agents and authors. He wanted first dibs on the best book projects. And he got them, publishing a steady stream of bestselling and award-winning books.

That's lead generation, specifically prospecting. You work your network so you can be the first in line for future opportunities.

The major lesson from the last chapter is that markets are living things, always moving. Every day you're in a buyers' market, the sooner you can expect the cycle to flip to a sellers' market. One eventually gives way to the other. While market conditions are out of your individual control, how you respond to them isn't. Agents who consistently lead generate have stable, growing businesses no matter the market.

Lead Generation 101

If lead generation is the stable foundation of your business, your **database** is the footing on which your lead generation stands. We like to say, "Your database is your business." It's that important. It will determine your productivity, your activities, and your profits. Your database is where you store names and contact information of leads and contacts. A good one will also record and drive your activities—who you connected with, what you discussed—and when to follow up appropriately. In the biz, they are often referred to as **CRMs (Customer Relationship Management** tools). They can be high-tech, cloud-based software platforms or simple analog notecard systems. The right CRM for you, quite simply, is the one you use.

While we're on the database, we should distinguish between leads and contacts. A **lead** is a person! Someone who might want your services, whose contact info you have, but with whom you haven't yet had a real estate conversation that positions you as their potential agent. All the names in your phone are leads until that important conversation happens. Same for all the people you know around town, from school, or from previous jobs. The conversation doesn't have to be about an urgent need to buy or sell. It can just be to create awareness of what you do and the services you provide. *Hi, Carly! It's Jay. I was just calling to let you know I've decided to start my career in real estate. I'd love to be the one you call when you or someone you know* *has a real estate need*. That conversation should conclude with their accepting your invitation to stay in contact about real estate–related stuff.

Once you've had "the talk" with a lead, they become a **contact**. Some of your lead generation activities will be to meet leads and turn them into contacts. Some of your lead generation activities will be to market to and connect with contacts about their real estate needs. The bigger your database and the more quality contacts it has, the better your chances of landing a client. You will grow your database through lead generation. And you will use strategic database touch plans and campaigns to stay top-of-mind with prospective and past clients.

Because your database is so important, we'll spend this chapter and the next two chapters walking you through the process of cultivating it, tending to it, and automating habits and systems around it.

Call to Action: Cultivate, Tend, and Automate Your Database

Conveniently, **CTA** stands for both cultivate-tend-automate *and* call-to-action. By cultivating, tending, and automating your database, you will prompt action from potential clients. This could be getting them to use a helpful resource on your website, engage in two-way communication, or attend an event you're hosting.

The Two CTAs: Call-to-Action and Cultivate-Tend-Automate

Figure 18

Think of your database like a garden: there's a lot of nuance and research required for success! To get started, you need to till the soil and plant seeds. This is **cultivation**. In real estate, this means generating more leads. Do this by reaching out to people in specific, effective ways. Then, you need to water your plants, trim back excess growth, and prune away dead branches. This is **tending**. It's about keeping your stored information accurate and up to date. Finally, you need to ensure your garden can grow in all seasons. It should keep perennials blooming year after year. This is **automating** habits and systems. It means using your database effectively by being consistent with your outreach and tracking your results. This chapter will cover the first step: planting the seeds of a thriving real estate business through cultivation.

Cultivate Your Database

As Rudyard Kipling wrote in *The Glory of the Garden*, "... gardens are not made by singing, 'Oh, how beautiful!' and sitting in the shade." A garden only yields when it is worked. Real estate is the same: You must connect with every lead, secure permission to stay in contact, and move them into your database. This is cultivating. You'll do it through prospecting and marketing—two types of lead generation.

The Rookie Lead Generation Model

Prospecting   **Marketing**

Leads

Contacts

Database

Appointments

Figure 19

Once in the database, you'll continue prospecting and marketing to your contacts to build relationships and to nurture connections. Over time, your work will bear fruit and your contacts will have real estate needs for you to help them with. That's when you set appointments to win the business and deliver your value proposition.

The goal in this section is for you to learn just enough about some proven prospecting and marketing activities to create a lead generation plan for your business. At the center of it all will be your database, which we'll discuss in-depth in Chapters 6 and 7. Make no mistake, to be successful you will need to include both prospecting and marketing in your plans.

Stay TCPA Compliant

There are several laws you need to be aware of and follow as a real estate agent. The Telephone Consumer Protection Act (TCPA) is one that we will bring up over and over when it comes to lead generation. The TCPA applies whenever you are telemarketing, that is, calling or texting someone to promote your services.[1] We may sound like a broken record, but we will do whatever it takes to avoid broken laws. There are also telemarketing laws that vary by state, and you will be educated on them while working to get your license. The law doesn't go away when school ends, so keep yourself aware of any changes or updates to the TCPA and your state's laws.

As an agent, you will rely heavily on contacting and connecting with people. Often, your first thought is to do this by phone. If you do not specifically have someone's permission to call them and they are on a

------

[1] In sum, you cannot call or text a number on the National Do Not Call Registry (or any other Do Not Call list) and cannot use an automatic telephone dialing system or an artificial or prerecorded voice without proper consent. We recommend that you contact an attorney to ensure your compliance with the TCPA and related state laws.

Do Not Call (DNC) list, you'll end up in serious trouble. There are plenty of other ways to get in touch with leads who are not contacts yet. Being on the right side of the law will save you in many ways, so it's important to keep your database updated in this respect. And if someone has requested to not be contacted by you in any way, it's time to remove them from your database.

Throughout the book, you'll notice this 📞 symbol. Anytime an activity includes TCPA compliance, you'll see 📞. We don't want to sound like a broken record and kill a forest of trees repeating the same mantra: "Always remember to do this in a TCPA compliant way!" So 📞 will be our signal to you.

Your First Leads: Reach Out to Your Sphere of Influence

Think of all the groups you're a part of: your family, friends, coworkers, parents in your kids' school, and the barista at your corner coffee shop who always spells your name with an extra vowel. Your existing network of personal connections is your **Sphere of Influence**, or SOI. This group will be of utmost importance to you as a new agent because they already have a connection with you. In fact, they are the heart and soul of your database. They are a natural first step when you start to build your sales pipeline, and some agents build their entire career on their SOI. Your sphere is all the people who are already connected to you and, importantly, they're the most likely to use you as an agent since you already have a relationship. You just have to convert them to contacts by sharing what you do and why they should consider working with you.

Whether you're new to town or are just starting out in the business, you already have a sphere of influence. Atlanta, Georgia, agent Joseph Eterno says his gym was a major source of business when he started. "I was just always around the same group of people, [the gym] community, people that just naturally knew me. And I wasn't trying to be sales-y with them, but they knew the business that I was in from conversations and following up on social media." By focusing on his existing relationships, Joseph closed twenty-one transactions in six months!

New agents are sometimes nervous about reaching out to people they know for lead generation. Crazily, it can seem safer to reach out to a total stranger. We get it, it can feel a little weird. Instead of seeing it as asking your sphere for something, think of it as offering them something. "If people don't know you're in real estate, they can't trust you with a real estate transaction," Jeff Reitzel, a Canadian mortgage broker from Kitchener-Waterloo, Ontario, says. "It's our job to tell everybody in the world that we know or that we meet that we're in real estate." Don't let your fear of being rejected get in the way of your ability to help. "If you're in a great relationship with these people, you're not just lead generating, you're having a conversation with a valued friend and helping them with all their real estate needs," agrees Jimmy Smith, an agent from Louisville, Kentucky. These are your people. It's so much better for them to put their trust in you instead of a random agent they met at an open house! You will take care of them like no one else.

Your initial focus with your SOI will be to let them know that you're in business, rather than asking directly for it. Don't be surprised if they say, "Wow, we were just talking about making the move!" Many younger agents have an SOI of people who aren't yet ready to purchase a home themselves, but that doesn't mean this kind of SOI is without value. An influential way that they can support you and your career is by referring you to people in their network who might need to buy or sell real estate.

The power of your sphere is clear when you go one step further and think about how each person in your sphere has their own sphere. Between your own personal network and the extended web of connections you have through each member, you already have access to tons of potential business. A referral is when someone recommends you to help someone with their real estate needs. This can be to their sibling, co-worker, neighbor, or anyone, really. Most agents eventually want to be in a referral-based business. Leaning on your SOI as a new agent is the best way to get there. According to the 2024 National Association of REALTORS® (NAR) *Member Profile*, 21 percent of agents get most of their business through personal referrals. Referrals, or "warm" leads, have high potential to set appointments. They come with built-in trust.

As you navigate real estate transactions, your network will grow. It will include professionals you work with, vendors like contractors and inspectors, and past clients. As your sphere grows, you'll need to organize those contacts and set up systems to connect with them on a regular basis. We'll cover these systems to keep you top-of-mind with the people in your sphere in Chapter 7.

Prospecting and Marketing

Now that you've identified who you will be lead generating to, let's talk about lead generation itself. More specifically, the two types of activities you can use to generate leads—prospecting and marketing.

Prospecting vs. Marketing: What's the Difference?

Did you or anyone you know have a job mowing lawns as a kid? Maybe you were a dog walker? A sidewalk snow shoveler? The best way to get business was always to go door-to-door in your neighborhood. A giant, braces-laden smile and a better deal than any big business in town meant you'd be revving up that weed eater or leashing up the pups in no time. This is **prospecting**. It's active and direct. You're connecting with leads to ask for business.

Maybe you weren't that kid who liked to get grass stains on their jorts, wrangle pooches, or lose feeling in their toes, but still wanted to make some extra cash. Chances are you had a lemonade stand.

You set up a table with little cups and a pitcher of fresh-squeezed liquid gold. You even got a lunch box to act as a makeshift cash register. Then you hit the neighborhood. You hung up signs that read, "Lemonade 25 cents, this way →" on every post you could find. Finally, you manned your station and waited for the customers to flock. This is **marketing**. Unlike prospecting, marketing is passive and indirect. You take a single action—like creating signs and flyers—that continues to bring leads to you over time.

There are endless options of prospecting and marketing activities that you can choose to implement in your business. Different activities work for different people. In this chapter, we will focus on a few tested activities. They are highly accessible for rookies and will help you get your business running as a new agent.

Prospecting and Marketing Activities ⊛

Prospecting Active and Direct	Both	Marketing Passive and Indirect
Quarterly Calls	Open Houses	Online Advertising
Text Outreach	Seminars	Offline Advertising
Apartment Canvassing	Community Events	Mail/Flyers
Networking	Social Media	Newsletters
Door Knocking	Email	Blogs/Vlogs

Figure 20

Focus Your Lead Generation

To reach your target clients, expand your database and meet your financial goals, you need to use a mix of prospecting and marketing tactics. You'll choose based on your existing skills and preferences to find the right combo. The good thing is you shouldn't, and can't, do all the things. As the saying goes, "A jack-of-all-trades is a master of none," and by spreading yourself thin, you'll burn yourself out. Instead, you should commit to mastering a few tactics. A rule of thumb is to focus on four lead generation methods. Make sure you have at least one prospecting activity and one marketing activity. Some are a mix, which makes things easier. Then, build them into your plan. We call this the Rule of Four.

The Rule of Four works because most agents get the majority of their business from their top four sources of lead generation. The following graph shows that, after your top four, results from other lead generation sources fall off.

The Rule of Four

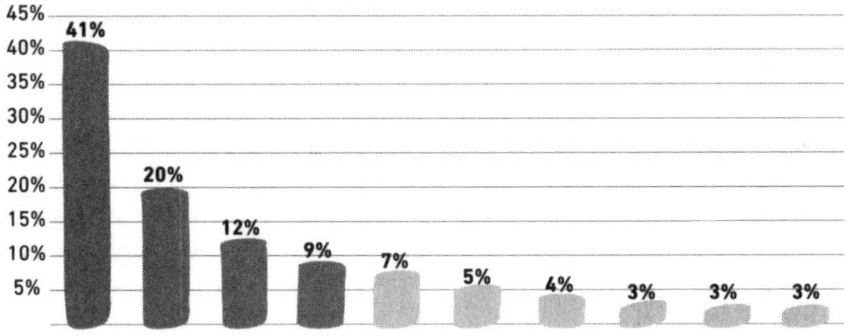

Figure 21

When you stick to the Rule of Four, you'll also be able to track your results more easily. If you find one lead generation method is not serving you over time, you can swap it out for another that catches your eye.

Build a Lead Generation Stack

With the Rule of Four in mind, you can create a lead generation stack. This is a mix of activities to prospect and market your business. Prospecting is usually cheaper and better at converting leads to clients than marketing is. So, we suggest that rookies use a prospecting-based, marketing-enhanced approach to lead generation. This may mean you pick two prospecting techniques, one marketing technique, and one technique that falls in the "both" bucket. However, you may want to adapt this based on your specific circumstances.

When choosing which tactics to focus on, remember that not every strategy is for everyone. You're entering your real estate journey with your own unique set of skills. Maybe you're an excellent designer and create beautiful, eye-catching graphics. Maybe you're tech-savvy and love to create educational videos. Or maybe you're like my sister who "never met a stranger" and build random relationships as effortlessly as a baker kneads dough. (I remember a time when Jan was giving the kid who sold her Slurpees™ rides home from 7/11.) Whatever you feel comfortable with and excited about, lean into that first. Focus on your strengths, but don't be afraid to experiment and try new things as you're getting started. After all, you may learn you like doing things you never thought you would.

1 Time vs. Money

Not every agent starts their journey in the same position. Maybe you're transitioning into real estate but won't go full time as an agent yet. You've been saving money and have a good long runway. In that case, you'll have more money at your disposal than time. Perhaps you're a recent college graduate living off ramen noodles with emptiness on your calendar that haunts you. In that case, you have an abundance of time, but not so much in the cash department.

Generally, prospecting costs less than marketing but takes more of your time. If you already own a cell phone, calling your sphere is no extra cost! Online advertisements, on the other hand, take practically no time but require more of an investment. By matching your priorities to your current resources, you can stay on track and not overextend yourself.

2 Market of the Moment vs. Evergreen Market

Lead generation is vital to your business. So, you must always generate leads. But the specific lead generation stack you choose may depend on the market of the moment.

Following the Great Recession of the late 2000s, The Housing and Economic Recovery Act of 2008 established a limited-time, $7,500 tax credit for first-time home buyers. A savvy agent may have seized on marketing to that market of the moment. They might have posted flyers for first-time home buyer seminars in local coffee shops and on telephone poles. First-time home buyers surged for a couple of years to around 40 percent of all transactions. The good news is that this is also an evergreen market. Historically, about 25 to 30 percent of annual transactions are first-timers.

During that same recession, a lot of homes sold for less than was owed on the mortgage. This is called a "short sale" and it requires some expertise to navigate all the moving parts. This was definitely another market of the moment, but it wasn't for everyone. Some agents chose to specialize in this market while others just referred their clients to them.

At the end of the day, you get to choose based on what is moving in the market, your current skill set, and your comfort level.

3 Enjoyment vs. Work

A lot of agents dread lead generation: there's a reason why we constantly have to remind agents to time block for it each day and get it out of the way early (more on this in Chapter 9)! But lead generating doesn't have to be a chore. One of the benefits of being an agent is the freedom to choose the activities you enjoy and are good at.

Extroverts might love to text or call their sphere ⊗, host events, or film themselves for social media. Introverts might love making market reports with colorful graphs. They might prefer to meet one-on-one or enjoy writing newsletters and crafting educational materials on creative financing. Boston, Massachusetts, agent Ashley Harwood advises matching your approach to your personality. Choose activities that match who you are or ease you out of your comfort zone. Too much friction and agents can fail to act at all. Find a good match and you set the stage for a successful, sustainable career.

Create a plan that fits your lifestyle and personality. It will make work feel less like work and more like a passion project. To help you create that plan, we're going to go over some essential prospecting and marketing activities.

Prospect Like a Pro

At its core, prospecting is about starting conversations with people who could use your guidance. It's about helping them see how you can solve their problems. These conversations may take place online, over the phone 📞, or in person.

There are two ways to generate relationships in this business—you either pay for those relationships with marketing, or you can put yourself out there with prospecting. Prospecting tends to take more time and effort and a little thicker skin than marketing does. You're going to see rejection, a lot of it. But there is usually less cost. Luckily, at this stage of your career, you can use all the practice you can get. Since you've adopted a growth mindset, you know that failure—rejection, in this case—is just another step toward your goals.

Quarterly Calls 📞

The top agents and leaders in the industry agree that making quarterly calls is one of the best lead generation strategies for rookie agents. This is the one tactic that we're going to suggest isn't optional. It would simply be a missed opportunity to neglect it.

Quarterly calls keep you top-of-mind with your SOI and past clients. They help you add new leads to your database when you ask if anyone they know is looking to move or needs to sell their house in a pinch. When we look under the hood of the most successful career agents, we almost always find some version of this tactic. The common refrain from the rest is that they wish they had built the habit in the beginning when their database was smaller and more manageable. We don't want you to have those same regrets.

Calling your entire database every three months requires a plan. Not sure what you'll say once you get someone on the phone? We'll cover conversation frameworks that can guide you in Chapter 8. In Chapter 6, we'll cover a system for organizing your notes on each person's life, anniversaries, and birthdays. This will help you connect with them beyond business.

Door Knocking

Face time is the golden ticket in real estate sales. Talking with people in person has advantages over computer screens and telephone calls. Your tone and nonverbal cues come across clearer and all parties tend to participate more. As a lead gen tactic that literally gets you face-to-face with potential clients, **door knocking** can be a powerful strategy. But we would be remiss if we didn't talk about real challenges that come with it. Knocking on doors takes a lot of time and physical effort. But there's more to it than that. Door knocking, like any activity that puts you in contact with strangers, can be dangerous. We wish we could say everyone will react with respect and at least common decency when someone rings their bell. Realistically, that's not always the case.

Getting out of your comfort zone and doing something that feels dangerous to you are two totally different things. So, here are some tips on how to best door knock if you choose to. But know that there are other ways to prospect and get face time with potential clients if this is unsafe or uncomfortable in your situation.

Before you start door knocking, first check your mindset. Don't spiral about how awkward it may be, or about getting turned away. Focus on the possible positive outcomes. The truth is, you could have an impactful conversation with a future client—and break down your walls while doing so.

Set specific goals and make an action plan before you hit the pavement. Perhaps you have set aside an entire afternoon and decide you won't stop door knocking until you have added ten new contacts to your database. If you're short on time, give yourself an hour. Knock on the doors of every house on a specific street in your neighborhood. You should also plan what you are going to say and think about the impression you want to leave with the people you speak to.

Door-Knocking Safety Toolkit

- **Tell someone what you are doing.** Let a friend, co-worker, or family member know what area you will be in and what your plans are.

- **Keep your phone charged.** Bring a travel charger with you and always have a way of getting in touch with someone. If you can, keep your location on your phone and check in periodically.

- **Check the weather.** Bring sunscreen, an umbrella, a personal fan, and anything you might need to help combat the elements.

- **Go during the day.** Like your mom always said, nothing good happens after dark.

- **Beware of "No Solicitors" signs.** If someone doesn't want you to ring their doorbell, don't.

- **Keep your distance.** After knocking or ringing, take five steps back from the door to remain at a neutral and safe distance. Let them see your feet through the peephole if there is one.

- **Have a friendly disposition.** Attitude is everything. Be friendly even if you are met with irritation.

- **Stay aware.** Trust your gut and keep your eyes and ears open for anything that makes you feel uncomfortable. It's okay to walk away.

- **Take no for an answer.** If someone says they aren't interested, don't be too pushy.

- **Know your exit plan.** Ideally, keep a line of sight to your car at all times. Have your car keys ready or plan another form of a quick exit.

- **Dress professionally.** But don't forget the comfy shoes.

Figure 22

Start Lead Generating and Cultivate Your Database 71

A great way to impress is to show up ready to discuss key market stats. Also, bring printouts of recent neighborhood "solds." Then, once you've started a conversation, be proactive. Collect people's contact info and note when and how you connected. They've allowed you to talk to them on their doorstep. So, don't be a nuisance by showing up to give them the same market report next week.

Texts ⊗

A conversation is a conversation, and texting is certainly a way of connecting in today's world. Texting is less direct than door knocking or calls. It doesn't promise as many true connections. But it's still a great way to reach your database. People often prefer to read and respond to them in their own time. Lots of people let calls go through to voicemail, which they later forget. This can be especially true if you cater to a younger or professional client base.

"Texting is my lead gen method of choice," says Augusta, Georgia, agent Josh Keck. "Part of it is that I'm a bit of an introvert, but part of it is that I've just found that it works better for me.

"Sometimes people don't pick up the phone because they don't know who it is or don't want to do a phone call. And if they missed that phone call, chances are good they won't respond back anytime soon. But if I text—it's sitting there waiting. They're going to get back to me."

Texting helps get your name in people's minds without taking too much time out of your day. Employ the same system you use on your quarterly calls to tackle texts. Or, you can automate a message through your CRM tool as long as you include opt-out instructions. We will discuss CRMs more in Chapter 6.

Agent-to-Agent Outreach

Rookies tend to overlook the symbiotic relationship they can have with other agents. Don't view them simply as competition. Instead, we should have an abundance mindset. Other agents are a key source of referrals. Chances are you'll meet many other agents in your day-to-day business or when attending large events. Get to know them. Exchange stories—along with contact information. Then, don't let that info sit in your phone. Every time you meet an agent, add them to your database. Plus, you can send periodic email blasts to remind agents of your services and great referral fees. And be sure to engage with anyone who reaches out to you, in return.

Master Marketing

Unlike prospecting, marketing is a passive and indirect way of attracting leads to you. It is a way to spread information to the masses about you and your value in order to build your brand awareness. With the internet, it's easier and cheaper to deploy tons of marketing strategies. It also builds your client pipeline. Leads will come to you as long as your marketing runs and people need a real estate agent—which is always!

Because marketing is passive, it may not generate leads as quickly as some prospecting techniques. This is because you're not in active conversation with potential clients, trying to convert them to appointments. Marketing also may cost more money, depending on what route you decide to take. A billboard over the local main street might cost a pretty penny. However, many avenues are free or low cost and allow you to reach a large audience in a short amount of time. As a rookie, use cheap but effective ways to show you are the best new agent in business.

Newsletters

You may find that you have more to say to your potential clients than you can contain in a caption to a picture or video featuring your newest listing. This is where a "link in bio" on your social media pages can come in handy. Here, many agents route their online audience to their newsletter—among other helpful resources.

Creating a newsletter is a solid way to develop your unique value proposition. They are also a great lead generation tool. When someone signs up, they provide contact info for your database.

You can start by doing a monthly market report that will keep people up to date on listings and prices in the area where you work. The monthly market report is the "quarterly call" of marketing. Almost every successful agent does it. As your business grows, you may choose to add a weekly "just listed, just sold" blast. Depending on who your audience is, you can stick with simple content like this. Or, if you get more interested in specifics, you may choose to focus on your niche. You might become the market's "Condo King." Your database relies on you for weekly updates on condo prices, remodeling hacks, and rentals. Whatever way you choose to market yourself, sending out newsletters will help you grow and get your name out.

Not everyone who subscribes and reads our newsletters will want to work with us right away. Some may never work with us. By providing useful info on home buying or selling, you'll be top-of-mind when it matters.

Other common marketing techniques are writing blogs or starting a YouTube channel. Some new agents do targeted direct mail, like "Golden Letters." A Golden Letter is a direct mail piece alerting homeowners that you have buyers looking for homes like theirs. Would they be open to the right offer? All of these marketing techniques can be done on a budget.

Have Your Lead Generation Both Ways: Prospect *and* Market

Two of the most necessary and beneficial lead generation activities you should focus on as a rookie agent are not prospecting *or* marketing. They're prospecting *and* marketing. Gotcha, didn't we? You must learn some key skills to build your database and find motivated buyers and sellers. They draw on both active and passive lead generation methods. Although there are many activities that reside somewhere in the middle, the two you should focus on when starting out are open houses and events.

Open Houses

As a new agent, an **open house** is a way to showcase a listed home to the general public in hopes of attracting motivated buyers. If you don't have a listing, there is a good chance someone in your office does and they'd be happy for you to help them market it. Open houses put you in the path of prospective buyers interested in properties nearby and potential sellers who live nearby and are curious about the competition. They also force you to get to know the inventory of the house's market and will help you gain industry knowledge. To put it simply, sitting open houses is a great way to learn. And, if you don't have a large SOI or database, they are a great way to capture more leads.

Open houses are a classic blend of marketing and prospecting. Holding them requires some planning, and their success relies heavily on marketing. After all, people can't come to an open house unless they know it is happening. At the open house, you can speak to people. The goal is to do business with them now or in the future; that is prospecting.

Open houses are such a key part of your rookie year that we've devoted a whole chapter to them later in this book (Chapter 15). Chances are, you'll be doing a lot of them, so prepare to get comfortable hosting.

Events and Seminars

When people start considering buying or selling property, they often have a ton of questions. As a market expert, you can connect with potential buyers and sellers by hosting events. They want to buy or sell but don't know where to start. Events and seminars put you face-to-face with potential clients and allow you to pour your resources and knowledge into several people at once.

As you learn more about your audience and your market, you will know which events and seminars best serve them. Additionally, as you do more business, you will find out what your specialties are. You may be excellent at finding mortgage hacks when rates are on the rise. Maybe you are amazing at helping people find a vacation home. Lean into these things and build events and seminars around them so you can provide high-value information to leads. These activities can be extremely low cost (people appreciate cookies and coffee just fine if you are giving them a quality experience) and can garner huge results. Focusing on hosting one event and one seminar each month will put you in a great position moving forward. And if you're feeling like a fledgling leading the flock, just remember one of the best ways to learn is to teach.

To generate leads, it's vital to provide quality information. If you work in an area of young professionals or new families, a first-time home buyer seminar could be just what you need. If you're interested in helping seniors downsize, you could host a local event where the first few rounds of Bingo are on you. By connecting with people and addressing their concerns, you will become their go-to agent when they decide to make a move. And leading a seminar positions you as an expert and taps into the built-in trust we have for teachers.

Like open houses, these activities require advertising and outreach. Seminars are more formal and informative. They focus on a specific topic in the home-buying or -selling journey. Events can be anything from a small vendor fair to a gathering at a local brewery. For Philadelphia, Pennsylvania, agent Jim Roche, it's all about fun. "Our Eagles tailgate is one of our biggest events of the year, and we always hear that people want to work with us because they want to get an invite to that."

Either way, the aim is to have people attend who you can add to your database and stay in touch with. Jim agrees, "Events are all about the outreach. I think people get more focused on the actual event, and not what the whole event is about, which is making contacts right and getting in front of them." With the right strategy, any and all of these people can transform into clients over time.

Social Media

Advice for every entrepreneur on the planet: take advantage of the tools around you. Everyone is on social media. Depending on your market, there is probably a platform of choice. Different platforms service different needs and clientele. You also probably have a knack for one social outlet over another. Your strategy will depend on your aim and your skills. But focus on a few things when marketing yourself and prospecting for contacts.

Something to note before you start your marketing portion of lead generating via social media is making sure you aren't chasing people away. Whether you choose to do branding on your personal page or create a separate business page, the main focus should be drawing people in. This may sound obvious, but it can be a bit of a dance when you first start lead generating on social. On the marketing side, if you only posted pictures of your dog, it may turn people off if you suddenly post only houses for sale and branded content. Finding a balance or deciding to keep your pages separate is a question of preference, but keep potential clients in mind.

If you keep your business and personal lives separate from online users, it's important to be approachable and relatable. You're an agent, not a robot. This doesn't mean share your deepest secrets and greatest regrets. But by giving people a glimpse of who you are, what your journey has been like, and other interesting things about you, you are building transparency.

Julianne Carney, an agent out of Memphis, Tennessee, has taken her social media followers with her along her real estate journey from studying for her licensing exam to now announcing her clients' sold homes. She says that people who followed her had confidence in her role as a real estate agent because she proved she had good character before and after getting her license. "Don't be a secret agent," she says. "Put yourself out there and use every opportunity that is given to you."

People do business with people they know, like, and trust. Especially when it comes to dealing with potentially the biggest transaction of their lives. This goes for people you know and don't know. Once you are a market expert, share some personal stuff. Post family photos, recipes, or anything that shows who you are. Showcasing a combination of these things is a great way to build your brand. And putting that brand out onto social media and the internet at large will build brand recognition.

You can run paid ads on some sites to boost your online presence. But social media marketing is usually cheap if you do it yourself. If it turns out that's where your main source of lead conversion is coming from, you may eventually hire someone to help manage your social media. But for your rookie year, running a hard online push with a thoughtful value proposition and targeted audiences can cost virtually nothing and get you up and running.

Another invaluable way to lead generate on social media is by directly communicating with your sphere online. Many use social media to connect more than via calls, texts, emails, or in person. For example, agent Joseph Eterno got his very first job as a listing agent because his wife posted to her social media that he had recently gotten his license. A woman direct messaged her because she knew and trusted their family even though Joseph was a brand-new agent. He sold her house, and six years later, they had to move again. Guess who they worked with.

Use your platform's direct connection feature to reach out to people you know. Tell them you are starting in real estate and can help with any questions they or their contacts have. Offer to give them an updated market analysis on their neighborhood. These reach outs can be better organized through your database plans, which we will talk about in the next chapter.

Social media, no matter the platform or strategy, is an incredible tool in both prospecting and marketing. Marketing yourself in a way that makes people remember you above anyone else will grow the amount of leads you are able to capitalize on. Western Michigan-area agent Margaux Drake ensures that her social posts showcase her value and personality. "I've had people from my sphere message me and say, 'When some people post they are presenting a problem. When I see your posts, I know it's going to be informative, uplifting, and funny.' An exceptional client experience begins with a great first touch." Your goal is to capture and retain the attention of the audience you are targeting. When you can do this, you can build a big business. If the biggest portion of your sphere is in your followers, don't ignore it. Create a system where you can get in touch with your contacts regularly. Using these tools to create brand recognition and talk to your leads at scale will help you get the leads you need. Then, you can set appointments and turn contacts into clients.

Get Ready to Build Your Database

We don't expect you to know which four lead generation activities you want to start doing just yet. By the end of the book, we think you'll have a better idea. In the next two chapters, we will discuss using some of these prospecting and marketing tactics on your leads and contacts in your database. First, we need to start by building that database.

CHAPTER 6

Build and Tend to
Your Database

To imagine your future, we're going to go back to the past. Think of a time when you had to go to a store if you wanted to catch the summer's new romcom or rent the latest slasher film. A place where VHS tapes and DVDs lined the walls, from floor to ceiling. Where life-size cutouts of Hollywood heartthrobs greeted you. A candy station overflowed with every choice imaginable. A place where the only laws were to return your rental on time and to "be kind, rewind."

While Blockbuster Video was a store that relied on physical media to exist, it was an early adopter of using consumer data for marketing. At its peak, the company maintained a database of over 40 million customers. The more than 9,000 Blockbuster stores nationwide fed it daily. Along with names, they collected member preferences as well as their buying and renting habits.

In 1993, the company's executives put their database intel to the test. They knew that many of the kids who frequented their stores would be gifted videogame consoles during the holidays. As any gamer knows, consoles don't come with a lot. And Blockbuster wanted to boost awareness of their broad selection of game rentals. So, they identified every customer in their database with a child and sent them a direct mail promotion. For most direct mail, the industry standard response rate was 2 to 4 percent. The flyers ended up seeing a 30 percent redemption rate! The executives were blown away.

That's the power of making targeted offers through a database.

Blockbuster, like many industry titans, might have flown too close to the sun. As technology advanced (hello, Netflix and Hulu) and local competition grew (uh, wow, people did use RedBox), Blockbuster's mighty hold on the rental industry faltered and fell. As of today, Blockbuster survives as a lone store in Bend, Oregon, and a feisty social media account. There are lots of lessons here, but the one we're focused on now is the power of building and tending to your database.

Built right, your database will allow you to reach the right people with the right message at the right time. Not only does this yield outsized success, it also avoids reaching the wrong people with the wrong message at the wrong time. We all get that junk, and no one likes it. Hotelier Conrad Hilton was famous for noting all his guests' preferences. It was not uncommon for regular guests to find their favorite flowers in their hotel rooms. People are telling us what they love every day. You order coffee together on Fridays. But how confident would you be to order for them when they are running late? Was it Splenda or sugar they liked? Two percent or oat milk? Your database allows you to capture the details of people's lives from birthdays and anniversaries to the names of their children and fur babies. Relationships can be reinforced on small, significant remembrances. Show others that you see them and know them. The "devil" is in the details and the details live in your database.

In the last chapter, we covered the basics of prospecting, marketing, and building your lead generation stack. This chapter is all about building and tending your database. To keep the garden metaphor working here, you'll choose a container to store your database in (a CRM), learn what to plant first (your SOI with the right contact fields), and how to tend to it (segmenting and tagging for efficiency).

First, let's review the fundamentals of a database and why it's vital for a successful real estate business.

What a Database Is and Why It's Vital for Success

When I got my first job, every professional had a Rolodex® on their desk. A Rolodex was the original way to organize your business contacts. The brand name is a portmanteau. Just as "motel" comes from "motor" and "hotel," Rolodex is a combination of "rolling" and "index." And those drab wheels of typed contact cards adorned desks world-wide from the 1950s to the early 2000s. The brainchild of Brooklyn inventor Arnold Neustadter, Rolodex is the precursor to the modern database.

If you wanted to sync your contacts back then, you had to type up a duplicate contact card. Today, we can sync our contacts across all our devices in a blink.

Your database is the container where you will organize your leads and contacts and collect all the details of your interactions with them, their lives, and their preferences. While you could go retro and outfit your new enterprise with an analog system like my old Rolodex, most new agents start with their contacts on their phone, their email, a spreadsheet, or a CRM system. "I lost out on a lot of business because I lost a lot of pieces of paper," confessed Asheville, North Carolina, agent Molly de Mattos. She eventually upgraded to a CRM and, today, Molly has such solid systems that she coaches others to database success. We encourage you to *start* with a great foundation and use a CRM.

A CRM is designed to collect all the needed information about your potential clients. It can also tell you when and why to reach out or follow up. Many include ways to automate the timing of your outreach and break your contacts into groups (segmenting and tagging). Just like with Blockbuster, tags and segments will make sure you're having the right conversations with the right people at the right time. Finally, as your business grows, CRMs are built for scale. Having a few hundred contacts on your phone or spreadsheet is one thing, it's quite another when you have thousands to sort through.

"He who counts on his memory has a fool for a filing system," says business author Harvey Mackay. We agree. Even the most social among us can't mentally track hundreds of relationships effectively. You can blame biology for these limitations. British anthropologist Robin Dunbar theorized that people can maintain effective social relationships with only about 150 individuals at a time. Today, that limit is known as Dunbar's Number. As you build your real estate database, you'll routinely add three to four times Dunbar's Number to your database annually. Your CRM will help you capture and keep track of them!

If you start with a CRM, not only will it help you overcome natural limitations, but it will also save you a lot of time! No more crumpled sticky notes. Say goodbye to adding calendar reminders for birthdays and anniversaries. Mailing labels and personalized newsletters will take a fraction of your time! Your database will help you get the most out of your time and the contacts you have.

"Connecting with" Your Leads and Contacts

In Chapter 5, you learned about leads and contacts. Both leads and contacts go into your database. Even if you have just a name and address, you need to input this information and keep track of it.

A database is useful because it administers touches to your leads and contacts. By "touching" your database, hopefully they will move from leads to contacts, contacts to appointments, appointments to agreements, and so on. A **touch** is a point of communication—one-way or two-way—between you and a lead or contact. When you stay consistent with your touches, you will be able to cultivate relationships with people in whatever stage of a real estate transaction they are in. By keeping an up-to-date database that you feed regularly, you can build touch plans and campaigns that will allow you to systematically reach out to the right people at the right time with the right information.

The point is, once you have organized your leads and contacts in your database, you can ultimately leverage your database to build relationships and generate new, repeat, and referral business. You do this by staying in contact, developing a connection, and delivering value.

Your database can also help you escape the "Today Trap." When we look at US housing research conducted by NAR, we note two key home-buying stats. First, on average, about 65 percent of households own their own home. Second, people tend to buy and sell about every ten years. That means that for the people in your database, only 6 or 7 percent will be buying or selling in any given year. When agents don't have a system for nurturing large numbers of leads over time to get consistent business, they are left searching for the proverbial needle-in-the-haystack buyer or seller. They're chasing "today" business to pay their bills and stay afloat. This is what David Huffaker, an agent from Mount Juliet, Tennessee, calls the "Today Trap."

In 2016, David attended a real estate training event where he realized, "If I don't figure out how to work a database successfully, I'm going to have to work as hard as I did that year every year for the next forty years." He came to the conclusion that there are two types of business: today's and tomorrow's. He had been wasting time chasing "today" business, transactions he could close in the immediate future. Instead, he should have been setting up a database that would help to naturally develop a business pipeline and grow "tomorrow" business. When David came home, he decided to get serious about his database.

The way out, as David discovered, is through your database. We sometimes refer to tomorrow business as **nurtures**. These are prospective clients who aren't interested in buying or selling today but do have a timeline in mind. Maybe they are waiting for their last child to go off to college. Maybe they need to save up for a downpayment or shore up their credit rating. Nurtures represent tomorrow business. They often have a defined action plan. For the couple waiting for a high school senior to go to college, you can set up a follow-up plan to stay top-of-mind with calls, texts, and emails between now and then. For the buyers saving up or shoring up, you can create appropriate follow-up plans and connect them to the right mortgage and credit professionals. You'll *nurture* them through the process, respecting their priorities and timelines. When you do this at scale, there will always be nurtures reaching the finish line each month, creating a steady flow of business for you.

Home Buying Over a Lifetime

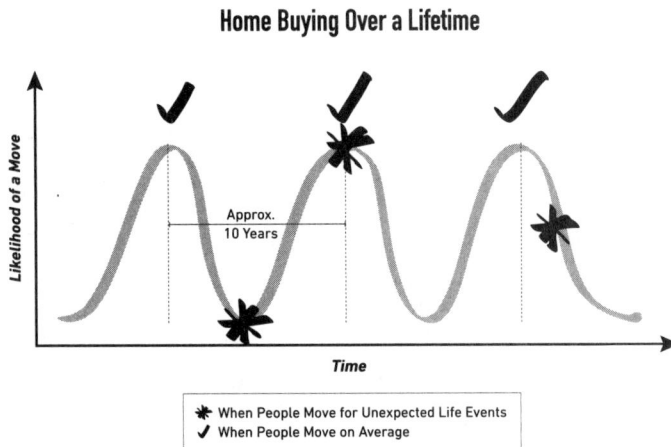

Figure 23

Life-altering events that can cause someone to move are not always easy to see. They can come out of nowhere. Events like having babies, getting deployed, or divorcing may prompt people to buy or sell. Andy Peters, an agent out of Atlanta, Georgia, says we can use national averages to help set a standard, but we can't always predict when people will move. It may be way sooner or later. "If we think of people's interest in real estate, it goes up and down. There are peaks and valleys," Andy says. "The peaks are where people are most interested in buying real estate, and the valleys are where they are least interested. We've got to make deposits in people's lives all through those valleys so we can capitalize on those peaks. We always have to be pouring into people." Your database helps you remain someone's agent of choice through the peaks and valleys.

Working your database is playing the long game to harvest both today's, and tomorrow's business. Over time, your sphere and past clients will refer you new business and your past clients will become repeat business. This is how database-driven businesses can grow rapidly over time.

In the next figure, you can see the relationship between the number of contacts added to Keller Williams's proprietary CRM system, Command®, and the GCI earned by agents. It also indirectly reflects time in the business. The longer you are in the business, the more contacts you will add to your database.

GCI in Relation to Contacts in Agent's CRM (Command)

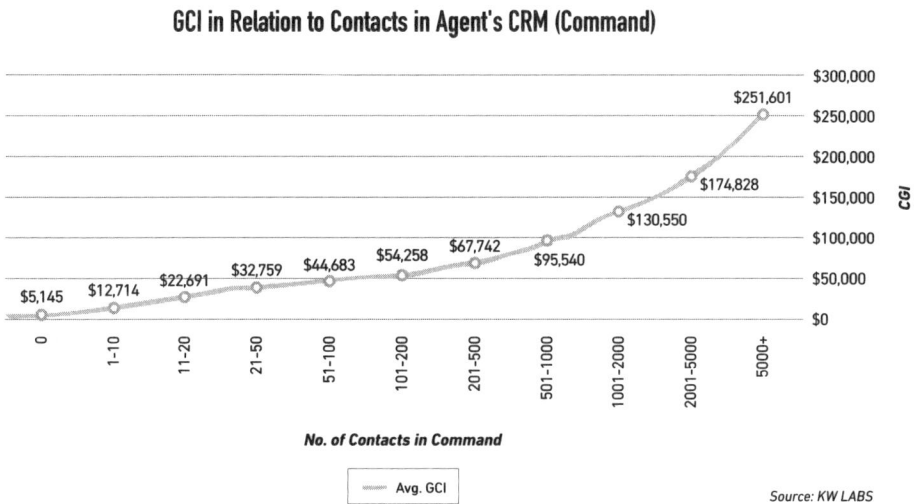

Figure 24

Our research on thousands of agents using Command shows that building and working your database with consistent habits can directly impact your GCI. At the start, there appears to be a direct, linear correlation between the number of contacts agents have in Command and their GCI. Then, when they amass 201 or more contacts in their database, their GCI takes off and grows exponentially. So, we can reason that your database goal should be at least 201 people. That's a little above average, but it's definitely doable. The average number of social media followers or friends someone has online is 338. That's already more than the inflection point in Command. You can also see that if your net income goal is over six figures, you'll need to aim for over 500 contacts. This data reflects more than just having numbers in a database. Agents whose GCI is growing along with their contact numbers are also taking action and staying in touch.

Build Your Database

Now that you know why starting with a database is so important, it's time to start building yours. There are two parts to building your database: picking your container and filling it. This means choosing which database platform to go with and what contacts and information to add to it.

When you start to build your database, think about your goals. Remember the math we did back in Chapter 3? To earn $100,000 a year, work backward from your average transaction commission/fee. This will show how many appointments, agreements, and closings you need to hit your income goals. The first milestone in the Economic Model is appointments. When you get the right number of leads and contacts in your database and then connect with them appropriately, that appointments milestone becomes far more predictable.

Your need to add new leads and contacts into your database is somewhat dependent on your current situation. If you have hundreds of connections from a past job or have a massive SOI, you may not need to work as hard to add new leads. The important thing is to take stock of what you have so you can build an appropriate plan to hit your goal.

Pick Your Container—Select Your Database Platform

As we've noted, all database platforms aren't all created equal. You can launch your business working leads and contacts in an analog system, on your phone, through your email, in a spreadsheet, or with a CRM. We recommend starting where most successful agents end up—with a CRM. That said, ultimately, the best database for you is the one you actually use.

Many an agent has built a spreadsheet that would make an Excel programmer blush with pride, only to abandon it for faster, easier tools on the fly. The same can be said for CRMs. An agent might invest big bucks in the latest enterprise software before getting bogged down in the complexity of the many options they offer before quitting. The goal is to start with a system that balances speed, budget, and ease of use with the ability to scale with your growing business.

The Speed and Scalability of Database Platforms

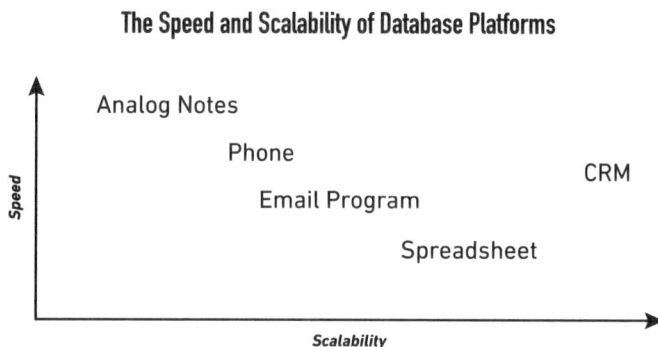

Figure 25

While I can't name a single agent who still uses an analog address book, note-cards, or a Rolodex for business, I'm sure they're out there. Both my brother-in-law and my late father-in-law clung to their flip phones until their carriers simply stopped supporting them. There is a kind of John Henry-esque valor in such commitment. But if you remember that old folktale of John Henry and the steam engine, it doesn't end well for John Henry. On a long enough timeline, technology wins. Jotting down handwritten notes is undeniably simple and fast, but this approach simply doesn't scale.

Phone and email programs are similarly fast. There's a close to 99 percent probability that you currently maintain all your personal and professional contacts in one or both. You've probably added lots of notes over the years, like birthdays and anniversaries. Email programs like Gmail and Outlook hold an edge in scalability. They can be accessed and updated via your phone or computer and offer lots of add-ons for mail merges, calendar reminders, and the like. The challenge is they weren't designed for a sales career. They won't give you a nudge to follow up with that soon-to-be empty nester without some extra work on your part. They don't automate touches. So, the tagging and segmenting features are rudimentary at best.

You could also import your phone or email contact list into a spreadsheet. This allows you to add unlimited tags, to segment and sort, and include whatever details you can imagine. But, unless you want to learn some programming, you can't sync reminders to your calendars or automate anything. I've seen it a hundred times. These database spreadsheets can quickly become as powerful and unwieldy as Thanos's Infinity Gauntlet. You may soon wish you could snap your fingers and make it disappear.

That's why it makes the most sense to start with a CRM or move there as soon as it's in your budget. While it will require you to learn a new piece of software, virtually all CRMs will sync to your phone, email contacts, and your calendar to create one seamless database system. A CRM makes it especially easy to keep up with every person in your database. With a CRM, you can create templates for emails and touch plans, assign them to contacts, and schedule them to be sent out automatically. It is a one-stop shop for storing information, scheduling outreach, organization, communication, branding, and, ultimately, business building. The key is to start with a simple sales CRM. Even with those, you won't need to set up every bell and whistle on day one. We'll walk you through a streamlined, start-up approach to your CRM in the following pages.

No matter which database you choose, we beg you to at least pick one! If not, you may find yourself dealing with a lot of potential business slipping out of your hands. "My database was on sticky notes, napkins, and notebooks and new leads were always coming in," says agent Mimi Bond. Once she was able to "organize all the chaos" into a CRM, her business became easier to run and she was able to close more transactions. Dozens of other agents had similar stories. So don't just take it from us—highly successful agents either credit their success to building a database and working it from the start, or regret time wasted with sticky notes and spreadsheets.

Fill Your Container—Add to Your Database Over Time

Once you pick your container, you need to fill it. When adding to your database, a good place to start is with your SOI. Remember, your SOI is all the people you already know and who know you—your dentist, your kids' teachers, co-workers, neighbors, friends, and family. Most email and phone contact systems have an export feature. Export all your contacts, select all the people you have in your SOI, and import them into your database of choice. It's also a good time to do some pruning, which we'll cover in a bit.

After you add your SOI, you have to continue feeding your database in order for your business to grow. How? Through lead generation. As you generate leads through prospecting and marketing, you will get new names and contact information to add to your database. We'll cover automating habits and systems for adding to your database in more depth in Chapter 7. Still, we want to instill this philosophy with you now.

If you have a small SOI, a good habit to build is adding two people to your database each weekday, or ten a week. Practicing this habit adds up to 520 new people in your database every year. Take that Dunbar! Be sure to segment them and tag them appropriately as you enter them. It's easy to say you'll do it later, but we both know how that goes. We procrastinate and delay until the task becomes so daunting we can't even start. Just like when moving, the best time to unpack those boxes is now. Otherwise, your database may start to look like your guest bedroom with boxes that date back to your college dorm room. Tag and segment as you go!

What Information Do You Need to Collect?

Before you can work your database or create campaigns, you need to collect essential information for each lead and contact. Without this information, you won't be able to connect with anyone, much less enter into two-way conversations.

Essential Information for a Database

1. Name

2. Cellphone number

3. Email

4. Address

5. Notes:
   - Wants and needs
   - Important dates
   - Price point
   - Pre-approval status
   - Misc.

The list in the preceding figure is in order of importance. You want to collect names first so that you can be personal and professional with your leads right off the bat. A cellphone number is often the preferred way to contact someone, once you've received permission. Email is almost as important as it allows you to share market reports, send calendar invites, and more. Next, an address allows you to do a home valuation, share a neighborhood trends report, or send a birthday or holiday card. These first four qualify as essential items to collect. The other key fields become more important as leads become contacts and nurtures.

Your CRM will likely have dozens of built-in contact fields that you don't have information for yet. Don't worry about immediately collecting all this detail the moment you meet someone new. After all, you might sound odd if you start asking a relative stranger about their spouse's birthday! Instead, make it your long-term goal to fill out this information. As you go, note what they share about their life, where they are in the home-buying or selling journey, and other information that will help you grow your relationship. These personal details help you build rapport and better serve your clients' needs.

Tend to Your Database

Remember when we compared tending to your database to tending to a garden? Tending to a garden is all about watering, making sure the plants get enough fertilizer and light, weeding, and pruning your bushes. Essentially, it means maintaining and caring for your garden. When it comes to tending to your database, the same is true. It means continuously adding to your database over time, segmenting and tagging, and making sure information is updated and accurate.

Segment and Tag Your Database

Would you talk to the cashier at your grocery store the same way you would talk to your sister? Probably not. How about your neighbor and your college roommate? Your boss and your dog walker? Didn't think so. The same goes with all the people in your database. Although they are all stored in the same container, they do not all have the same relationship with you. It doesn't serve you to communicate with them all the same way or in the same cadence. Some people in your database (leads), may not even know you well or that you're in real estate. That's why you need to correctly organize and categorize people within your database. It's gardening 101.

Segmenting Levels in a Database

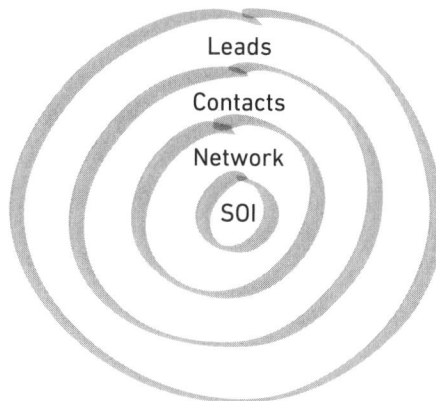

Figure 26

Figure 26 shows different levels of people who will exist in your database. These are **segments**. At the core is your SOI, the people who won't think twice about doing business with you or referring you to their own SOI. Then there's your network—people you know but aren't necessarily in your close sphere. There are contacts, who know you and who've given permission to stay in touch about real estate, and leads, who you are working to get permission to have those conversations with. This is basic database makeup. Within all these levels are people who have different interests, wants, needs, and personal ties to you. You can use these differences to create specific, informed, high-quality, and effective communication.

Since we are assuming you're using a CRM or are quickly on your way to one, let's talk tagging. **Tags** are labels that you add to contacts that allow you to sort them into different buckets. The tags you use will help organize your database, activities, and messaging. It's one thing to touch your database regularly. But providing valuable information to the right people at the right time will help your business go the extra mile. By segmenting and tagging people appropriately, you can become deliberate and personal with your approaches, resulting in more steady and ready business.

Popular Database Tags for Rookies

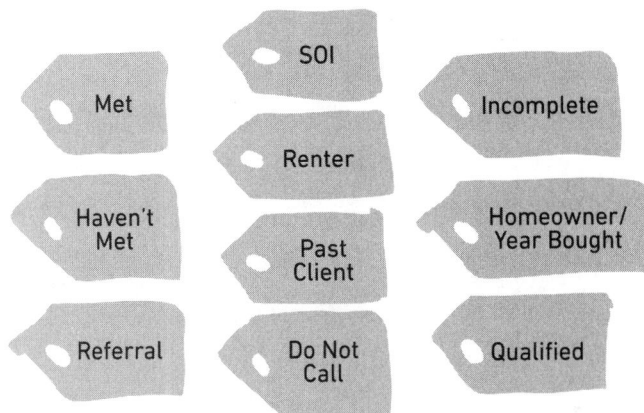

SOI

Met

Incomplete

Renter

Haven't Met

Past Client

Homeowner/ Year Bought

Referral

Do Not Call

Qualified

Figure 27

Tags can really be anything. They can start as simply as people you have "Met" and people you "Haven't Met." They can be a "Homeowner" or a "Renter." Tagging can start simple. It can become more complex once you've found your real estate niche, be it a geographic area or demographic. One important tag to consider when building your database is "Incomplete," meaning a contact that has blanks in important fields. Tagging someone as incomplete can help you track the work you need to do on your database and remind you to spread the love beyond your usual favorites.

Other tags can include whether people are past clients or referral contacts, if they are qualified leads (have been approved for a mortgage loan) or unqualified and need direction, or anything that will help define when and how to connect with each person. If you're an avid player in your local pickleball league, you can create a tag for that group. Maybe you're leaning into your spiritual community; you can add tags for your church or synagogue as well. Just don't overdo things. There is a tipping point where tags become overwhelming.

Here's how segments and tags might work together. If you wanted to alert your database to a first-time home buyer seminar you're hosting, you'd obviously want to start by filtering for your "renter" tag. For your SOI, Network, and Contact segments, you could create an email focusing on the details of the seminar and what they will learn. For renters in your Leads segment, you'd need to add almost as much detail about you, the host they have yet to truly connect with. Then you might send to your SOI homeowners asking if they know any young professionals or couples who might want to attend. With a well-tended database, you just created awareness for your event with three different groups in appropriate ways. The right message to the right people at the right time!

These tags and segments will be integral to building out campaigns. Sorting people into these buckets lets you send customized mass messaging. As your database grows, the tags you use may change or evolve, which is another part of tending to your database.

Maintain

Part of tending to your database is ensuring that the information within it is well-maintained. This means it's up to date and accurate, properly filled in, and isn't overflowing with unfruitful leads. These three areas are non-negotiables when it comes to keeping your database in the best shape for your business.

The Three Non-Negotiables for Database Maintenance

1. Update information and check for accuracy
2. Fill in the gaps
3. Purge

1 Update Information and Check for Accuracy

While you'll be adding new leads and contacts to your database consistently, don't forget to make updates for people who have been in it for some time. People's lives change constantly. Someone who was unmarried or living alone before might now be engaged and ready to start a family. Another person could have recently gone through a divorce and is now looking to downsize. Leads will turn into contacts as you continue your prospecting and marketing strategies. The point is the people in your database evolve and you want your database to keep up with them. A database is only as good as it is accurate.

As you tend to your database, also make it a habit to check whether people who are already in your database have been added to the DNC list. You can access this list at Telemarketing.DoNotCall.gov but be aware that the list is updated monthly, so build a habit to sync your database with an updated version of the list at least every 31 days. Simply tagging them as such will help you stay in compliance with the law. When we get permission to hold two-way conversations with people over the phone, you can remove the tag, but only then.

Just like the people in your database are likely to change, so is your business! Hopefully you start off strong by appropriately segmenting and tagging every lead you add to your database. But, over time, the way you use these tools will likely change as you adopt new strategies to cater to your market. As your tags and segments change, make sure to update each lead with your new system—otherwise it won't work.

2 Re-engage and Fill in the Gaps 🔍

Chances are there are people in your database who you haven't heard from in a while or have missing information for. These are great opportunities to connect, fill in any gaps, and see if people still want to hear from you. A re-engagement campaign would be a series of calls, texts, and emails with the purpose of getting someone to re-engage with you. As Atlanta, Georgia, agent Letrissa Frieson explains, "My rule is I have my [database tagged] as a 'jersey wearer' or a 'benchwarmer,' and my 'jersey wearers' are getting in the game."

As you engage with your contacts, build the habit of glancing at their contact card before or during the call. This will allow you to spot missing information and ask for it. Social media also helps. People tend to post about big occasions like anniversaries, birthdays, and promotions. These posts should all be "stop the scroll" moments for you, where you pause and update their contact card with the new info.

3 Purge

A **purge** is a way to clean up your database and should probably be done every six months. It's inevitable that some people won't want you to contact them anymore. They will unsubscribe from your newsletter and won't return your messages. That's business. But what about the people who haven't done any of these things and are just sitting idly in your database? It's possible these leads already feel spammed by your emails or other attempts at contacting them, they just haven't said so. Maybe their information isn't correct. If a lead is unresponsive for a long time, then it may be time to purge.

Think of purging your database as weeding your garden. A purge includes people who haven't connected with you or opened your emails. Reaching out to people who don't want to hear from us can harm our business. Weeding out these individuals is best for the sake of the other thriving flora. It means we're giving our resources to relationships that we can cultivate. The last thing we want to do is put effort where it doesn't belong and fail to be effective where it matters. This doesn't mean you shouldn't be persistent with those who aren't ready to do business with you. It's nuanced, so stay vigilant when purging.

Optimize Your Time with a Virtual Assistant

If you find early success as an agent, there are parts of working your database that you can get help with. We urge you to do this only with earned income, a solid plan, and a budget. It's important to hold off on hiring before you've earned the right to.

After you set rules to tend to your database, you have the option of hiring a virtual assistant to tend to these day-to-day tasks for you. This will allow you to spend more time generating leads and working with clients. Bringing on a virtual assistant is not a one-size-fits-all solution. What works for some agents might not work for others. As you become more comfortable managing your business, think about what you want your business to be and do. Where is it heading? This will help you decide when to hire and who to take on board as you and your business grow.

Make Tending a Habit

You'll have to tend to your database consistently so that you get the most out of it. Regular maintenance, along with adding to your database over time, will keep it running smoothly.

You've built your database, added to it, and will continue to add to it. You've made a maintenance plan to keep it in good shape. Now, it's time to really work it so that it can work for you. This will be done through automating systems that will allow you to touch the right people at the right time with the right information. Read all about that in the next chapter as you finish the database CTA plan and reap the fruits of your labor.

When you know what's working and what's not, you can make better business decisions.

CHAPTER 7

Automate and Work Your Database

Gerald Stratford is the one of the world's biggest gardeners. We mean that literally. Gerald grows record-breaking, enormous vegetables. This mild-mannered British retiree grows carrots that are over three feet long, zucchini over eighty pounds, and pumpkins, one reaching 150 pounds. From his small garden in Nottinghamshire, Gerald regularly sets Guinness World Records with his "big veg." How does he do it? He works his garden, paying attention to which plants are giving him the best results, and then he cultivates the next season from the cream of the crop. Gerald is a man with a plan, a plan for gargantuan veggies.

Now that you've built your database, it's time to roll up your sleeves and work it. To get the most out of it, be like Gerald and create a plan. Just as you wouldn't scatter seeds in your garden without caring about the sunlight or shade, you'll work your database purposefully.

In this chapter, we'll discuss how to put your lead generation tactics into action with your database. We'll cover touch plans, campaigns to focus your efforts, and automation to help your business scale.

Discover Touch Plans and Campaigns

It's highly possible that another agent along your real estate journey has given you a copy of *The Millionaire Real Estate Agent*. If you read it, you've heard of a 36 Touch or a 12 Direct. These are famous touch plans that help you prospect and market to your database. **Touch plans** are systematic and automated touches based on a potential client's needs and the value you can offer them. The 36 Touch and 12 Direct are broad, annual touch plans intended to cultivate your Mets and Haven't Mets. Both will be OG staples in your database arsenal.

If you're focusing on more short-term strategies, you'll be using campaigns. **Campaigns** are strategic plans of action usually focused on a single idea, event, or goal. They are usually oriented toward getting a segment of your database to take a particular action. You can have a campaign within a touch plan, if the touch plan is big enough.

"When I think of campaigns," says Champaign, Illinois, agent Ashley Miller, "I think of intense activity for a specific period. You can have generalized touch plans that are going on year-round, but if you're looking to create a specific campaign, that's a little like politics, right? There's a certain season where there's a lot of activity looking for a specific result. Our lead generation campaigns should be the same thing."

Your touch plans and campaigns will vary based on your database's segments and tags. They will differ in communication, frequency, and content. But the important thing when you're doing either is being intentional. Touch plans and campaigns work best if you think them through.

Master the 36 Touch Plan

To help explain how touch plans and campaigns can take your lead generation from average to outstanding, let's make a 36 Touch Plan. This plan uses thirty-six touches, or outreach attempts, over the course of a year. The point is to try to interact with each person in your database that many times. A 36 Touch is about cultivating your contacts, people with whom you have already connected and know you're in real estate. You've had the "talk." Many choose to narrow it even further to their SOI, past clients, and anyone who sends them referrals.

A 36 Touch Plan Template

Quarterly Calls	IIII
Personal Cards and Notes	IIII
4 x 4 Events or Giveaways	JHT JHT JHT I
Monthly Newsletter	JHT JHT II

Figure 28

Thirty-six touches may seem like a lot of moving parts at first glance. You're actually layering different touch plans and campaigns to staircase your way to the goal of thirty-six touches. You can start with the first step, and when you feel you've got it in place, climb up to the next one. You'll note in Figure 28 that the quarterly call is the first step. Our research shows that if you could only run one database touch plan, this should be it. It's just that effective.

Next, we have personal cards and notes. This could include holiday cards, birthday and anniversary cards, or maybe a "homeaversary" note for past clients. Events and giveaways take a little more planning, so you can add them later. The monthly newsletter will likely be the last to complete. You can knock out one each month or pre-write a few if you're so inclined. Next year should be that much easier when you have twelve months of experience!

So, take heart and take heed. It's time to walk through how you can plan out your 36 Touch.

Quarterly Call Plan (Four Touches)

The first layer of your 36 Touch is the most important: your quarterly calls. For that, we suggest using the DTD2 quarterly call system.

Imagine you've got 200 people in your database you want to call each quarter. Now you do the math. Since there are thirteen weeks in a quarter, that means calling about fifteen people a week or about two each workday. Totally doable!

Start by dividing your database into thirteen groups, one for each week of the quarter. A helpful tool for dividing up groups is to call "two letters" of your database each week. This is where the DTD2 name comes from. How convenient that there are twenty-six letters in the alphabet! San Antonio, Texas, agent Steve Schlueter organizes his list by pairing up last name initials in a particular order. Looking at Figure 29, it may just seem like a clever pairing of familiar letters (A&W like the root beer, B&E from your favorite crime show, or the P&L for your business). Schlueter says he created it this way for another reason. Last names aren't evenly distributed. Do you know anyone whose last name begins with X? Some weeks, like winter holidays, you'll want to be lighter than others. These pairings ensure a more even spread of calls throughout the quarter with a lighter load toward the end when you may be wanting to take some days off or plan for the next quarter.

The DTD2 Quarterly Call System

Q1

Week:	Call:	Text:
1	A&W	N
2	B&E	S
3	D&O	P
4	H&V	T
5	C&K	I
6	F&G	Y
7	M&X	X
8	N&R	A
9	S&U	B
10	P&L	D
11	T&J	H
12	I&Q	C
13	Y&Z	F

Q2

Week:	Call:	Text:
1	A&W	R
2	B&E	U
3	D&O	L
4	H&V	J
5	C&K	Q
6	F&G	Z
7	M&X	W
8	N&R	E
9	S&U	O
10	P&L	V
11	T&J	K
12	I&Q	G
13	Y&Z	M

Q3

Week:	Call:	Text:
1	A&W	N
2	B&E	S
3	D&O	P
4	H&V	T
5	C&K	I
6	F&G	Y
7	M&X	X
8	N&R	A
9	S&U	B
10	P&L	D
11	T&J	H
12	I&Q	C
13	Y&Z	F

Q4

Week:	Call:	Text:
1	A&W	R
2	B&E	U
3	D&O	L
4	H&V	J
5	C&K	Q
6	F&G	Z
7	M&X	W
8	N&R	E
9	S&U	O
10	P&L	V
11	T&J	K
12	I&Q	G
13	Y&Z	M

Source: Ops Boss Coaching/Steve Schlueter

Figure 29

You'll be touching each person in your database four times over the course of the year. Not only is this a critical component of your lead generation strategy, it's also a crucial part of maintaining great relationships! Plus, if you're worried about what to talk about, the other components of your 36 Touch have you covered ("Did I mention we have a family movie night coming up next month?") "Each touch should feel like it leads organically to the next one," agent Ashley Miller says. "If you're reaching out to your database to do a quarterly call, then ask them if they've read your monthly newsletter."

An added bonus to quarterly calls is that they naturally yield lots of information to fill in gaps in your database. The simple question, "How are things?" can lead to conversations about aging parents, growing kids, upcoming graduations, and milestone birthdays and anniversaries. Because you're committed to building great database habits from day one, take five minutes after each call to update your contacts with new knowledge to enrich the relationship.

Personal Cards and Notes (Four Touches)

Among my mother's many superpowers is her ability to have a birthday card be delivered on your actual birthday. She could also hear conspiring teenagers through multiple closed doors and spot stains on a dress shirt from a thousand yards. But that's not the point. She always championed the handwritten thank-you note, thoughtful holiday cards, and never forgetting a loved one's birthday or anniversary. In a digital era, don't underestimate how impactful physical correspondence can be. It simply stands out.

That's why our basic 36 Touch includes four personal cards or notes. You probably already have a holiday card list. That's one touch. Secure your contacts' birthdays from social media or a quarterly call and you're halfway there. The other two are entirely up to you. Each month, you can sort your database by birthday, anniversary, "homeaversary," or whatever you choose. I'm a fan of gratitude notes. A gratitude note just lets folks you know you enjoyed seeing them at an event, chatting with them on the phone, or simply that they are a part of your life. You can also leverage social. When it's time to write someone in your 36 Touch, scroll through their social feed and see if something doesn't pop up. Maybe their youngest just started kindergarten or their oldest ran a personal record at the cross-country race. Like gratitude notes, these "thinking of you" notes stand out in a special way. The odds are close to zero that anyone else reached out with a note for that particular reason.

One final note on notes. While I'm a fan of the handwritten variety, text messages and email work, too. Just avoid the generic. The goal is to stand out. Every year, my wife and I reach out to our friend Amy on the anniversary of her birthday when we met twenty-seven years ago. We wish her a happy birthday and thank her again for being the reason we met. Boom! Gratitude and birthday wishes in one note!

Event and Giveaway Campaigns (Sixteen Touches)

The next steps in your 36 Touch are events and giveaways. You may choose four events or four giveaways or any combination of the two. That's up to you and your 36 Touch plan. We'll tackle events first since they each require a different approach.

Hate sounding sales-y? Events are a great way to connect with your database and generate business by offering a fun experience. For each event, you'll be doing outreach to your database before and after, and you'll be able to rack up high-value touches each time. While your mileage may vary depending on your messaging, these are the basic touches for an event campaign:

Essential Event Touches

1 Save the date

2 Day before the event reminder

3 Day of the event reminder

4 Thanks for coming/Sorry we missed you

Pay particular attention to number four. Many agents swear that the touches after the event have the greatest success. This makes sense when you think about a "thanks for coming" touch being a follow up to a face-to-face convo. You've probably talked about something at your event and can revisit whether you think the Patriots or Cowboys are really America's team. A "Sorry we missed you" is also pretty powerful. Seth Godin in his TED Talk about his book *Tribes* rightly asserted, "Do you know what people want more than anything? They want to be missed. They want to be missed the day they don't show up. They want to be missed when they're gone." People may be busy and unable to come to your shindig, but they will always remember that you missed seeing them.

Our Keller Williams Realty International team hosts hundreds of events each year, from our annual conventions with tens of thousands of attendees to local in-person trainings with dozens. I am very clear that I will never be an event planner. But when we say events, forget about convention centers and keynotes, and think more along the lines of parties, get-togethers, or small classes. When my wife Wendy was starting out, she wanted to work with investors. We hosted "Millionaire Meals" at our home for a dozen or so friends. They were potlucks. She'd also host "Millionaire Mochas" at a local coffee shop or "Millionaire Margaritas" at the neighborhood TexMex. Small events can be done inexpensively and don't require an event planner's expertise. You can also host classes online with tools like Zoom or Google Meet.

Text at Scale with Text Replacement

During Covid, my wife used this hack to quickly create a ton of lead generation energy for her business. She could send fifty-plus text messages to her sphere in less than an hour. Over the course of the day, recipients would text or call her back. Done right, it's a powerful form of reverse-prospecting. Getting the right message to your sphere will make your phone ring (or, in this case, vibrate).

So what does text replacement mean? When you type "TY" in a text message your phone will autocorrect it to "thank you." We're going to leverage that feature to autofill your entire conversation. In the settings of your smart phone, you can create a custom text replacement for any message you want to send.

1. Write up your message.
2. Copy and paste it into a new text replacement in your phone's settings.
3. Create the shortcut that will prompt the autofill.
4. Use the shortcut to text your list.
5. Follow up with the replies.

I recommend including an unusual character (like #SeminarInvite) so the shortcut isn't triggered accidentally. Once you've got it set, you're off to the races!

We've seen other new agents host first-time home buyer classes (and the like) at local breweries on a slow night, their brokerage office after hours, or at an area community center. As your business ramps up or your network expands, you can consider bigger events like movie nights, pie days, and pumpkin patches. Let your ambition grow with your experience and your income. So, as you are planning, here are a few examples of events held by highly successful agents to get your creative juices flowing:

1. Holidays

Sometimes, an event can be as simple as offering something for free as a token of appreciation. It keeps you top-of-mind, shows that you care about your clients, and is a great way to get referrals.

Many agents put on a "Pie Day" event each Thanksgiving. They reach out to their database and offer a free pie for anyone who wants to come pick one up. It's good to ask for RSVPs. This lets you buy the right number of pies. In general, about 10 percent will not show up. You can drop one off the next day if you end up short. If you have extras, you can give them away. Our college-aged son loves when we have extras! Remember the goal of your event: to connect with your sphere. As you hand out pies, ask your contacts what they're up to, wish them a happy holiday, and ask if you can help them or someone they know with a real estate need. Pie days done well can generate oodles of referrals.

As your business continues, annual events around Independence Day, Thanksgiving, or Christmas can come to be traditions that your database looks forward to every year. This kind of reputation builds invaluable connection and loyalty. While it requires an investment, the return is usually worth it. When you plan your year of lead generation through a 36 Touch, you can plot these campaigns on a calendar. Then, share your favorite holidays with your database.

2. Movie Screenings

In many cities, local movie theaters will let you to rent an auditorium for private screenings. Agent Kelly Henderson out of Phoenix, Arizona, says she rents out an auditorium that seats about a hundred people for $1,000! The theater staff will take care of most logistics, giving you more time to worry about mingling with your attendees. While not everyone can come to a brewery or wine bar because they have young children, Kelly says theaters are a family-friendly event venue. Always be mindful of who is in your database to ensure a great turnout and happy clients.

3. Micro-Events and One-on-Ones

After a certain amount of time, your database will recognize you as the real estate market expert that you are. But they may not be ready to ask you questions about real estate because they aren't planning on buying or selling a property soon. So, how do you offer a low-pressure way for them to ask those questions without them feeling like they're booking an appointment? Many of Wendy's "Millionaire Mochas" turned into one-on-one advice sessions around wealth building through real estate. Wendy will tell you that hosting these events has cemented her reputation as an agent with a *latte* of knowledge (dad joke for the win).

4. Seminars and Learning Events

Don't have the time for one-on-ones or simply want to scale learning opportunities? That's what seminars and other educational events are for. Hosting a seminar for first-time home buyers or a class on the basics of real estate investing can educate your database and reveal who is ready for your services.

As you set up your classes, don't forget to ensure that people provide their contact information when they register. If someone has a question during your class, tell them that you'll reach out afterward with a personalized answer. Even if they no-show, you can circle back with them and make sure they know you can help them.

Some agents record their seminars and have them available on demand. If you go this route, we still urge you to collect registration info. Then, follow up to make sure that you create a personal connection with your potential client.

Giveaways (Four Touches+)

After events, you can consider adding giveaways to your 36 Touch. A giveaway campaign is a great way to get your name out in the community, add to your database, and gain future clients. As with open houses, a single giveaway can generate multiple touches. They are a powerful component of your 36 Touch. Additionally, if done right, you can even get your database to do a lot of the marketing lift for you.

An example of this is a giveaway campaign by Atlanta, Georgia, agent Lesley Peters, which she called "Ready for a YETI®?" The premise of the campaign was to give a free YETI cooler to a lucky winner and gain referrals and brand recognition in the process. First, Lesley's team sent out a free koozie to everyone in her database. The koozie was printed with her business information and directions for entering the giveaway. "Our goal with all mailers is to send something that will outlast a piece of mail," she says. "Nicely printed party invitations sent out a month in advance will remain on their cork board or refrigerator. An SEC football schedule they can keep up all fall also does the trick." Then, she sent her database into a frenzy by coordinating her mailer with social media promotion. Her followers spread the word about her business by taking selfies with their koozies and using the #readyforayeti hashtag, in hopes of winning the cooler. All summer, Lesley's team sent out reminders via postcards and emails. At the end, they announced a lucky winner.

As you plan your giveaway, here are basic touches you can build into your campaign:

Essential Giveaway Touches

1. Piece of mail or email with giveaway instructions
2. Confirmation of entry
3. Reminder: Final day to enter and win
4. Announcement of the winner/ Thanks for participating

A good giveaway campaign is a brilliant way to create a buzz. Lesley built her plan around a YETI, but we've seen successful giveaway campaigns around less expensive items, like a monthly $20 gas card giveaway. You don't have to break the bank. You can also focus on popular items that are hard to come by. If you camped out to get your niece a coveted Stanley Cup for her birthday, go ahead and buy two. One of my co-workers reserves tables at prized restaurants many months out. If he and his wife can't use them, he sends out a message to his SOI offering to transfer the reservation.

A giveaway done right makes your phone ring or blows up your texts or email inbox. People reach out to you because they want what you're offering. The magic happens when you turn those inquiries into real estate conversations.

Monthly Newsletter (Twelve Touches)

You can hit a large portion of your database through newsletters. When you're building out your 36 Touch, plan to send a newsletter out each month. The monthly newsletter is basically a modern version of the classic 12 Direct. Back in the day, agents printed and mailed them. You still can, but email newsletters are easier on your budget, seem to be preferred by clients, offer you rich data on open rates and click-throughs, and, heck, they save paper.

Not sure what to write about? Morehead City, North Carolina, agent Mary Cheatham King is the queen of content creation. She advises that if you're overwhelmed by too many topics, create "buckets" for your content. For example, you could pick listings, market updates, a community spotlight, and information about you or your team. Each newsletter would have content that falls under each bucket, making it easier to be consistent in your message and execution. Mary Cheatham's team sends their emails every Thursday at 6 p.m. to their list of over 22,000 subscribers using their content strategy and free design websites. It's remarkably inexpensive for a strategy with such enormous reach.

Don't forget, even if we're marketing for our business, in the end the story isn't about us. "I think agents forget sometimes that you need to market yourself as a fiduciary, a guide. You aren't the hero of the story," Mary Cheatham says. "Your clients are."

Because our clients are the main characters, we can't forget to allow people to opt out of our newsletter so that we avoid spamming them.

Automate Habits and Systems to Scale Your Database

It's easy for us to tell you to cultivate and tend to your database. But actually doing these activities, and doing so effectively, is a whole different story. You'll need habits and systems. Bear with us while we share one final garden metaphor—even if you *might* feel uprooted when they're gone!

A novice gardener can raise beautiful, thriving plants with little to no practice. If they read up on botany, gather the right materials, and care for their plants, they may have a successful harvest. The difference between a hobbyist and a professional farmer is scale. A hobbyist is doing it for fun (and fresh food), while the professional has to earn a living. Guess which kind of database gardener you are? That's right. You're a pro.

A professional farmer cultivates crops with a timed irrigation system. A gardener uses a watering can. A farmer has tractors to help them sow acres of seeds.

A gardener has a hoe and a dream. What we're saying is the professional here not only levels up their techniques, but they also employ automated systems and tools. Likewise, you need to automate habits and systems for your database if you want to take it to professional grade.

Drip Campaigns

So, you've learned that a campaign is a focused touch plan that is used to cultivate relationships and future business with the contacts in your database. If most campaigns are short-term and focused on a goal, then drip campaigns are specifically designed to turn unmet leads into contacts. We call them **drip campaigns** because they send information to a lead based on the action they take from your CTA. A drip campaign can only realistically be done using automation.

For instance, let's say you include a CTA in your monthly newsletter like, "Are you interested in seeing what homes are selling for in your neighborhood?" You could just reply to everyone who says yes, or you could use your CRM to create a trigger that puts every "yes" on a drip campaign. The CRM would tag them appropriately and subscribe them to receive "Just Listed/Just Sold" data for their zip code each month.

Example Drip Campaign

Are you interested in seeing the value of your home?

Yes   No   No Reply

✔ Have them fill out address info.

✔ Send the most recent market update for neighborhood automatically.

✔ Subscribe them to future calls, market reports, newsletters. 📞

Figure 30

Building out these follow-up systems will take time, but once those systems are built, they allow you to do less task work in the future. Saratoga Springs, New York, agent Christine Marchesiello says that being intentional about systems is what made her business strong. "We have a system behind everything we do," she says. "People think that it's overwhelming to systematize and that they lose a sense of freedom with it. But it's actually very freeing to systematize your business and database. It's a teeny bit of work up front, and then it's bulletproof and runs itself after you set it up." Eventually, your database will be working for you. You can build your drip campaigns so that they collect information and funnel people into the right buckets. This will ensure you're providing them with immediate value for engaging with you.

Re-Engagement Campaigns

No matter how well you structure your touch plans and campaigns, there will always be some people in your database that will appear non-reactive. They don't respond to your emails and never come to events. If you find yourself wondering if these are real people or zombies, don't panic!

The first thing to understand about the silent people in your database is that just because they aren't engaging doesn't mean they aren't getting any value out of what you're sending them. Don't worry if it seems like no one is listening. People can reach out after years of radio silence. They'll get your monthly market updates. They see what you're posting. They're aware that you're out there still working and, when they need you, they'll show up. Silence isn't always absence, it's just means that it's not yet time for them to act.

We helped my high school guidance counselor, Betty Copeland, buy a home in Austin to be closer to her kids and grandkids. Ten years later, we helped her sell it. She let us know how much she appreciated all the invitations we'd sent her over the years. "The timing just never worked," she said. She hadn't responded for ten years but called us when it was time to list her home.

The second thing to know about the colder leads in your database is that they may not be engaging because you haven't offered them the right value. Or they don't believe that you are paying attention. Either way, before you purge someone from your database, you should try to re-engage them.

Re-engagement campaigns don't have to be complex. You can simply send an email that asks if the person is still interested in hearing from you. If not, you'll unsubscribe them to spare their inbox. All your emails will offer the chance for recipients to unsubscribe. A re-engagement campaign should also have a link to re-subscribe. That's the goal. If they get around to reading that "Is this the end?" email months later, but actually do want to hear from you, they can re-engage with a simple click.

Track Your Results to Stay on Top of Your Game

Every activity you need to do as a rookie agent—and a veteran agent, for that matter—is informed by your conversion rates.

As we discussed in Chapter 3, conversion rates track your success in converting leads to appointments, appointments to agreements, and agreements to closings. You will use campaigns to cultivate your database and move clients down your pipeline, so you should track how effective your touches are. What activities are producing the best outcomes? What kind of information and types of touches are people reacting to most? Knowing this will allow you to create strong database campaigns. It may take you a while to figure out exactly which strategies are working and at what rate they are converting. As you get more comfortable doing business, you will develop better strategies that fit your market and business plan. But it's still important to track your numbers from the beginning. When you know what's working and what's not, you can make better business decisions.

A CRM can track this information for you. If you have a virtual assistant that tends to your database regularly, they could also keep track of these statistics and rates for you. But it's up to you to study them and come up with plans to get your business where it needs to be.

If you've built your database and practiced your CTA plan, but aren't tracking your results, even your best efforts may not get you to your goals. We want you to work smarter, not harder. Tracking your database results is crucial to your success. You need to know:

1. How many contacts to import weekly.
2. Your email open rate.
3. Your lead-to-client conversion rate from campaigns.

Knowing your results is not just a good business practice, it's the only way you can reach your net income goals. And if something's not working, you may simply need to change the way you're speaking to potential clients. And you're in luck! We happen to know the best ways to spark conversation, keep people engaged, and convert them to clients. And we're talking about it in the next chapter.

CHAPTER 8

Practice Role Play and Conversations

Knowing what to say, how to say it, and when to say it is vital to a successful sales career. Almost everyone agrees on this point, but most people misunderstand *why* conversations and role play are so important. Many over-index on memorizing "scripts" like they imbue salespeople with Jedi-like powers. We have two challenges to that thinking. First, conversations are living things, and memorization won't get you far. Second, our job isn't to persuade or, worse, manipulate. Our job is to educate our clients so they can make great decisions.

Practicing conversations builds experience with having technical, emotional, and strategic conversations with clients. That practice yields confidence. Forget Jedi mind tricks: Confidence is the real magic! Great salespeople focus more on frameworks and phrases. Frameworks are like scaffolding—they guide us through conversations so we can ask the right questions and convey the correct answers without skipping anything important. If memorization plays a part, it's often around key phrases and questions that serve to move conversations forward, allay common fears or misunderstandings, and to bring precision and accuracy to our counsel.

You will hold conversations to help explain the complex home-buying and home-selling processes to first-timers who may feel lost or unsure of where to start. You will use them to walk buyers and sellers through the complex process of closing a sale. And you will use them in consultations to better understand your clients and their needs. That's why it's so important for us to know what to say, how to say it, and when to say it so that we are always providing the best service and advice for our clients.

Maybe the biggest benefit of role playing conversations is that when we're confident we know what to say, we can give all our attention to listening.

Conversing Is Listening

At least half of any conversation is listening. It's a reciprocal exchange. Alabaster, Alabama, agent Danielle Turner says impactful conversations are all about being present. "Tell your story and let them tell theirs. Real estate agents love to talk. But you have to listen, let them make their own decisions, and let them know that you're there to support that decision," she says. As much as our conversation frameworks are about knowing what to say, a crucial tool for you to leverage is not speaking at all. Listen and learn.

Sales vs. Service

At the start of your real estate journey, you may feel like an imposter as you ask for business. The truth is that sales and service are just two sides of the same coin; they don't have to be in opposition. But, if you focus on service, you won't feel bad about asking for business. Snellville, Georgia, agent Danny Emmett takes customer service very seriously, which is how he gets his clients to keep coming back. "I used to think about commissions all the time when I first started," Danny says. "But really, it's all about service from the word 'go.' I ask people about their hobbies, their favorite flower, their favorite sports team. I get them whatever vendor they're looking for. Service is how you build lasting client relationships."

Some conversations will happen organically. But there are also plenty of muscles you can exercise to get comfortable talking with people. You can strengthen your "conversation muscle" by practicing frameworks with other agents. Frameworks and role playing will help you know your stuff so you can focus on listening and learning. It's all about knowing what to say and how to say it. Before we get to the practice portion, let's walk through conversation frameworks that are vital to your business.

Master Conversation Frameworks

Many buyers and sellers have similar hesitations and questions. That's why agents use frameworks to address common problems and similar situations. Just like solid foundations create long-lasting houses, frameworks offer a base on which to build a strong real estate career. Though **conversation frameworks** have guidelines, they can be easily tweaked to fit a client's situation. There are many different frameworks, and the ones you should focus on are the ones that are vital to your lead generation plan.

Vital Conversation Frameworks

1 FORD

2 LPMAMA

3 Feel, Felt, Found

The frameworks we are discussing can be used in various situations and at each point of conversion throughout the client journey. Based on your lead generation and outreach, you can use these conversation frameworks to help move buyers and sellers along the path from appointments to contract-to-close. In Chapters 11 and 12, we will talk more about the buyer and seller consultations, where you will use frameworks to help address your client's wants, needs, and fears.

These three vital frameworks may be classics, but they are not the only frameworks out there. You can probably find a conversation framework for the most specific circumstance if you look hard enough. However, these three areas will come up a lot in your career: uncovering people's wants and needs, qualifying leads, and educating people around misconceptions in real estate.

1 FORD

FORD stands for Family, Occupation, Recreation, and Dreams—the foundational things in people's lives. When we put them into a real estate context, they can help us solve people's problems. By running through FORD, you can uncover what truly matters to someone as they look to buy or sell.

The FORD conversation framework is like a multi-use tool in your pocket. It is handy in all kinds of situations. As an agent, you can use FORD to fill in your database. It can help you form new relationships and learn what people are motivated by. It can also help you reconnect with clients throughout the transaction and at any moments of truth. Richardson, Texas, agent Heather Kobs says while real estate is always the main point of any conversation she has, she wants to build relationships that are personal and not just transactional. "We have other things to talk about when I get to know them on a personal level," she says. "Real estate is the hook. That's their association with me. But I want to know their kids' names, I want to know where they're from, I want to know what brought them to Texas or why they want the house. So, for me, it's a lot more than just a transaction; they let me into all parts of their lives." By diving a level deeper, Heather can build relationships with her clients that help them know she is focused on their needs.

The FORD framework builds trust and connection. The topics are universal, so you can bring them up in almost any situation and people will relate.

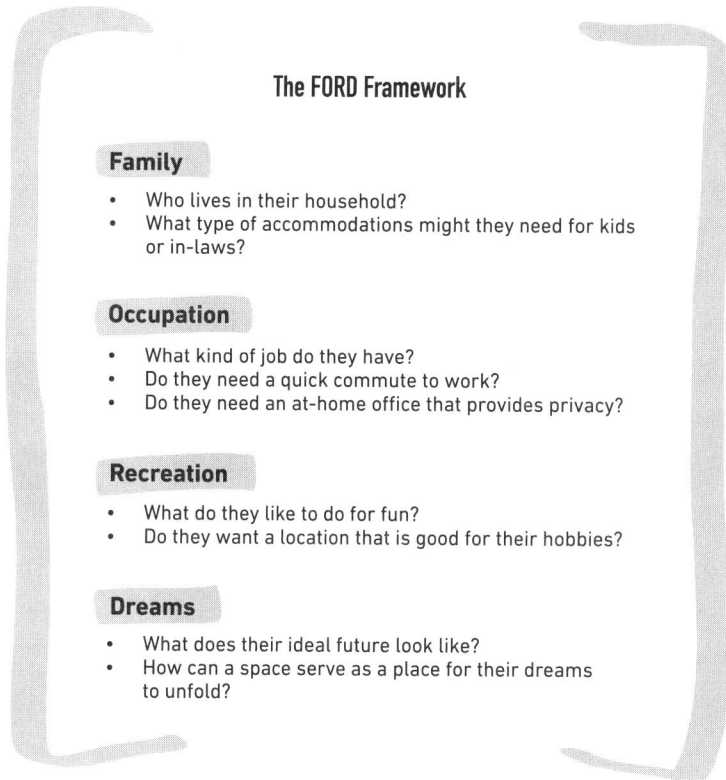

The FORD Framework

Family

- Who lives in their household?
- What type of accommodations might they need for kids or in-laws?

Occupation

- What kind of job do they have?
- Do they need a quick commute to work?
- Do they need an at-home office that provides privacy?

Recreation

- What do they like to do for fun?
- Do they want a location that is good for their hobbies?

Dreams

- What does their ideal future look like?
- How can a space serve as a place for their dreams to unfold?

Figure 31

Family

Learning about someone's family is crucial to helping them with real estate choices. *Who* they live with is one of the main things that affects *the kind of home they choose.* But beyond what's happening in someone's life right now, it's also good to learn about what might happen later. A client might be moving in with a partner, but do they plan on having kids or will their elderly parents move in down the line? Each would require more space and different accommodations. When you ask about family, you learn about someone on a personal level, which will inform how you serve their real estate needs.

If you're going to ask about family, be mindful that it can be a sensitive topic. And families are not all the same. Some are community, not biological. Some are complex and require thoughtful solutions. And some people may not consider family an important part of their decision-making. Knowing where someone stands with family will help you be a better fiduciary for them in the long run.

Occupation

Someone's occupation can bring up both personal and business-related questions and concerns when buying or selling a home. A career takes a lot of time and energy. It may be a passion, a way to earn money, or both. Questions about occupation are also questions about values, long-term goals, and what someone might need out of their home.

Finding a place for someone to live that helps them do the work they need to do is part of your job. If your client is the CEO of a tech company, they might need a large home office. Or perhaps they commute and don't need or want the extra space but want to live close to work. Is your client up for a promotion or looking into relocation? Asking questions about their circumstances will get you the information you need to best help.

Recreation

If a buyer is passionate about cooking and meal preparation, they probably want a chef's kitchen. Or maybe your client is a powder hound who drools at the thought of living close to the slopes. With information about what your client likes to do for fun, you can strive to match their home to their heart.

Knowing someone's hobbies and interests will help you interact with them before and after a transaction. Perhaps you just added someone new to your database and they tell you that each year they plan a vacation around visiting a winery in a different state. What a coincidence! You already put on a quarterly event for your sphere at a local wine bar. Why not add them to your event invite list? They're sure to appreciate the personalized attention. Or, if someone loves hiking and the outdoors, you can point them to a newsletter in your archives where you've listed the best trails in town. Recreation creates common ground, allowing you to speak someone's language and take the focus off sales.

Dreams

Potentially the most personal and informative of the FORD framework is the final letter: D, which stands for dreams. You may not start a conversation talking with someone about their dreams. But, when you do eventually hear about them, they're a treasure trove of information. They affect and are affected by someone's family, occupation, and recreation.

Asking people about their dreams is the best way to gauge their future. Dreams are about long-term goals and visions. People need homes they can grow into. They also need areas that support their personal, professional, and recreational pursuits. Some people dream about a growing family. Others might pine for a place where they can foster pups. Discussing dreams helps solidify your connections with people. It gives you a deeper look into who they are and what they want. Green Bay, Wisconsin, agent Alex Young reminds us, "There are emotions and people behind every single decision in real estate. So the faster you can understand that and the faster you can learn to connect with people there, the more successful you'll be."

When using the FORD framework, remember to share as well. Simply powering through the questions can feel one-sided, and no one welcomes an interrogation. As your clients open up to you, you can respond in kind. Keep track of the important stuff in your database as you go. If you gather all this information and it doesn't go anywhere, it does you no good. Burlingame, California, agent Caroline Huo keeps the mantra "show me you know me" close to heart with her clients. She always keeps track of what she learns about the people she serves. She uses those insights to inform her future conversations and touches. It shows she listens to her clients and cares about their lives.

2 LPMAMA

If you are using the **LPMAMA** conversation framework, someone has shown interest in working with you to purchase a home. However, you may not know if working with them is worth the full investment of your time just yet. LPMAMA can get you those answers.

LPMAMA (said like LP-mama) is not the latest record store. It's an acronym for Location, Price, Motivation, Agent, Mortgage, and Appointment. These are ultimately the nitty-gritty details for someone looking to purchase a home. LPMAMA helps identify promising leads. It does this by asking questions based around those six topics. (And while all together it works for potential buyers, broken into parts, it can be used for sellers as well!).

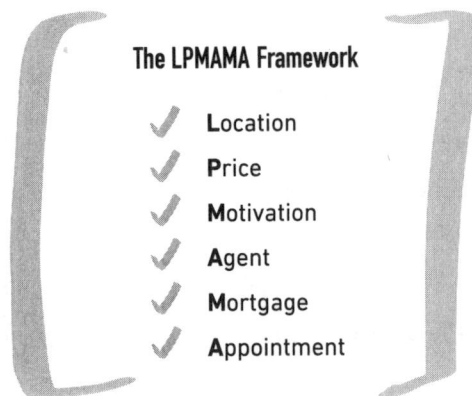

The LPMAMA Framework

✓ **L**ocation
✓ **P**rice
✓ **M**otivation
✓ **A**gent
✓ **M**ortgage
✓ **A**ppointment

Figure 32

Location

"Location, location, location!" We say it three times in a row because it's *that* big of a deal. Place is one of the main things people consider when searching for a home. But the question, "Where do you want to live?" might be too big. You may have to start by asking smaller-scale questions like, "What type of neighborhood are you looking for?" or, "Does school district matter?" If a client still doesn't know these answers, chances are they know what they *don't* want. They *don't* want a noisy highway nearby. They *don't* want to live in the middle of nowhere. They *don't* like that their current home is in a busy neighborhood. Sometimes, knowing what they don't want is just as informative as knowing what they *do*.

Price

Warren Buffett once said the home he bought for $31,500 in 1958 is the third-best investment he ever made (only behind his two wedding rings). But the Oracle of Omaha also warns that "a house can be a nightmare if the buyer's eyes are bigger than [their] wallet." As your client's fiduciary, your job begins with knowing their budget so you can find a house that fits their financial circumstances.

Motivation

The FORD framework showed that people's motivations are key to setting expectations and fulfilling needs. Everyone who moves is motivated to do so for a reason. Whether it's to downsize, upsize, relocate, or invest in a first home, use the keywords "why" and "when" to unlock the details of their circumstances. Understanding motivation and urgency will help you set expectations and create a plan of action.

Agent

Although this letter comes fourth in the acronym, you might want to address it first. Ask your potential client if they already have an agent.

If they don't have an agent, you can ask what they are looking for in an agent and discuss your value proposition.

If someone is working with an agent, you can ask if they have signed an agreement to work with them. If not, they can choose to sign one with you. If yes, you can still follow up and see how their purchase went. Some clients fire their agents, and others are ghosted by them after the transaction. If you're playing the long game, you can stay in touch and be ready when they need your help.

Mortgage

Finding out whether someone has been pre-approved for a mortgage loan can help you identify who is truly ready to do business with you. Pre-approved buyers have taken a legitimate step toward homeownership. This shows that they're not only serious but also motivated to start their home-buying adventure.

If a buyer has not been pre-approved for a mortgage, but is serious about starting their home search, you can guide them in the right direction. Part of your value proposition is who you know. Getting them in touch with a lender is a good way to get them on track to an appointment. You can ask whether they've been approved or not, about their savings for a downpayment and what they feel they can afford for a monthly payment. Talking about money is not always fun, or comfortable, or natural. But, ultimately, home buying and home selling are financial transactions. You'll need to be aware of someone's money situation if you are going to work with them.

Appointment

The second A and final letter in LPMAMA stands for appointment. Now that you've qualified a client, you can pursue the real goal of this frame-work—to set an appointment that results in a signed representation agreement. If they are ready to go ahead and sign you as an agent without an appointment, that's even better! If they seem unsure about signing with you or are hesitant about anything, let them know that you can go over any questions with them at an appointment. After all, appointments exist so that you can address any concerns they may have and set expectations for the transaction process.

If someone still isn't ready for an appointment after you practice LPMAMA, that doesn't mean they aren't potential business. Add them to your database and sign them up for nurture campaigns you have for potential clients. An Austin, Texas, agent on Wendy's and my team, Warren McEnulty, once followed up with a lead for six years. For the last two, all of his outreach was met with silence. He got no replies to his texts, emails, voicemails, and invites to pie days and events. 😣 Toward the end of the year, he reached out to wish them well and ask if they might be ready to start looking for a home in the new year. The silence was broken. They replied back and were ready to meet. Warren shared, "Remember, other people are busy. It's our job to follow up, not theirs!"

Staying top-of-mind is the best way to get business with people who can't seem to commit in the moment. Either way, you've started a solid relationship with someone. You now know where they are at both personally and on their home-buying journey.

3 Feel, Felt, Found

The **Feel, Felt, Found** conversation framework is best used to educate someone who has a misconception about real estate. It allows you to talk with them in an emotionally intelligent way.

The three parts of the Feel, Felt, Found conversation framework are in the name. First, you want your client to know that you have listened to them and understand how they *feel*. Then you want them to know that other people have *felt* the same way they have. Finally, you tell them what others have *found* when presented with the right perspective or solution.

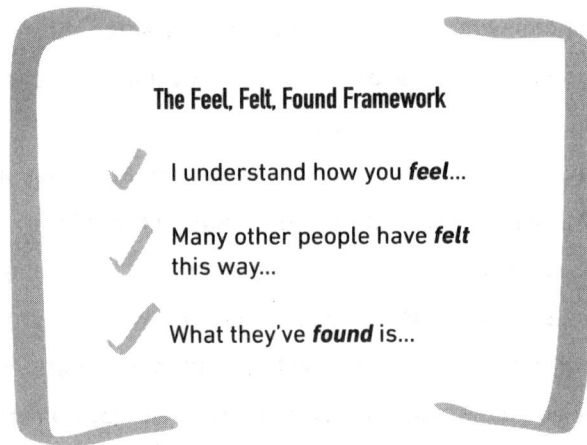

The Feel, Felt, Found Framework

✓ I understand how you **feel**...

✓ Many other people have **felt** this way...

✓ What they've **found** is...

Figure 33

Buyers and sellers will likely have different objections while you work with them. Whatever someone's objections may be, to move past them, you need to understand where they are coming from. Feel, Felt, Found can help.

Potential clients often feel like they are getting the runaround when talking with salespeople. Like no one is considering their needs. They may fear that an agent simply wants to get their business and land a check. By using Feel, Felt, Found, you can actively listen to your client's concerns and address them accordingly.

Now, as you're working with this framework, remember to be honest about what you can do for your clients and keep your integrity. But if you can meet their wants and needs and allay their fears, this type of conversation framework often makes people feel ready to move forward. At the end of the day, people want to work with someone who has their best interests in mind. Be that team player.

Practice Makes Personalized

Having purposeful conversations with potential clients is like flexing a muscle. And the best way to strengthen that muscle is repetition. We know that sounds simple, and that's because it is. Remember, simple and easy are not the same thing.

Take WNBA rookie Caitlin Clark. As of 2024, she is the highest scoring NCAA Division 1 basketball player of all time. This includes men's and women's records. In 139 games played for the University of Iowa, she scored 3,951 points. She did not achieve this feat by showing up to games cold, having taken no practice shots. Famously, Caitlin takes 300 shots at every practice in the off-season. One hundred three-pointers (her specialty is a long-range three from the logo), one hundred free throws, and one hundred midrange shots. And this is in the off-season. As a rookie professional, she broke the record for assists with 337 and scored the most points by a guard in WNBA history. Practice paid off. It's no wonder she earned WNBA Rookie of the Year honors.

When we practice, we grow and can achieve what we want to achieve. As real estate agents, when we know what we want to say and how we want to say it, we become confident and we can have constructive conversations with people.

Conversation frameworks will help you build connections with potential clients. But the thing is, they aren't necessarily effective if you are reading someone questions off a list and filling in answers as you go. They need to feel natural. The conversations you have will provide you with information on how to best do business. If you aren't practiced enough, you may go into them feeling too self-conscious or unprepared and miss all the good stuff. If you don't remember what to say, you'll be too focused on what question comes next to truly listen to someone's answer, which is where the gold is! By practicing these conversation frameworks, you can get to a point where they flow naturally, and then you can use them effectively.

Role Play and Real Experience

We don't need a bunch of bells and whistles to practice, or role play, conversations. All we need is a few partners who are willing to sit down with us or answer the phone or respond to our texts. Tim Bilbo, an agent out of Raleigh, North Carolina, says he and the agents he works with will randomly call each other and say, "Hey, I'd like to sell you a house." They practice common buyer and seller scenarios as well as topics that they haven't come across in real life so they can prepare for what might pop up in transactions. "We just want that familiarity of answering that stranger's call or being that stranger on the other line. It helps us better communicate when we do get those calls," Tim says. "If we run into something we haven't seen before, we talk about it in our group text. And then we review and work together to see how we can answer things correctly."

New agents should take a page out of Tim's book. Take turns switching roles and conversation frameworks until you get so comfortable with any hesitations that you can pivot, explain, educate, and guide with no problem. You'll probably end up having answers to the wildest objections because of all your practice. The goal is to listen to the other person, learn about their issues, build confidence in your own skills, and then take the right actions, as illustrated in the following figure.

Role Play Your Way to Growth

5 Action

4 Confidence

3 Learning

2 Listening

1 Practice

Figure 34

The best real estate agents in the world role play and practice throughout their careers. It's what keeps them at the top of their game. When you practice your conversation frameworks, you'll be able to focus on both the business and the personal.

Practicing leads to personalization. In the beginning, you have to memorize the frameworks or consult your notes. After a while, you internalize the basics and can bring your own flair and personality to the conversations. As you gain experience, practicing that is what makes a real difference.

Make Practice a Habit

A real estate transaction has many conversion points. These moments are where the transaction is at its most vulnerable. That's when you can look to conversation frameworks like these to help you navigate these conversations. Some frameworks are better suited for the beginning of a relationship, others for when trying to get an appointment or getting a transaction to close. Over the course of your career, you'll likely be collecting the best conversation frameworks to add to your toolbox.

You will be glad you know these frameworks when you enter a buyer or seller consultation. But you need to be purposeful about building habits that serve your success. If you role play and practice your conversations once in a blue moon, you're not going to be prepared to make hay when the sun shines. In the next chapter, we're focusing on creating the habits that will be the cornerstones of your career.

The best of the best not only set big goals and design big plans, but they also allow themselves to be held accountable to them.

CHAPTER 9

Build Success Habits

Starting a career in real estate probably isn't like any job you've had before. You likely won't arrive on a Monday morning, trusty travel mug in hand, to start onboarding with the HR team. You wake up, get ready for work, open your laptop, and, voila, you're at the office! You're your own boss. Now, you have a choice. You can lose yourself in the freedom and flexibility that being an agent offers or you can build your career on a schedule for success. We recommend the latter.

Like any new work opportunity, it takes time to ramp up and get truly busy. Those early weeks are actually your opportunity to practice living the schedule of a highly successful agent. Live it long enough and it becomes routine. Not in a boring, robotic way, but rather in the sense that your natural reflex is to move from the right thing to the right thing. The alternative is to pinball through your days reacting to random texts, emails, and invites. Sure, there will be periods of chaos when you have to juggle three closings, Jenga appointments with prospective clients in between, and race over to the Underhills' soon-to-be home to see if the laundry hookups are gas or electric.

A real estate agent often is asked to do a bit of everything. Time is not necessarily on our side, but it is possible to find order in the chaos. Developing habits today will prepare you to navigate those days with clarity and purpose. While it takes a while for habits to gel, the good news is, once established, habits work *for you*.

One of the best ways to tame the chaos is to schedule the stuff that matters. Over time, you'll want to build habits around lead generation, role play, database management, your finances, and your education. It's okay that you don't have established routines in any of these areas today. The point is to put them on your schedule. Depending on the activity, you'll schedule daily, weekly, monthly, quarterly, and annual check-ins. What I'm describing is what we call "time blocking." Think of it as making appointments with yourself to do your most important work. It's simple and surprisingly effective. Research suggests that the simple act of scheduling an activity makes you about three times more likely to do it. That's why the first habit you should add to your arsenal is time blocking.

Time Blocking

In Tolkien's *The Lord of the Rings*, Sauron created one ring to rule them all. The habit equivalent to the "one ring" is time blocking. You build the habit of scheduling your priorities and then live your schedule like your success depends on it.

Time blocking is a method that treats your time like the precious resource that it is. Instead of allowing a to-do list to set the agenda of the day, time blocking means creating a schedule around what's most important to you. You set appointments with yourself dedicated to what you want to accomplish. This simple habit will enable you to take control of your life and your business.

If you could steal a glance at the schedules of the most successful people in the world, you'd find a common thread. They time block their priorities. Agent Jimmy Smith says consistency is better than intensity when it comes to seeing results in your business. "If you do one hundred push-ups in the gym, what's going to happen? You're going to be sore and not go back the next day. But if you do what's needed, day by day, you'll stay at it and reach your goals," he says. "Time on task over time and being consistent breeds success."

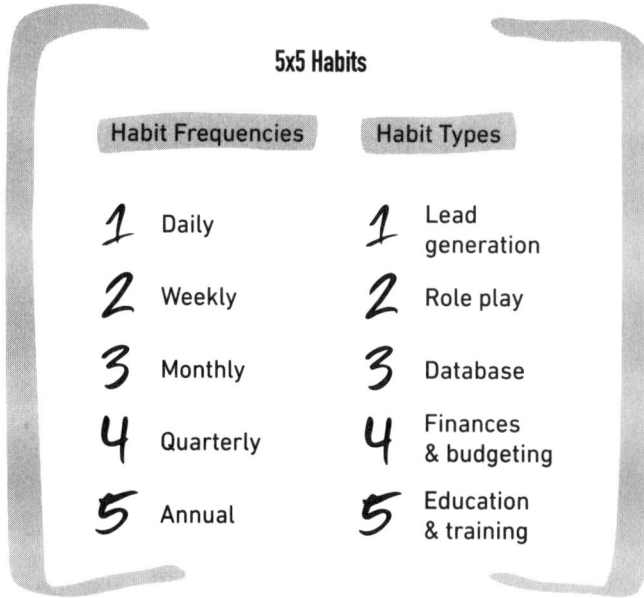

5x5 Habits

Habit Frequencies	Habit Types
1 Daily	*1* Lead generation
2 Weekly	*2* Role play
3 Monthly	*3* Database
4 Quarterly	*4* Finances & budgeting
5 Annual	*5* Education & training

Figure 35

To help you establish your habits, time block them into your days, weeks, and months so that you stay on track to meet your goals. Your key habits fall into five categories: lead generation, role play, database, finances and budgeting, and education and training. Within those five buckets, you follow five frequencies of repetition: daily, weekly, monthly, quarterly, and annual habits. Think of them as your **5 x 5 Habits**.

Design Your Schedule, Live Your Schedule

Your days will look different depending on who you are working with and where you are in your various transactions. However, there are things you need to do every day to build a successful business. An easy way to divide up your time in your daily schedule is by doing it in four sections: early morning, morning, afternoon, and evening. The hours these quadrants fall into depend on your lifestyle choices.

Daily

The early morning is the time before work when you prepare for your day. The morning is the first part of your working hours. The afternoon is the last part of your working hours. And the evening is your time after work, before bed. Not all of these hours will be spent on work. A lot of them will be spent on your personal life, and we encourage you to prioritize these hours and time block them as well. Building habits around your schedule doesn't have to strictly pertain to your professional life, and honestly, it shouldn't.

EARLY MORNING

You can use your early morning hours to prepare for your day. Big success requires big energy. That's why we encourage you to embrace the Rookie Energy Plan. It's a habit stack, a series of rituals that the best adopt to launch their days with energy and focus. Each day, you'll engage in a series of activities to foster spiritual, mental, physical, emotional, and business energy. Think meditation and prayer, reflection, exercise, nutrition, and family time, as well as planning and time blocking.

The Rookie Energy Plan

1	Meditate and pray for spiritual energy
2	Journal and reflect for mental energy
3	Exercise and eat for physical energy
4	Family time for emotional energy
5	Planning and time blocking for business energy

Figure 36

Early morning is when you get ready to launch each day as your best self. Habit stacks can serve as a buffet. You pick the pieces that matter to you and assemble them into a daily ritual. Where one person prays, another meditates, and another just takes a moment to unplug and be. Feel free to build your own unique stack. I've helped thousands builds habits and the one that had the most startling impact was planning and time blocking. When you start your day with a review of your goals and schedule, you get clear on your priorities. And when you're clear on what you need to say yes to on the path to your dreams, it becomes infinitely easier to avoid distractions and stay on track. If you start your day in your inbox or on social, good luck. You've just immersed yourself in everyone else's priorities!

MORNING

Your mornings will be spent working "on" your business, doing all the things you need to do to build it. Every single day, this should include lead generation, follow-up, practicing presentations, and role-playing conversations. Without leads and effective tools to convert them, you have no business. Doing these activities first ensures you are staying on top of what will make your business thrive. Plantation, Florida, agent Laurie Reader says to practice your buyer and listing consultations as much as possible. "You want to be paid like a professional? You better practice like one," she says. "Record yourself and listen to the painful recording so you can get better. Once you become really good at it, you'll internalize it. And then you can personalize it."

AFTERNOON

Your afternoons will be spent working "in" your business. If you have appointments or current transactions, this means working with buyers and sellers and on contract-to-close duties. There will be days without client appointments. Use that time to build your skills, prepare for future appointments, and maintain your business. This could mean scheduling weekly activities on your slow days or previewing inventory.

EVENING

While you might work some evenings, usually your nighttime hours are where you time block personal things into your schedule. Think dinner with friends, walking your dog, reading your favorite spy novel. It's also a great time to reflect on your progress, record your wins, and identify the brights spots in your days. At the beginning of your career, you may have less personal time. Make sure that the things that really matter don't get overlooked. Eventually, your hard work will give way to more free time if you prioritize and leverage intentionally. With this in mind, here is an example day for an agent who time blocks effectively.

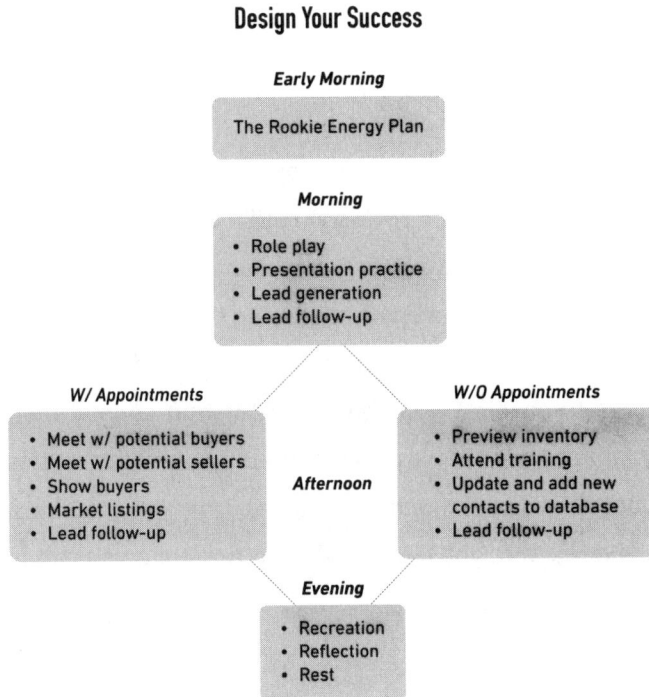

Design Your Success

Early Morning

The Rookie Energy Plan

Morning
- Role play
- Presentation practice
- Lead generation
- Lead follow-up

W/ Appointments
- Meet w/ potential buyers
- Meet w/ potential sellers
- Show buyers
- Market listings
- Lead follow-up

Afternoon

W/O Appointments
- Preview inventory
- Attend training
- Update and add new contacts to database
- Lead follow-up

Evening
- Recreation
- Reflection
- Rest

Figure 37

Weekly

Although necessities like lead generation and role playing will be on your schedule every day, there are other things that need to be done weekly. Time block your schedule to reflect your weekly needs. This habit will help you stay on top of important, but less frequent, tasks. Some weekly things to time block include reviewing your goals, scheduling priorities, and updating your database.

Staying on top of your database is crucial to successful lead generation and conversion. As methodical as you are about working your database, you need to be just as systematic building it and maintaining it. You'll add new contacts to your database, make sure the information is up to date, and set up and run systems within it.

You may also take extra time each week to review your long-term schedule against your goals and make sure you're on track. Ask yourself what you did last week that you want to do better this week. Make sure your answers are reflected in your time blocking. If you want to dedicate more time to preparing for an open house so that your attendance is better, block in your needs each day to make sure that happens. Also, check your upcoming vacations or days off and make sure you are scheduling around any dates you won't be working.

Weekly Schedule

	Sun	Mon	Tues	Wed	Thurs	Fri	Sat
Early Morning		The Rookie Energy Plan					
Morning	Recreation / Reflection / Rest	• Role play • Presentation practice • Lead generation				• Role play • Lead generation • Closing!	
Afternoon		• Open house follow-up • Preview homes for buyer	• Show buyer • White offers • Prep for listing appointment • Lead follow-up	• Listing appointment • Open house prep • Lead follow-up	• Buyer consultation • Update database • Seminar prep • Lead follow-up	• Seminar follow-up • Open house prep • Budget work • Inspection	Open house / Show buyers
Evening		• Recreation • Reflection • Rest			Host first-time home buyer seminar	• Recreation • Reflection • Rest	

Figure 38

Monthly

Each month, you'll have to take care of a few big-picture items. These include examining your budget and P&L, reviewing your pipeline, and again checking to see if your goals align with your schedule. Remember the "One Habit" is time blocking. When your schedule reflects your goals and you commit to living your schedule, your goals will feel like a foregone conclusion. You do the activities, and eventually, you'll enjoy the outcomes of your labor.

You probably think that a budgeting session would be a yawn festival, right? Admit it—you wouldn't be alone. Most agents just can't get their heads around the fact that a budget is a powerful financial-planning tool. They tend to see budgets as a necessary evil, more of a record for income tax purposes and audits than anything else. But when a top agent looks at their budget and P&L, they're in their fighter plane cockpit, and they see two tools that will help them make better decisions faster. This superpower starts with your monthly check-in. It will help you ensure that your expenses aren't sinking your business faster than your income stream can keep it afloat. Review your budget, your bank accounts, and your active clients to get a sense of your financial health and trajectory. If things look like they are starting to trend in one direction, you'll have a better idea of what's working for your business and what's not. Think about any budget changes you need to implement to stay solid. If you use a bookkeeper to help you review your P&L, you should schedule appointments with them monthly.

Knowing your numbers is an important skill to build. At the beginning of your career you may not have many transactions to input, but having a monthly check in with your finances is a big part of being successful.

A pipeline review is the process of identifying clients you're working with, assigning timelines, and estimating the odds of closing the commissions you might earn. You create a spreadsheet and add in your active clients. Estimate the timeline you expect them to follow. For buyers, you weigh their motivation, financial readiness, and price point. For sellers, you consider their motivation, home price, and home conditions. You have A, B, and C clients (you'll learn more about this soon). Your A clients represent likely future closings. The Bs and Cs not so much. Considering the commissions and fees you've negotiated, you can start forecasting your income. For example, maybe you're working with your best friend's parents who have great income and credit, have saved up a large downpayment, and are highly motivated to move to town before their first grandchild arrives. And you've negotiated fees and a commission that should add up to $13,000 for the homes in their price range. There's lots of inventory in the area of town they want to live, and your best guess is that they will close in January. Your pipeline report would show $13,000 earned in January. Each month as you update this, you'll have a better sense of how to navigate your finances.

The last step of your monthly check-in is comparing your pipeline report to your monthly and annual goals. Make sure your calendar reflects the schedule needed to achieve these goals. If you're behind, you may need to block more lead generation time! Ensure that your time blocking is aligned with your needs, and rearrange anything that isn't.

Quarterly

About four times a year, or quarterly, you need to time block for higher level check ins. These include your education, performing a lead generation audit, and doing your quarterly taxes.

Even with your daily and weekly conversation practice and role play, you should keep up to date with the market knowledge you need. Education is key to staying on top in an ever-changing industry. Check for classes that your market center or brokerage is hosting and sign up for the things you would benefit from. You should have a goal of reading or listening to a book or podcast that can help you tackle new challenges in your business or mindset. Learning to earn comes from many sources, and you can't rely on someone else's calendar to bring you solutions if you need information now.

In most regions, you'll need to focus on staying current with your continuing education (CE) in the fourth quarter or early in the first. You'll have to make time to take these classes or risk having your license lapse! Many an agent has had to cancel their plans for a weekend to cram in dozens of hours of CE before the deadline. Don't let that be you!

Every quarter, you want to check in on the results from your lead generation and database. With your P&L in hand, check to see what activities are reaping rewards. We don't recommend switching tactics often on lead generation. But look to see if you're spending enough time on your activities to get the results you want. If you don't know what is bringing in and converting leads, you may be wasting time and money. Audit your lead generation plan at least four times a year and get your database activity aligned with your goals.

Finally, and certainly not least importantly, you need to pay your quarterly taxes. Put reminders on your calendar for when your quarterly taxes are due. A quick huddle with your bookkeeper or CPA at these times will help you pay taxes on time and avoid unnecessary penalties. Staying on top of your taxes will save you a lot of unnecessary grief.

Annually

A birthday can make us reflect on the past year. It can also inspire dreams for the next one. Like birthdays, it's important for us to have time, at least once a year, to reflect and set goals in our business. (Cake optional but encouraged.)

Time block your daily, weekly, monthly, and quarterly check-ins. Make sure your daily priorities are adding up to purposeful weeks, your weeks are driving your goals for the month, and so on. Are your goals the same as they were last year? Do you need to set your sights higher?

When you have a business plan, time blocking and working the pieces is the best way to make sure that plan comes to fruition. Allen, Texas, agent Jason Otts says his calendar with time blocks keeps him accountable to his goals all year. "I know what I need to do and when I need to do it," he says. "I know when I need to lead generate, when I need to make videos. My goals are all worked into my calendar." While you are discovering and building out your goals, make sure your calendar reflects them. Often, we think we are using our time to do what's best to reach our goals when the reality is different. If your goal is to buy your dream car, you need to earn a certain amount of money. Then you need to align that income goal with the time you spend on your business. In Chapter 3, you calculated the number of appointments, agreements, and closings you need to meet your financial goal for the year. How you time block your calendar will determine whether you meet this goal or not. If you aren't generating enough leads or honing your skills, your calendar will show it. Consistently check in with your goals and your calendar so that they are aligned.

Your schedule will change as you take on new clients and try different prospecting and marketing methods. But you need to establish the habit of working on your business basics year-round. This will keep things from falling behind. Sticking to a schedule and time blocking your duties will build the habits you need to run and grow a successful business.

Your annual goals can be both monetary goals and life goals that answer to your Big Why. You may not know all the details of your goals yet, but by the end of this book they'll start to take on a more recognizable and actionable form. Doing a big check-in annually will set you on the right path from the start. Below is a helpful overview of all the success habits you will build over your first year. If it feels a little overwhelming, don't fret. When you schedule these activities and follow your schedule, the habits will form over time.

Success Habits to Time Block

Daily	Weekly	Monthly	Quarterly	Annual
1. The Rookie Energy Plan 2. Role play 3. Presentation practice 4. Lead generation 5. Lead follow-up	1. Review goals 2. Create plan 3. Time block 4. Maintain database	1. Review budget 2. Review P&L 3. Pipeline review 4. Track budget	1. Quarterly taxes 2. Education 3. Lead generation review	1. Review & reflect 2. Goal planning

Figure 39

Establish Accountability

The best of the best not only set big goals and design big plans, but they also allow themselves to be held accountable to them. **Accountability** can come from a variety of sources: friends and family, coaches and mentors, tools, and even from within yourself! Self-discipline can take you far. But voicing your dreams aloud to someone else is one extra step toward bringing them to life. Many brokerages offer services specifically for accountability. You can choose to partake in these services or find an accountability partner among your peers, or both. There are also tools like apps for goal tracking that can keep you focused.

Whatever you decide to do, make sure you are using a system that has consequences. If your accountability partner couldn't care less whether you meet your lead gen goal for the week, you should probably look elsewhere. Though you may not have the funds for it right away, it might be in your best interest to budget for a paid coach so that you're more likely to stick to your plan. When there's money at stake, we tend to follow through more diligently. Think about that gym membership bill that comes each month. It probably motivates you more than the cobweb-covered treadmill in your garage.

Accountability needs to be built into your business plan. Write out what you need to be held accountable to in order to meet your goals, and schedule weekly check-ins to go over your progress. There shouldn't be much excitement or surprises to come from these checks. They all boil down to one thing: consistency. Austin, Texas, coach Monica Reynolds says looking at your goals daily will help you stay on the right path. "You have to be willing to do what it takes and keep your goals visible every day and look at them. Post them everywhere," she says. "And then get your accountability partner to keep you on track. You must be willing to be persistent knowing it will be hard at first until you build the habits."

The only thing between you and success is your commitment to habits that will help you achieve your goals. When you have a vision for yourself, you must be committed. Design your goals to fulfill that vision. Establish habits to meet your goals. Hold yourself accountable. And success will come.

Be the Master of Your Time

Inevitably, when you start working with clients, people will demand your time. You'll need to start protecting your energy. Time blocking your calendar creates boundaries to protect your success habits from the start. When someone wants to meet during your lead gen time, you can honestly say, "I already have a commitment at that time. Can you do 2 p.m. that afternoon or on Tuesday?" No one ever asks what you're doing. You're a busy professional, just like them!

You've probably heard about "speed-to-lead," which is the practice of contacting leads as soon as possible. This is a best practice, but it's also not always possible or sustainable. Sure, checking your phone and emails throughout the day will be a large part of your job as a new agent. Quick responses will help you build a client base and a good reputation. However, we need to set boundaries to build authentic relationships. It helps us stay professional and happy, too. Misti Herring, a director of sales based out of Princeton, Texas, uses time blocking to help her balance her schedule. "In order to do what I do professionally and still have the life I choose to have with my family, I have to follow a time-blocked schedule," Misti says. "In my business, I am the product and the service, so it's about my energy, too. It's critical to set boundaries so I can maintain and have energy left for my family." We can't let leads rule our lives. We won't create the impression that our client is a top priority if we check our texts every thirty seconds during their appointment. Also, when we're at home eating dinner with people we love, it may not be the best idea to get up and take a call from an internet lead we haven't even spoken to yet.

At the end of the day, the only person who can set your boundaries is you. "Learn early to set boundaries. If you tell people it's okay for them to call you at nine o'clock at night, they always will," St. Augustine, Florida, agent Kendra Scott says. "It's okay to say no and to protect your boundaries. Protect your time and protect your personal time." Use time blocking to your advantage to be the master of your time while building a business you love.

Objections usually come up because people have unanswered questions.

CHAPTER 10

Set Appointments

Setting appointments may be the most dollar-productive activity you will ever do as an agent. Over the last ten years, about 70 percent of buyers and more than 75 percent of sellers only interviewed one agent before deciding to hire them. "Yes, I'd love someone to help me," says almost no one in a clothing store. That is until they need a size they can't find, want access to a changing room, or need to check out at the register. Likewise, most buyers and sellers are "just looking" until they aren't. Your ability to connect with buyer and seller leads early in the process, follow up regularly, and identify when the time is right to meet will be essential to your success. Building those skills is the focus of this chapter.

In Chapter 5, you learned the difference between leads and contacts. Leads are people you are able to connect with but who may not know you or that you are in real estate sales. Leads become contacts when you engage them in a two-way communication and tell them what you do, and they agree to future communication. It can happen at first contact, or you may be reaching out for weeks, months, or longer to make this essential connection. This is when you share what you do and who you serve. A few will announce they are ready to sign an agreement to work with you on the spot. Most will take longer.

A first-time home buyer likely needs information about the process and their financial readiness. A move-up seller is more likely to want to know the current value of their home and what properties cost where they're looking. Luxury buyers... well, you get it. Each lead or contact is like a little mystery to be solved.

When someone agrees to meet to discuss their real estate needs, you move to the appointment where you clarify their wants and needs and offer your services. Appointments are also special because they mark the beginning of your official relationship with a client. "Appointments are important for a million reasons, but two in particular," says New Orleans, Louisiana, agent Liz Edgecomb. "First, they help you become a human being. Before now, you might have been a picture on a sign or a number on a website, and so the appointment is where you can become a real human being for people.

"Second, the appointment is where you become a real estate professional," Liz explains. "Especially if you're working with someone who came to you through your sphere of influence, the appointment is where you get to say, 'Here's all the things I do!' If they're not familiar with you as a professional, you have the opportunity to showcase all your expertise."

In the following pages, we'll cover the logistics of setting appointments by quickly contacting qualified leads and scheduling a time to meet. This chapter also shares techniques for improving the rate at which you convert leads to appointments. As you practice, you'll get better at addressing key concerns and showcasing your value. That will both generate better returns on the time you invest and maximize the positive impact you can have in the communities you work in.

The Three Steps to Set Appointments

Appointments are often called "buyer consultations" or "seller consultations," or "strategy sessions." You'll follow these three simple steps to set an appointment:

The Three Steps to Set Appointments

1 **Connect**

2 **Qualify**

3 **Schedule**

You connect with your leads by contacting them quickly, building rapport, uncovering their needs and motivations, and showcasing how you can serve them. To avoid wasting your time or theirs, you also need to make sure your potential client is ready, willing, and able to do business with you. That's qualifying. Then, you can focus on scheduling an appointment. If you find they still aren't ready to make an appointment with you yet, that's fine! You can continue to nurture them and stay top-of-mind when they are ready to take the leap.

1 Connect

Connecting with clients is really all about two things: contacting them quickly and addressing their wants and needs. If you make this connection in a timely manner, chances are you will be able to sell yourself and gain a customer.

Optimize Speed-to-Lead

When it comes to converting leads to appointments, speed is the name of the game. As we shared earlier, between 70 and 75 percent of buyers and sellers will sign with the first agent they interview. There is a huge advantage in being first, so you will want to connect with them as fast as practically possible. How quickly you contact a potential customer is "speed-to-lead."

Many gurus will share studies that show responding to internet leads in the first five minutes greatly improves conversion rates. They are correct, but you should take them with a grain of salt. Those studies are all around internet leads not SOI, open houses, or other warmer kinds of leads. Your friend, your co-worker, the cool couple you met at the open house—they don't expect you to be hovering over your keyboard hitting refresh on your inbox. They imagine you are a busy professional, out serving other clients. Respond as fast as you are able. Within a few hours is great for a solo agent. Same-day replies meet most expectations. Within one business day is likely fine. Build habits to check your inbox and messages a few times a day and be responsive to your current and potential clients.

These studies show that optimizing speed-to-lead is key to landing more appointments. If you connect quickly, the odds lean in your favor. Especially early in your career, when you likely have less on your plate, do your best to optimize your speed-to-lead.

Uncover Wants and Needs

Once you have connected with a potential client, you can take your connection to the next level. Remember the LPMAMA conversation framework from Chapter 8? This framework will help you determine if someone is ready for an appointment or if a better way exists to meet their needs.

The best agents are willing to be curious a little longer. They ask more follow-up questions and listen for clues to what's really going on. "I connect with people by asking questions and really listening to them, because typically the first answer I get isn't the real driving force of what a buyer or seller is looking for," says Alisha Fickert, an agent from

Chico, California. "So, by really asking great questions and connecting with them, I find the root cause of why they're wanting to move or why they're wanting to buy." Be like Alisha!

Most people will only buy or sell a home a few times in their life. They don't know exactly what they want. Part of an agent's job is helping clients get clear on their wants and needs. This can often take some patience and persistence on your part.

Practice asking open-ended questions that extend the conversations. "Can you tell me more about that? Why do you need to move to Denver? Why is a back yard important to you?" Questions that lead to a direct yes or no, often will. They are useful when you need a black and white answer. "Are you currently working with an agent? Have you been prequalified by a mortgage professional?" There is some art to connecting with and qualifying leads. You'll get better and better with practice.

The answers you get from your initial connection with leads will help customize your seller or buyer consultation later. If they have serious objections to scheduling an appointment with you, it may take some further discussion and connection. Los Angeles, California, agent Richard Schulman says connecting with the right intention can make all the difference. "We are never reaching out to make a sale. We are reaching out to add value to people's experiences," he says. You'll learn more in the handling objections section of this chapter.

2 Qualify

Even if you've found out a lot of information from a potential client, you'll need to qualify them. So, it's time for **qualification**. For you to prosper, you can't invest lots of time in buyers or sellers who aren't yet ready to transact. You need to focus on the leads that are more likely to end in closed transactions. The rest, you nurture.

It is essential to qualify buyers and sellers to discover their goals, timelines and motivation before you meet and commit your valuable time. A simple framework for a qualified lead is that they are ready, willing, and able to move forward. **Readiness** is about personal motives for wanting to buy or sell. It means a contact is motivated to make strategic decisions now. Do they need more room for their growing family? Are they relocating for work? If they're just curious as to how much their home could sell for, they may not be ready to hire an agent.

Willingness is how urgent someone is to make a decision in the current market. Is their readiness so strong they might be willing to brave a multiple offer situation to secure their next home? A willing seller is one that might need to do some renovation work in order to market their home for sale. A great question to ask is: "What happens if you don't [buy or sell]?" If they answer with a shrug, they probably aren't willing. Willing buyers and sellers usually have a deep motivation driving them. Maybe their kids *need* to be in a new school district to prosper, they need be closer to an aging parent to provide care, or the financial status quo simply doesn't work.

Finally, **ability** to buy or sell a home lies in financial capacity. Do they have funds available for a down payment and are they pre-approved for a loan? Do they have enough equity in their home to sell without writing a check to close? Ability is the most straightforward of the three. It's usually about debt and for buyers. For sellers, it can be about whether their net will cover their existing mortgage. Sellers may also need to net enough from the sale of their property to cover their next move.

During the qualifying stage of setting an appointment, seek more information and avoid making assumptions. Some people may be ready and willing but haven't been pre-approved yet. They may just need some guidance on this, especially if they are a potential first-time home buyer. "I always ask a potential client if they are prequalified," says Austin, Texas, agent Joy Powell. "I ask because I will always say that we should speak to a lender before we show homes so they can know their true budget." Likewise, you can do a seller net sheet (see Chapter 16) to determine if their home sale will end in a net positive or a loss.

If other things, beyond pre-approvals, are holding a potential client back, they may need to return to your nurture pipeline before scheduling an appointment with you. You can and should keep in touch with them for future business. If they don't qualify right now, ask if they have your permission to follow up with them in a few months. Then you can add them to a drip campaign and your newsletter or market report so that you stay top-of-mind for when they do become qualified.

ABC Clients

Another way to think about qualifying clients is to think about what "group" they may fall into. Some agents label potential clients as A, B, or C. You can group people into one of these categories by asking questions that address key points.

A Clients are the closest to doing business with you. They are ready, willing, and able to buy or sell a home. Another way to think about these clients is that they are "hot." Like a fresh tray of cookies out of the oven, they are best served as soon as possible. If someone is ready to move in the next few months, they qualify as an A Client.

B Clients might be ready and willing, but they aren't financially able to buy or sell right now. They lack one of the three key ingredients to do business in the near future. There are myriad reasons why someone might not be able to do business right away. You need to uncover why when you talk with them. They may need to wait for their youngest to graduate, get their credit repaired, or perform maintenance on their current home. When you find out what their hurdles are, you can give them the right resources and stay in contact in the meantime. That ongoing service-based communication is what we call nurturing.

C Clients have no immediate need to purchase or sell a home. Maybe they've shown up to an open house in their neighborhood out of curiosity. Or, maybe they still have nine months left on their lease. They can be cultivated for later business if you have the right follow-up plans in place.

ABC Clients

	Qualification		
A Client	✓	✓	✓
B Client	✓	✓	
C Client	✓		

Figure 40

If you've quickly contacted your leads, connected with them and learned critical information, and qualified them, it is time to head down the conversion trail. B and C Clients can continue to be nurtured in your database. A Clients are ready for a consultation, so it's time to get scheduling.

3 Schedule

Moving from a conversation with a real estate agent into an "official" relationship via an appointment may be a turning point for some leads. Many qualified clients will be ready to meet with you, no questions asked. Others may need some follow up. Even so, it's important to outright ask for the appointment. The worst that can happen is someone says no or not now. Remember your value proposition and stay positive.

It's best practice to assume a client wants to meet with you. If you appear to be on the same page, you can say it's time for a meeting. Perhaps start off by suggesting something to do during the consultation. Then, offer two to three options for appointment times and ask which works for them. This takes out the question-and-answer portion of setting up an appointment. Instead, they have to come up with a reason *not* to meet with you. Most of the time, if you really are on the same page, they will choose a time you've offered. Assume the yes.

The moment you believe they are ready, willing, and able, you can ask, "Thanks so much for sharing. I think the next step is to meet. Would [time and date] or [time and date] be more convenient for you?" So many times in life—whether asking someone out for a first date or asking for business—we make things more complicated than necessary. Just ask. If they still aren't ready, they will tell you. Sometimes, their reasons are valid and you tap the brakes. Other times, they simply need more information.

People want to know why you're a good person to work with. If you explain this up front, you're more likely to get into an appointment with them. You should be able to clearly state the benefits of working with you—even if you haven't worked with many people. Be confident.

You can personalize your pitch for an appointment by offering what they say they want. If your buyer is eager to see houses, you promise to bring all the properties that match their criteria when you meet. Many sellers are eager to know the value of their home. For them, you can promise to work on some comps to provide a preliminary valuation when you meet.

Handling Objections to Setting an Appointment

Objections usually come up when people have unanswered questions. Instead of feeling defeated, take the opportunity to identify and address any fears you can help a buyer or seller overcome. Manhasset, New York, agent Kristin Scanlon says addressing concerns and handling objections comes with practice. "Every case is unique. I look at people's personality types and respond based on what I think fits their needs best," she says. "The more you practice, the more you hear, and the more you're able to adapt to the situation and understand it deeper." Combined with practicing your conversations and role playing, you can use the following four-step system to help you handle these objections.

The Four Steps to Overcoming Objections

1 **Ask questions**

2 **Empathize**

3 **Identify the real issue**

4 **Offer a solution**

1 Ask Questions

Often, people don't know how to articulate their wants and needs. They might be better at telling you what they *don't* want, or perhaps they just say, "I know it when I see it." That's why it's important to seek details. If they hint that something is holding them back from setting an appointment with you, dig deeper with follow-up questions. Then you can address the specifics and help them find answers. Ask them to explain in detail what their situation is and what they are concerned about. Usually, their answers will provide a clue to what the issue is, even if they don't give you the whole reason. Questions that help people open up like, "Can you share what you mean by that?" may end up being all you need. "Clarity is power," says Naples, Florida, agent Denny Grimes. "There really are no bad questions in real estate. When we ask questions and help people verbalize their thoughts, they move from emotion to logic, and we can serve them better."

2 Empathize

Your client wants to know that you understand how they feel. This goes back to the Feel, Felt, Found framework (see Chapter 8). For someone to trust you, you must establish that you know where they are coming from and can help them. If you can't get on their level or see their point of view, it will be a struggle for you to work together. Open those ears and imagine how your potential client may be feeling; empathy is the key to understanding and, eventually, trust.

3 Identify the Real Issue

Often, the issue preventing someone from getting to a meeting with you is different than the one they think it is. For instance, if a potential client says they don't have time, chances are their schedule is adaptable, but they are hesitant for another reason. This is why the first step is to ask questions. You may uncover a root cause of an objection that even the client is unaware of. But just listening isn't enough—listen and see if you can identify patterns or hear something new. If a buyer has mentioned finances several times, they may be struggling to afford a down payment. Maybe they do have enough saved, but no one in their family has ever bought a house and they fear taking that leap. You'll never know unless you ask questions and listen.

Whatever you are asking, make sure your question sounds like it's coming from curiosity, not judgment. We rarely can know with 100 percent certainty what someone else is thinking. Instead of saying, "There's an issue with money isn't there?" frame it instead as something like, "You've mentioned that you're nervous about the amount needed for a down payment. Could you explain a little bit more about your hesitation?" Be open, curious, and lead with what you've heard. Once they've either confirmed your question or explained what the real issue is, you can work together to move past it.

4   Offer a Solution

Once you've asked questions, empathized with the client, and identified the real issue, you can offer a solution. Say a couple wants to move to be closer to their grandkids, but they are hesitant about losing a low mortgage rate that they locked in several years ago. Remind them of their true reasons for wanting to move. People often think they have a problem that can't be solved or that they must solve on their own. Help guide them toward the right solution to their problem. And remember, you don't have to know everything all the time. If a potential client asks you something that you don't know, tell them that you will find out and get back to them quickly. They will appreciate your honesty, and you will get to grow your knowledge!

Overall, your clients will be happy for your help. You have solutions or connections that could greatly benefit them. So, when you've reached this stage, ask again to set up an appointment. You may have shed light on previous misconceptions and gained more trust. Once a meeting time is set, it's time to prep for your consultation!

Pick Your Path

Whether you're setting appointments with buyers or sellers, there is a process. Here's where you can pick your path. For the buyer consultation and servicing buyers, go to Chapters 11 and 13. For the listing presentation and servicing sellers, go to Chapters 12 and 14. Or, better yet, keep on reading and learn about both sides of the transaction.

CHAPTER 11

Master the Buyer Consultation

Prior to the 1990s, buyer agency was pretty much unheard of in real estate transactions. There was no such thing as a buyer representation agreement. Clients believed their buyer's agent was their legal representative. Those agents may have had their clients' best interests at heart, but they were legally beholden to the seller. Since listing agents were the ones operating with an agreement, buyer's agents were technically acting on the listing agent's behalf. This meant they had a fiduciary duty to the seller, not the buyer. This created a host of issues, like a lack of confidentiality, among others. Real estate professionals back then knew it was a problem.

According to *HousingWire*, real estate agents were the ones who stepped up to solve those issues in 1992. They introduced a system where one fiduciary agent could represent a buyer and another could represent a seller under separate agreements. Each agent would have a fiduciary duty to their own client.

At this stage, your goal is to get a signed buyer's representation agreement. This will allow you to represent your client as a true fiduciary (and get paid for your work). The best way to do this is through a buyer consultation.

When holding consultations with potential buyers, you should keep a few objectives in mind. You need to educate the prospective buyer about the home-buying process. You'll explain what you do for your clients and why it helps them achieve their goals, discuss how you'll get paid, and answer any questions they have about the road ahead. Generally, a buyer consultation will take on the form of a presentation and consultation. Some agents choose to lean heavily on the presentation itself, others use the time to consult deeply with their potential clients. You can do a mix of both if you choose. Your personal style will become clear through practice. The main outcome should always be that you deliver necessary information, become aligned, and get a signed buyer's agreement.

Agent Laurie Reader says your main duty as an agent during a buyer's consultation and throughout business is to serve. "If you're not here to serve, there's really nothing the consumer can't get on their own," she says. "There's the internet today, they'll find their own answers. So, if you can't set powerful expectations and ask important questions, there might not be space for you. Because that's what they truly need from agents." To meet expectations, you have to take yourself seriously. Don't let wishy-washy buyers give you the runaround. That's why a buyer's agreement is crucial for both the client and the agent, and why you are going to learn the best ways to secure one.

Before we get into the steps of securing a signed buyer's agreement, there's a few things you need to know. First, you should understand the benefits of working with buyers. Then you need to know what buyers look for in an agent so you can deliver on their expectations. Finally, getting clear on the core services of a buyer's agent will help you align what clients want from you with what you can best provide. With this knowledge and your skills, you can create a great experience for every client. You'll also convert leads to clients more easily.

Three Benefits of Working with Buyers

There are many positives to working with buyers and having a buyer-based business. When agents first start out, chances are they will be mainly working with buyers. While their goal will often be to move toward a listing-based business, the virtues of working with buyers should not be overlooked.

Three Benefits of Working with Buyers

1. Lasting relationships
2. Little to no expense
3. Learning the market

1 Lasting Relationships

When you work with buyers, you're creating potential for long-lasting relationships. You're getting to know their wants and needs during each transaction and spending time in their lives. If you do your due diligence and act as a fiduciary, you'll keep in contact with them as they grow and change. "What I love about working with buyers is being able to make a difference in their lives," says Tesha Shannon, an agent from Dallas-Fort Worth, Texas.

Buyers, particularly first-time buyers, are about to make a life-changing investment. Clients may want to purchase multiple properties in their lifetime. You have the opportunity to be their agent of choice each time. Or they may be interested in purchasing investment properties.

Canadian agent Omar Kiki in Ottawa, Ontario, says, "Building wealth for people and helping people brings me a lot of joy. It's not a monetary value, it's more. It's about making a positive impact in their lives." Your relationships with buyers will be some of the most important ones in your real estate career.

And here's the clincher: When you help someone buy and stay in touch, who do you think they will call when it's time to sell? Today's buyer is tomorrow's seller. If you tend to them well, they will help grow your business consistently.

2 Little to No Expense

Unlike working with sellers, buyers cost very little to work with. Aside from your normal marketing, advertising, and some gas money, you shouldn't have large out-of-pocket expenses while working the buy side of a transaction. This is no small thing when you are launching your career. Every penny you save between getting your license and earning your first commission check extends your runway to achieve lasting success.

3 Learning the Market

Working with buyers educates you about what is desirable in your current market. Buyers drive demand. By knowing buyers' tastes and what they seek in a home, you can better advise the sellers you work with. Buyers also ultimately determine what homes sell for. A seller can list their home for any amount they choose. It will ultimately sell for what the buyer is willing to pay for that property in that location in that condition in that market. Essentially, you are getting unfiltered feedback on what demands top dollar in your market.

What a Buyer Wants...

You need to know what clients are looking for when you're preparing your buyer consultation. What exactly should you bring to the table? Of course, you have your unique value proposition. But some things are non-negotiables when it comes to clients choosing to work with you.

...In an Agent

A decade of research by NAR shows that buyers' desired traits in an agent have remained steady. Each year the association publishes a *Profile of Home Buyers and Sellers*. When we surveyed the annual reports from the last ten years, there were evergreen trends. Across the board, buyers put honesty and integrity above most other qualities as what they look for in an agent. Because buyers will be working with you on such a monumental purchase, they want to trust you. So be true to your word!

...From an Agent

Job number one for buyer's agents is clear: Find the *right* property that *meets* their clients' timing needs and get it at the *best* price with the *fewest* number of hassles. They also want help with negotiations and pricing. NAR reports from the same decade showed that buyers fundamentally want their agent to assist them with finding the right home to purchase, negotiate the terms of the sale, and negotiate pricing.

What Buyers Want from Their Agent

Find the *right* property...

...that *meets* their client's timing needs...

...and get it at the *best* price...

...with the *fewest* number of hassles.

Figure 41

By offering services that meet your buyers' goals, you show your value. Keep the qualities they seek in an agent at the forefront. Both of these things will show them why they should sign an agreement with you. And now that you know what buyers look for in and from an agent, let's dive into the core services buyer agents offer clients throughout the transaction process. When you are giving your consultation, you'll know to cover these main areas.

The Four Core Services of a Buyer's Agent

To get a buyer to work with you, your buyer consultation should touch on all the services you provide. There are four distinct services you supply during a buyer-side transaction that you'll need to discuss during your consultation.

The Four Core Services of a Buyer's Agent

1 Help clients make a great decision

2 Search for properties

3 Tour houses and decide to buy

4 Make offers and negotiate the contract

The consultation is when you explain how you will tackle the items should the buyer choose to work with you. While these may be the basics, you should highlight anything you do in these areas that is above and beyond the norm. This will remind them of both the importance of working with an agent and, more specifically, working with you!

Let buyers know they can expect you to perform well in these areas. Many buyers may not have purchased a home before or even met with a real estate agent. The consultation gives clients an overview of what to expect throughout the home-buying process and what you will help them with. Washington, D.C., agent Keith James says that building this rapport with your potential buyers from the start will serve you throughout the transaction. "If they trust you during the buyer consultation, they'll trust you during the offer process," he says.

1 Help Clients Make a Great Decision

The highest goal of a fiduciary is to do what is best for their client. As a real estate agent, your goal is to help your buyers make a great decision about what property to buy to fit their needs, timing, and budget.

Let your buyers know that as soon as you've got a signed agreement, you'll start talking strategy. To develop a strategy, you first need to understand who your clients are and what they are looking for in a home. Start with a Wants and Needs Analysis. To help them get to the right decision, you need to understand their motivations. As Rob Howard, an agent from Knoxville, Tennessee, says, "My favorite part of working with a buyer is sitting down and finding out exactly what they are looking for. The fun little give and take of the conversation where you hear about their dreams, the top five things they want in their home. A lot of times people talk about their forever home." This conversation is the foundation of your working relationship.

The Wants and Needs Analysis will provide a clearer view of their current living situation and life circumstances. It will also reveal their dreams of an ideal home and lifestyle. The Wants and Needs Analysis is a form for buyers to fill out before the consultation. Or, you can fill it out together after getting a signed agreement. Once your *potential* clients are your *official* clients, you will dig deeper into this information, which we will talk about in Chapter 13.

Many brokerages provide Wants and Needs Analysis templates you can use. If you take a less formal approach and simply have a conversation with your clients about what they want and need, be sure to write notes later so that you don't forget!

Try an Assumptive Close

Some people may come to your appointment ready to do business with you. Maybe they were referred to you and they trust and know the person who referred you, and they are excited to get started. They may not need you to go through the entire consultation before they sign an agreement. You can test the waters, "I know you've been pre-approved and are ready to start looking at homes. If you want to get straight to work, let's review and sign the paperwork so we can start looking at homes."

Present the buyer's agreement for them to sign. If they need some more information, it's a good thing you have the presentation ready for them! But, if it's not needed, it's all the better to get to an agreement right away and start working.

Explain Your Process

Be prepared to talk about what *you* do as a real estate agent that makes you a great investment. Before you start taking buyers through the journey ahead of them, slow down and explain what the experience of working with you will be like and what "special sauce" you offer. "Educate the buyer so that they can invest in your strategy to find them a home," says Tampa, Florida, agent Kate Conroy.

When you're in your consultation, you will also be explaining to your buyer how much you charge for your services and who will be paying you. Showcasing your value and how it benefits your buyer helps them understand how you earn your compensation.

How you get paid for your services will vary depending on your market, brokerage, and the transaction at hand. Your compensation is always negotiable, and you agree on it with your client. Your negotiation may not be back-and-forth. It may be as simple as saying, "These are the rates I charge for these services." Then, they choose which plan to sign up for. In the end, your fees are transparent, and the buyer will have agreed to them.

The value of your services is dependent on the value you provide. Show up as a professional and your clients will respond to you as one. Know how to communicate your value and you'll be able to maximize your earning potential. And they will be able to charge the most over time. Being excellent at what you do is a solid business decision.

Explain the Home-Buying Process

It doesn't matter if you've helped a hundred clients buy a home or if it's your first rodeo. The steps in the home-buying process generally follow the same path. Most of the buyer consult will be explaining what's ahead and how you will work through it together.

Describe how you'll need a mortgage pre-approval, break down properties to look at, and then view homes. Once you find the right place, you'll craft an offer, negotiate on their behalf, and lead them all the way to closing.

Just remember you might be able to navigate the path with your eyes closed, but never assume your client knows the way.

Pre-Approval

Buying a home is the single largest financial transaction many will ever experience. As an agent, part of your value is to help your client stay within their budget. You should also advise them to make the best decision with their money. You learned the process of vetting potential clients for readiness, willingness, and ability in Chapter 10. This stage of the buyer consultation is where ability comes into play.

To move any further in the home-buying process, clients will need to provide proof that they're "able" to buy. Hopefully, they will come to the appointment pre-approved for a mortgage or be able to obtain one quickly. Besides stressing the pre-approval's importance, this is your chance to ask more questions about their financial situation. What lender are they working with and who is their mortgage loan officer? What financing options do they offer? What is their desired monthly payment? How much cash do they have for a down payment? What's their overall home-buying budget? These answers will inform the home search and keep your clients on track for a smart and affordable home purchase.

It's best to be direct when talking about financial matters. You could say, "I know you spoke to a lender, were you able to get pre-approved for a mortgage loan?" If the buyer replies saying something like, "We're having trouble with our lender. Do you have someone you could recommend for a second opinion?" you can flex your network and offer various solutions. If your potential buyer replies that they are pre-approved, you can ask bigger financial questions like, "With your mortgage approval in mind, what kind of budget are you looking at? And does that amount include all other costs or do you have some wiggle room for home improvements?" Price dictates purchasing for most buyers, so having a firm grasp on what they want and can afford will put you in the best position to get them into a home.

2 Search for Properties

The home search is where the fun starts for the buyer. During the consultation, you will need to describe this process and come up with a communication and search plan. Tell your buyers that you can set up a home search for them. It will show all the homes that fit their needs and budget, since you know what they are looking for.

Explain How You'll Share Property Listings

You're going to find and share **property listings**—descriptions of available properties—with your buyers almost daily. Your job is to filter the available inventory against their buying criteria. Let them know that when they are your clients, you will discuss how they want to review those listings and give you feedback.

3 Tour Houses and Decide to Buy!

During your consultation, you'll need to cover the plan for when it's time to get into action. Tell the buyers that, after reviewing the listings that you've sent, it's time to hit the road. They can also share any homes they found on their own.

But there's more to a buyer's agent than access to a lock box. Let your potential clients know that part of your job in facilitating the home search goes beyond showing houses. You will provide ongoing updates to new home listings, including price changes, and if any homes they like have gone off market. And, of course, once your clients have found a home they love, you will help them make an offer.

4 Make Offers and Negotiate the Contract

You've now reached the point in your explanation of the home-buying process where you can tell your clients how you'll help in the high-stakes stage of making an offer. Explain that because your client has made the excellent choice to work with you, you will provide guidance and expertise throughout the offer-to-closing phase of their transaction.

Let them know you'll be there to communicate what's going on and keep them comfortable, and move the process along.

Making an offer is often one of the most nerve-wracking parts of the home-buying process for clients. That's why you need to let your clients in on exactly what this looks like. Your explanation should include what finances and paperwork will be needed, how you will pull relevant comps to determine your offer amount, and how you will submit a smart offer. This will often be followed by some back and forth, maybe a counter-offer or two. This is when you help them negotiate with the seller to arrive a final executed contract. More on this process soon.

When you go over this service area in your consultation, tell the buyers that once you come to an agreement, you'll fill out the purchase offer contract and present it to the seller and their agent.

Buyer's Agent or Master Negotiator? Be Both

When a buyer's agent presents an offer to a seller, they are responsible for negotiating on the buyer's behalf. Many clients are relieved that the agent will act as their representative and be at the negotiating table instead of them. In your description of this service area, tell buyers you will listen and do your best to advocate for both their interests and their wallet. Maybe a buyer is nervous about doing any work on a house and feels like they are already at the top of their budget. If they find a house they love, but it needs some work, tell them they should still put in an offer. Then you can do the labor of negotiating for repair work or concessions at close. That's what you're here for!

Your consultation should help bring some peace-of-mind to this step in home buying. Reassure them you'll keep in touch so there are no surprises.

Four Steps to a Signed Buyer's Agreement

An agreement serves as a form of protection and makes sure you are putting your time and efforts in a place that is beneficial to your business. Having a client sign a buyer's agreement protects you as an agent. Although people can terminate their agreement at any time, for as long as it is signed, you are the sole agent they work with.

Getting a signed agreement is sort of like wearing a seatbelt. It outlines what actions you or the buyer can take and what will happen should a buyer choose to no longer work with you. As long as the relationship is going smoothly, the agreement and its terms generally don't show up again. But if things go south, this document can be a lifesaver.

A signed agreement is a must-have. So, the buyer's consultation should happen at the start of your work with a client. The agreement must also be signed before an agent can show a property. Your consultation is a perfect time to make your client-agent relationship official before you hit the road.

We will take you step-by-step on how to conduct the most successful consultation. Using your value proposition, you can design and host the best buyer consultation that fits your skillset and caters to your client's needs. And remember all that time we spent talking about role playing in Chapter 8? That's *actually* Step Zero here. We urge you to put in a significant amount of time role playing your consultations. If you dedicate time to preparing and practicing, you'll be as ready as you can be to present your appointments and close to agreements. And then, you'll get better and better with time and experience.

The Four Steps to a Signed Buyer's Agreement

1 **Prepare for the buyer consultation**

2 **Present the consultation**

3 **Share the buyer guide**

4 **Secure an agreement**

1 Prepare for the Buyer Consultation

The buyer consultation is the best way to get a signed buyer's agreement and give potential clients a preview of what a working relationship with you looks like. You want to make sure you're organized and ready to go on meeting day.

Confirm Logistics

When someone agrees to meet with you, set a time and place for your consultation right away. Then, as the date approaches, confirm the attendees, meeting place, date, and time. You want all decision-makers at the appointment. Having all the important parties present ensures the buying process doesn't get stalled. If a couple is looking to buy a home but only one member of the party can make the consultation, reschedule for a time everyone is available.

For a buyer's consultation, the meeting place can be your office or any comfortable, neutral location. If you are meeting at a client's house, be sure to follow safety precautions and let someone else know where you are. Keeping it easy for the client needs to be balanced against driving all over town. Scheduling meetings in your office sets you up to meet multiple people for consultations without adding commute time into your schedule. Whatever you decide to do, arrive promptly, be prepared, and stay safe.

2 Present the Consultation

The goals of the buyer consultation are to showcase your value proposition, and get a signed buyer agreement. While the hoped-for outcome should always be the same, you can personalize your approach.

Some agents choose to focus heavily on the consultation, while others lean more on the presentation itself. If you want, you can do a combination of the two. At this stage, it's really up to you when it comes to presenting. And there are benefits to all three strategies.

Buyer Consultation Styles

Approach	Focus	Methods
Consultation Heavy	Signed Buyer's Agreement	• Powerful questions • Discussion focused • Emphasis on buyer
Presentation Heavy	Signed Buyer's Agreement	• Detailed information • Education focused • Emphasis on service
Balanced Consultation/ Presentation	Signed Buyer's Agreement	• Strategy session • Education and discussion • Emphasis on partnership

Figure 42

Agents with a presentation-heavy consultation will focus on educating their buyers. They give detailed information on their services. Some agents use this consultation style because they want their clients to feel well-informed at the beginning of their relationship.

Some agents lean a little more toward presentation mixed with conversation. When they first meet the buyer, they go through the buyer's presentation, but don't read line by line. If you go for a more balanced approach, you will likely combine the two and hold what we like to call a strategy session, where you are both discussing and educating.

Whatever path you take, remember to touch on the agent core services and keep the goal outcome in mind. By educating your potential buyer about your services, you're sure to get that agreement signed and move into action.

3 Share the Buyer Guide

A **buyer guide** is a document you create that educates the buyer and shows your credibility. Depending on how you've decided to present your consultation, it could also guide most of the presentation. If you're presentation heavy, this is likely the case. If you are more focused on the consultation, it might be something that you give to your buyers after your consultation for them to keep. You should be prepared to show it when necessary for your client's needs. In general, it showcases and walks through the agent core services and your transaction process.

The guide can be presented as a PowerPoint or you can print handouts for your clients. It should cover a few areas that are significant to every client. It needs to go over timelines and processes, your credentials, a market analysis, testimonials, the process, the market, and your value proposition.

As you create the buyer guide, have some things on hand: brokerage assets like logos and addresses, your photo, and your contact information. Include a section toward the beginning that sets expectations with your clients and uncovers their communication preferences. Everyone likes to be contacted in different ways, so ask for their ideal method and give them yours.

Now, we've put sharing the buyer guide as the third step in your buyer's consultation. But it can come before you even hold your appointment. Many agents like to send their guides ahead of the consultation to help their prospective clients discover what questions they may have.

4 Secure an Agreement

Just like the buyer guide, we've put this step at the end because it's the end goal, but it doesn't always have to come last when you're holding your consultation. If your buyer is ready to sign their agreement at the top of your meeting, don't make them wait! Whenever it is natural for them to sign with you, make it happen. With electronic agreements, signatures can be done within minutes, whether you're in-person, on a video call, or connecting through email.

For the sake of this chapter, though, let's say it's now. After you've presented your consultation, it's time to get the agreement signed. Hopefully you've answered any questions the buyer has asked and worked through any hesitations. They may still feel unsure about signing an agreement for whatever reason, so go back over why an agreement is good for both of you.

A buyer's agreement protects your time and the buyer's investment in you. If you invest the time to show a buyer multiple houses, but they buy a house with another agent who has a contract with them, you get nothing. Having an exclusivity agreement between a buyer and an agent prevents this from happening. Most buyers will understand this reasoning. If you need to, use any of the closing strategies we went over before. You can apply them in multiple scenarios. What's most important is you let your buyers know how you will advocate for them throughout the entire transaction. You will help them with any issues, celebrate wins with them, and negotiate on their behalf. You're their guide along this exciting journey, and that's why an agreement is needed.

Sometimes, even if you've done the best buyer consultation of your life, people still may not want to work with you. That's okay. Put these people on a touch program and nurture them. They may become ready to work with you over time.

What's Next? Moving Forward

When you succeed in getting a signed agreement, let your client know the next steps, what you need from them, and what they can expect from you.

Set Expectations

Once you've established your communication preferences, plan out your next points of contact. Gather all the materials you need to send in order to get them on the right home search.

You'll want to ensure that every question is answered. Prepare them for after the executed contract, into the inspections, and on to title and then closing.

We will go over the activities that come next when working with buyers in Chapter 13. Sometimes, buyers may have another job for you. If they aren't a first-time home buyer, are they also selling their home? You may be able to get both sides of a commission and work each part of the transaction. Obtaining a listing agreement is similar to getting a buyer's agreement, with some extra pieces along the way. Don't worry, the next chapter explains.

CHAPTER 12

Ace the Seller Consultation

Winning new clients is a challenge. It can be expensive both in terms of your time and your money. That's why making "clients for life" is a common goal among real estate agents. You want to deliver so much value to your clients that you become their default choice for all things real estate. Repeat clients arrive as warm leads and everything tends to be just a little easier. Your phone buzzes and it's that couple you helped purchase a first home years ago. They are ready to move up and will need you to help them sell their current house and buy a new home. By delivering on the initial client experience, you've earned lots of future business (and probably referrals, too). Keep delivering and, eventually, you'll have a loyal customer. They don't just prefer you, they won't consider working with anyone else.

First-time clients are essential. Repeat clients are precious. Loyal clients are invaluable. It's a little like your childhood merry-go-round. It's hard to get it going. You have to lean into it, step-by-step, as it slowly builds momentum. Then suddenly it's spinning on its own! As the handle spins by, you time each push to make it go faster and faster. Like any flywheel, once spinning, it requires less and less to keep it going. With repeat customers, each transaction is another opportunity to deliver an amazing customer experience. That experience is another push on the merry-go-round.

The best way to gain clients for life is to put service above any potential sales. That's why you need to showcase the service you plan to provide from beginning to end during your seller consultation. This appointment is also referred to as a "listing presentation." We prefer the term "seller consultation" because it puts the focus on the person you are serving and refers to the fiduciary discussion you have with them, as opposed to a one-sided presentation.

When you are focused on service, you'd be surprised what you can accomplish. You may even land a listing you think is out of reach. Plano, Texas, agent Carol Thompson got her first listing this way. "There was someone in my sphere who was going to be buying her parents' house. I gave her step-by-step advice on how to do several remodel projects, even after she told me she was going to list with someone else who was her friend in the neighborhood." Carol wasn't helping so she could get business. She had time and wanted to be of service as a licensed agent. "Well, she called me one day and said she was impressed with what I had done for her and asked me to list her house. I got the listing, but without a culture of contribution, I couldn't have done that."

In this chapter, you'll learn how to host a winning seller consultation. Let's revisit why sellers are important for a successful business and examine what they are looking for from an agent.

Four Benefits of Working with Sellers

A listing-focused business has many benefits. Listings are the most efficient way to earn money for the time you work. They increase your marketing opportunities and build your business because more clients will come to you through each listing.

Four Benefits of Working with Sellers

1 **Marketing opportunities**

2 **More business**

3 **More income for your output**

4 **Pricing and market knowledge**

1 Marketing Opportunities

A seller listing provides marketing opportunities for both the property and your business. Think about it. When a buyer signs an agreement with you, you don't put a sign in their yard. But that's exactly what you do with sellers. They are hiring you to market their home. Holding your own listing open is a perfect win-win. With open houses, you get to market the property and your practice! Whether or not you hold an "open," you'll have chances for directionals, direct mail, door hangers, and more—all with your name and business in a prominent font!

2 More Business

Ultimately, working with sellers breeds more business. Because of the marketing opportunities listings create, you'll reach more leads. If you properly market your properties, you will undoubtedly bring in buyers who need an agent. According to ten years of NAR real estate industry surveys, 39 percent of sellers used the same agent that sold their home to help them buy a new one.

One of the truths of real estate is that those who control the listings, control the market. Finally, all those sold signs add up to a reputation. When you grow the listing side of your business, your business will grow. It's that simple.

3   More Income for Your Output

Leveraging listings can mean big returns for your business and your time. Working with sellers allows you to take on a greater volume of clients. Listings simply aren't as time intensive. As a solo agent, you might struggle to work with more than four or five active buyers at a time. How many homes can you show in one weekend? But lots of successful solo agents will carry dozens of active listings at once.

Listings give you more control of your time, so you have the potential to earn more. After all, being able to set your schedule and not limit your income are two reasons people become agents in the first place. What's not to love?

4   Pricing and Market Knowledge

As a listing agent, you get to be on the front end of pricing and market knowledge. You will know the area's inventory before other agents do. You'll be the first to know when the market shifts. Having your finger on the pulse of where the market is headed helps you better serve clients. You'll become someone people depend on when they want to know what's happening in their area or want to sell their house for the biggest return.

Now that you know the benefits of working with sellers, we will show you how to deliver value to your clients based on what they want.

What a Seller Wants...

To prepare for your consultation and to provide exceptional service, you need to understand what qualities sellers want in an agent and what duties they expect of you.

...In an Agent

Sellers look for agents who have a good reputation and who are honest and trustworthy. They also prefer to work with a friend or family member. You can't help whether you're related to a potential client. That's just the way cards are dealt. But understand that people hire agents who they know, like, and trust. Relative or not. Real estate is a relationship business!

Agents with more transactions under their belt have an advantage in the reputation area. But every one of them started with one listing and built their reputation, one home at a time. As a new agent, you can also lean on the statistics and reputation of your team or brokerage. This may be your first listing, but how many has your team or office sold? You can leverage their experience to win business and to deliver it. Being a part of a larger team or office can be an advantage. Anytime you are stuck, you can "phone a friend" and get the answer. Always focus on offering and delivering great service. In the end, a spotty reputation could be worse than having no reputation at all.

A surefire way to build a solid reputation and establish honesty and trustworthiness is to always act as a fiduciary. Miami Beach, Florida, agent Kathrin Rein says that when you come from a place of contribution, that's when people want to work with you. "When you approach sellers with the mindset of coaching them, helping them, and providing them with value, you are already different from so many agents," she says. When people see you are committed to this ideology, they won't forget it.

...From an Agent

People have diverse reasons for selling their homes. They need a bigger or smaller space for their family. They got a new job and are moving across the country. They won the lottery and can finally afford that chalet with three fountains in the front and the infinity pool in the back. No matter the reason, sellers tend to want the same things—to net the most amount of money with the fewest number of hassles in the least amount of time. Some want all three. Others may want one more than the rest. For example, a seller who needs to move quickly may be less focused on financials.

What Sellers Want from Their Agent

To net the *most* amount of money...

...with the *fewest* number of hassles.

...in the *least* amount of time.

Figure 43

To accomplish this goal, you'll need a solid marketing plan. Knowing the market and pricing strategies is critical. If you run your marketing plan well and present the house to the right audience, you could receive multiple competitive offers. That means you can sell the house quickly and for top dollar. You should also have B2B connections if they need help with any home fixes prior to listing. Look! You've already checked all the boxes of what a seller wants from an agent.

Now that you know what a seller wants, let's walk through the essential services listing agents provide. Your consultation should cover these areas so your potential client knows you are an expert and will be a fiduciary at every step.

The Four Core Services of a Listing Agent

To get that listing agreement signed, use the seller consultation to explain what you do. Understanding your focus as a listing agent is crucial to doing your job well. There are four core service areas of a listing agent that, when done at the highest level, put the seller in the best position to accomplish their goals.

The Four Core Services of a Listing Agent

1 **Advise and educate the client**

2 **Market the property**

3 **Negotiate the contract**

4 **Close the sale**

At this point in the relationship with your potential clients, you aren't doing most of these jobs yet. However, you're showing what these steps will look like if a prospect does decide to sell and work with you. At each milestone, share your value proposition. Highlight the unique benefits of working with you and explain how you will help guide your clients.

1 Advise and Educate the Client

For a client to work with you, you need to align on expectations and goals. This will ultimately help you advise and educate them to make the best decisions around selling their house. Ask about their wants and needs. Then, do a home walkthrough. This will help set expectations about your plan to sell their house. A lot of this is outlined in your pre-listing packet, which is covered in the next section.

Sometimes, your seller consultation may end up with the clients deciding it's not the best time for them to sell. As an agent, you've done your job. You helped them make a good decision. Next, you need to stay in touch so you'll be there when they decide to sell. Add them to your nurture pipeline and keep showing your value over time.

2 Market the Property

Marketing the property is one of the primary services clients want from their listing agent. It is also one of the core services you provide. Chapter 14 covers marketing strategies in depth. While we won't get into specifics now, know that you need to show your clients a solid marketing plan during your consult.

3 Negotiate the Contract

The primary window for negotiations happens when a buyer makes an offer on the property. Whether an offer is over, at, or below asking, you have a duty to present it to your seller. When the offer doesn't match your clients' needs, you get the opportunity to bring your negotiation skills to bear. Negotiation isn't just haggling over price. It's knowing all the options to find a win-win. Where are tradeoffs that meet your sellers' needs and satisfy the buyers? Do the buyers need more concessions to pay closing costs or make repairs? Do your sellers need a leaseback to accommodate their timelines? Can the terms, price, or what conveys be tweaked to everyone's satisfaction? Asking the right questions and discovering the answers is a big part of the value you deliver in negotiations.

4 Close the Sale

After you've helped them with everything else, your last core service is to help clients close the sale. You will coordinate with title companies and attorneys, depending on where you operate. Walk the sellers through the closing process. Tell them what timelines to expect. If you offer any special services like helping people move or clean, showcase that during your consultation. Anything that makes you stand out from the crowd is a must-share!

There are many benefits to working with sellers. That's why you need to give your sellers the time, energy, and commitment it takes to meet their needs and successfully sell their house. This level of service will win you referrals. To do these things, though, sellers need to sign your representation agreement to go from being your potential client to your actual client. Now, we're going explain how to put on the best seller consultation that will get you that signed agreement.

Three Steps to a Signed Listing Agreement

Your primary goal with the seller consultation is to secure a signed listing agreement. That said, there are other wins to be had. Some sellers want to list now. For others, the best decision may be to wait. Occasionally, it makes sense for a prospective seller to keep the property as a rental. In our experience, consulting with them to make a great decision is always the right move. When you earn their trust, they will often choose to work with you when the timing is right. For the rest, just follow these three steps and get that signed agreement.

Three Steps to a Signed Listing Agreement

1 Share a pre-listing packet

2 Prepare for the seller consultation

3 Host the consultation and secure an agreement

At this point in the relationship with your potential clients, you aren't doing most of these jobs yet. However, you're showing what these steps will look like if a prospect does decide to sell and work with you. At each milestone, share your value proposition. Highlight the unique benefits of working with you and explain how you will help guide your clients.

1 Share a Pre-Listing Packet

You don't need to wait for the consultation to start providing value to your potential seller. A **pre-listing packet** builds trust and answers questions sellers may have ahead of the consultation. Done well, it communicates your professionalism and value. It should be fairly short and to the point. You don't want it to feel like "homework." It's more of a brochure that highlights your best attributes and answers common questions. In general, your pre-listing packet will accomplish a few things. It should pre-sell your services, save time, and state your value.

Pre-Sell Your Services

A pre-listing packet markets your services to your potential clients. It highlights your plan and the benefits of working with you. "When you drop off the pre-listing packet, you're setting the expectations for a seller and what they think is going to happen through the process," says Nancy Chu, an agent from Montclair, New Jersey. Sellers use an agent because they need advice, expertise, and support. Sharing the pre-listing packet with the seller ahead of time will help them decide if they are interested in working with you. Then, at the consultation, you can explore deeper concerns and motivations.

Save Time

Another thing a pre-listing packet can do is save you time. An informed client will have fewer questions and objections. This can make the consultation smoother and likely shorter. In the best circumstances, it may erase the need for a full consultation altogether.

However, most busy adults typically don't crave homework. If you give them something to read before your consultation—like a pre-listing packet—they might not look over it. Either way, you gave them the option to get a head start on the process.

A Pre-Listing Packet Shares...

1. **Who you are:** Start with a short bio with your photo, your contact info, and any testimonials you have.

2. **Your promise to the seller:** Lay out your commitment of a five-star experience for your sellers. Another testimonial wouldn't hurt!

3. **The selling process overview:** Include an overview of the home-selling process from start to finish and your standard marketing approach. Definitely highlight areas that are your strengths.

4. **General pricing information:** Provide pricing trends for houses like theirs and their neighborhood. Let them know you will provide a detailed analysis and comps at or after the consultation.

5. **Your value proposition:** This may echo your earlier promise, but clearly state your value proposition. What special programs, services, or expertise do you provide that sets you apart?

6. **Vendor partners:** Include any vendor partners you, your team, or your brokerage have that are relevant to a seller. Think: staging vendors, photographers, contractors, landscapers, etc.

Overall, your pre-listing packet should be error free, well written, and have an appealing design from its first page to its last. It reflects who you are and how you conduct business, so it needs to be professional and accurate. Unsure if you're hitting the mark? Ask other agents to look over it for edits or suggestions.

Deliver your pre-listing packet to your potential client once you've set an appointment with them. This gives them time to review the content and think of any additional needs or questions to ask at the consultation. And, like we said, a pre-listing packet could replace the consultation if it provides significant value.

2 Prepare for the Seller Consultation

One part of preparation will be checking things off a list so that you're ready to meet with the sellers. Another part will be practicing the consultation itself, just like you would for buyers.

We spoke a lot about time blocking and role playing in Chapters 8 and 9, and we want to remind you about it here. Practicing your presentations will improve your skills and better your business. Plymouth, Michigan, agent Jeff Glover says, "A lot of agents do it backwards. They spend too much time focusing on generating the lead and not enough time getting better at the presentation. That's what is going to give them the confidence and energy to know how to go and find listing business." Take Jeff's advice and don't make this mistake! Practice!

When you feel practiced enough, there are a few items to check off your list before consultation day.

Review Pricing Data and Presentation Materials
As you learned earlier in this chapter, sellers want an agent to effectively price their home. To do this, you need to do two things. First, pull comps from the MLS and run a comparative market analysis. You must check the recent active, pending, and sold prices of similar houses nearby.

Buyers tend to compare homes on a lot more than price and square footage. They look at condition, location, features, and amenities, too. Note these details with those comparable listings. Later, when you do a walkthrough with the seller, you'll see first-hand what the home has to offer buyers in comparison to the rest. Weston, Florida, agent Sandra Rathe says you need to show, not just tell, your clients how their house compares to others. She says, "They need to experience it and come up with the decisions on their own, based on what you're showing them." If all the comps have three-car garages but the sellers only have a carport, try to get them to see that difference from a buyer's perspective. Sandra recommends using pictures and data to help paint a picture.

You can also pull information from any other resources you have. If you got the listing from another agent or a team member, they may have information about the seller and property for you to review. You asked questions and got information from the seller when you set the appointment. Now is the time to go over it. If you know why they want to sell, you can tailor your strategy to their needs. Sandra advises, "Always prepare your presentation for the person that you're meeting with. Be able to adjust based on their background and personality." Knowing the sellers' motivations and preferences will help you set expectations and answer questions.

Finally, make sure any materials you plan to use during the consultation are updated and accurate. Have your listing agreement either printed out or available electronically. This is the reason you're meeting, so don't forget it!

Confirm Appointment

Once you've pulled comps and prepared all your materials, confirm your meeting details with all decision-makers. Include the seller (or sellers) and anyone they deem important to the transaction. Anyone who could influence the final decision should attend the consultation. This saves time and ensures no one misses critical conversations.

Ideally, seller consultations will take place at the seller's house. This is because you need to do a walkthrough of the house ahead of listing it. Having the consultation right after the walkthrough is convenient. Sometimes, however, appointments in another location can't be avoided. Either way, confirm the details of your meeting like the location, date, and time.

As always, be safe! It can feel scary to meet with someone you don't know very well in their house. Tell someone where you will be, when you will be there, and who will be in attendance. Consider bringing another agent along if you feel hesitant. Agents are always here to help each other out, especially when it comes to safety. Check with a title company or the assessor's website to confirm who owns the property. And if you have any bad feelings, leave immediately. Even a multi-million-dollar listing is never worth the risk.

3 Host the Consultation and Secure an Agreement

This may seem forward, but when you arrive for your consultation, start off with a trial close. Ask if they are ready to sign the agreement so that you can launch your marketing plan and recommend a listing price. If they loved your pre-listing packet and feel comfortable about moving forward, they may not need a presentation or have any objections. It could save everyone some time and get the ball rolling. If they need a little more from you, go ahead and proceed with the consultation. Good thing you're already prepped!

If the consultation proceeds, you'll do a walkthrough of the house. This will let you recommend a proper listing price.

Your goal in this first meeting is to make a good impression. You want to build the seller's confidence in you. Showcase your expertise and let them know how you will show up throughout the home-selling journey. Use the listing presentation to show the seller you are the best agent to help them achieve their goals. When you do all these things, you have a great chance of walking away with a signed seller agreement.

Conduct the Walkthrough

The home walkthrough will help you write the property's listing description and inform your pricing strategy. Here are a few best practices for doing a walkthrough.

First, if it's possible, do the walkthrough alone. This allows you to come to conclusions without the homeowner's input. They have a biased view of their house, and you need to be objective when thinking about your plan. Vanessa Pollock from South Orange, New Jersey, uses an interesting tactic. She tells her clients, "I'm going to look at the house by myself because you might have either rose-colored glasses or overly critical glasses on about your home. Let me see the house as a real estate professional. Then I'll come back and tell you my plan and my opinion." When she returns, Vanessa says, "Great news! Your house is definitely going to sell!" This lets them relax before she details her action plan.

Remember, if listing on the MLS, certain data is required, so keep a checklist handy while you survey the house. You might add other items to the checklist that you think makes the home stand out.

Note that some sellers may not be completely realistic about their property. A lot of the time their house is their baby, and they're a little too close to home (literally!) to be objective about the situation. They may think they have three bedrooms, but one room is missing a closet and cannot legally be listed as a bedroom. They may think no updates are needed and want to price their house high, but it's got blue shag carpet and leaky faucets. You can explain your strategy and support your reasoning with facts while remaining understanding of their concerns. Let them know your thoughts and the logic behind them.

You want to be both helpful and honest; it will set the right expectations for your relationship.

Go Over Your Process and Set Expectations

After the walkthrough, sit down with your potential clients to share your thoughts about their house. Throw in a compliment! Ask lots of questions. "Did you plant this tree?", "Were the cabinets custom or did you add them later?" Explain your process and describe your journey together should they sign an agreement with you.

As you're setting expectations, give details about your plan. Ask if they have preferences around how and when you'll provide updates. Share when you're available and how to best contact you. Agree on how often you'll be in touch. Clarify what you will be working on for them when they don't hear from you. They want to know you will do right by them. Many people may not know the ins and outs of selling a home, so be informative.

Discuss Pricing

If you give a price recommendation after the walkthrough, include your reasoning. Explain how that price will get their house sold in a timely manner and for the most money possible. The seller will ultimately determine the listing price based on your recommendation.

If you choose to wait to discuss a price, you can still inform them of your approach to pricing. Make a strong case for your pricing strategy, even if you choose not to reveal your recommendation until the agreement is signed. Talk about the market, your knowledge, and tell stories about any satisfied clients. After all this, why wouldn't the seller want to list with you?

Write a Thank-You Note

Whether a seller decides to list with you or not, it's a good practice to send a hand-written thank-you note immediately after meeting. The note shows the seller you appreciate that they took time out of their busy lives to listen to you and consider working with you. Also, handwritten notes tend to standout positively in our digital age.

Showing gratitude benefits both you and the thank-you note recipient. Win or lose the listing, you've gained the experience. Put this habit into practice for every consultation you go on. It will build your reputation and get you future referrals. If someone does decide to work with you, your relationship starts on a high note.

Discuss How You Get Paid

Now that you've discussed the house's pricing, you need to discuss your fees. As a listing agent, your value can determine your compensation. There are two ways to present your value and charge for it—bundling and unbundling.

Bundling is when you take all the value you provide and the outcomes you achieve and charge a set fee, percentage, or combination of the two for those services. In this case, you'd say, "I will take care of everything for [your commission charged]."

Unbundling is when you separate your services and charge an amount or percentage for each one. It is *à la carte* pricing based on outcomes and services you provide. An example of this would be you charge X amount if the seller brings the buyer, you charge Y amount if you bring the buyer, and so on. Whatever you decide, the terms must be understood by all parties from the beginning.

Most agents get a giant case of the nerves before their first conversation around signing an agreement or discussing how they get paid. That's totally normal. The good news is it's easier than you think and every time you do it will be easier and more comfortable. Just remember the stats are on your side. More than 75 percent of sellers on average will choose to work with the first agent they meet. That agent would be you. The very fact that you're reading this book makes me imagine you're not "average" and will achieve even better results.

Sign the Agreement and Inquire About Buying

The time has come! You have put in all the work toward gaining a client and the opportunity to sell their home. Now you can trust that you've done the best you can do, have given all the relevant information necessary, and are ready to carry out the task at hand. You can say, "The next step is to review the listing agreement, answer any remaining questions you have about it, and then sign so we can get to work." Best practice would be to review the agreement, to make sure the seller understands what they are about to sign. With practice, you'll find the best ways to explain the agreement clearly and efficiently. At the end, you clear any remaining questions and everyone signs. *Huzzah!* You have a seller client!

The next words out of your mouth should include gratitude for their trust in you and some version of "Here's what happens next." Whether with a lead or a client, every meeting or conversation should connect with a future action or communication. "This was so great, here's what you can expect next . . . " Let them know next steps and what to expect in the upcoming days.

Pro tip: When someone sells their house, there is a great chance they will need to buy a new one. Always inquire about both sides of a transaction. If you can gain a seller and a buyer client at the same time, your business will thank you! If they are moving out of your area, you can refer them to a local agent in their new spot. If they want to work with you for both, you can walk them through your buyer representation agreement.

You're now well on your way!. When potential clients become official clients, it's time to do the work. And that's what the next two chapters are all about.

Lead with compassion, knowledge, and integrity.

CHAPTER 13

Work with Buyers

In his book *Give and Take*, Adam Grant explores success. He examines the paths to success taken by three types of people: givers, takers, and matchers. There are successful and unsuccessful people in each category. Takers want to get as much as possible from others, matchers want to trade evenly, and givers split into two very different paths. Grant found that givers tend to be at the bottom of the success pool and, paradoxically, at the top as well. Givers who give too much often find themselves struggling to advance, but those who are at the top are givers with a strategy. These "strategic givers" know how to give in a way that deepens relationships. Grant writes, "It's the givers, by virtue of their interest in getting to know us, who ask us the questions that enable us to experience the joy of learning from ourselves. And by giving us the floor, givers are actually learning about us and from us, which helps them figure out how to sell us things we already value." Truly successful agents know that givers have an edge over their competition because service is at the core of real estate. They use their giving to better deliver value.

The best agents don't go into business thinking about what they can gain or how much money they can make. They focus on building solid relationships with their clients. In turn, business comes to them because they are trustworthy, honest, and full of integrity. When working with buyers, continue to have a strategic giving mentality and your business will expand.

Know Your Clients

Every client that you work with will be different. The personalities change, the properties change, and the market changes. But two truths remain: You work for your client and you want to provide the best experience. Use the differences of each transaction to inform how you can provide the best service.

Dig Deep into the Needs Analysis

In Chapter 11 you learned that filling out a Wants and Needs Analysis will help you develop a strategy for a buyer's home search. It's your opportunity to dig deep and understand not only what your buyers are looking for, but why. For example, if you don't know your buyers well, things that seem mundane to you may actually be a meaningful factor in their home search. If your buyers say they are looking for a property with a big kitchen, ask why that is important to them. Perhaps they love to host dinner parties. Maybe their dream is to teach cooking classes out of their home. With this information, you may ask if they want to prioritize properties with ample entertaining space. Maybe a backyard patio for grilling or an open layout with expansive dining and living areas would wow them. Don't just ask one question. Asking deeper questions can give greater clarity to the kind of homes you should look for.

For Philadelphia, Pennsylvania, agent Alison Simon, questions are key to service. She says, "Asking probing questions will always make me shine because it shows that I care about getting my buyers exactly what they want."

For her market, this means Alison must think about not only the right home for her buyers, but also how they commute. "Many of my buyers don't have cars, so they need to be within a certain distance of public transportation," she says. "I dig deeper to find out if a bus route will suffice or if it needs to be a subway stop."

On our team, Wendy teaches our buyer agents to end the Wants and Needs Analysis by identifying the client's top five wants and needs. She asks, "After everything we've discussed, what are the top five things you want in your new home?" If she's working with a couple, she will ask them to create their top five lists separately. Once done, they'll discuss, and she will help them agree on a top five wants and needs for their home search.

Know the Market

Once you know your clients' needs and experience, consider how the market will affect their transaction. Depending on the market you're working in, the way you show homes and work with clients will be different.

You learned in Chapter 4 that there are different realities and strategies for working with clients in a sellers' market and in a buyers' market. You also need to understand a few key things about the different markets when working with buyers. The following figure illustrates them.

Buyer's Agent Strategies for the Market

Buyers' Market	Sellers' Market
1 Identify the best matches among many options.	1 Highlight the best matches available
2 Establish tight criteria.	2 Establish expectation for speed.
3 Prioritize desired concessions.	3 Clarify strategy for multiple offers.

Figure 44

In any market, you can look for sales trends in current listings, days on market, pendings, and recently solds. This will help you set expectations with your clients about what is on the market and which properties are moving. Even slow buyers' markets often have neighborhoods and price points that move quickly. And in a sellers' market, prices may be rising quickly. A home in your client's price range may no longer be affordable in a month or so.

In a **buyers' market**, there is a surplus of homes available in relation to buyers. That means there will be a lot of choices. Because of this, you'll have to establish tight criteria with your buyers about what they are looking for. Narrow down the options into "Yes," "No," and "Maybe" categories. Then, honestly, throw out the noes and the maybes too. When there are this many choices, a maybe just isn't going to cut it. It will only waste yours and your clients' time. Then, narrow down the yeses even further. Establishing detailed standards here will make the process smoother and quicker.

In a **sellers' market**, the options may feel few and far between. You have to tap into your clients' true wants and needs, and potentially focus mostly on the needs. It also means the best properties will move fast, often with multiple offers. Establishing an expectation of speediness when trying to get your clients the best house for them is crucial. Otherwise, they may misunderstand their situation and miss out on the perfect home because they don't know when to pull the trigger.

Knowing where the market is and where it is headed is key to providing the best service.

But we can't tell you what your market looks like. We don't know when or where you are reading this book. We can tell you, though, that you have to stay on top of market trends if you want to be a successful agent that clients refer to their friends and family. If you truly understand your local market, every other part of your job will be easier. You'll be able to show the right homes, understand why your buyers are hesitating, and advise their decision-making. Jennifer Kelly, an agent out of Fort Collins, Colorado, says it's your job to set realistic expectations and fill in any holes to help them make decisions. "I won't quote payments, insurance, or guess on any numbers because your clients will always remember what you told them," she says. "I want them to get information from the source so it's true and accurate." They will lean on you for market knowledge and trust that you can educate them on the circumstances. Fight on their behalf and guide them toward a win-win decision.

Remember, buyers look for agents to demonstrate honesty and integrity above all else. They also want agents who can find them the home that fits their needs. Combining these wants and coming from a giving mindset will allow you to deliver service that will earn you clients for life.

Show the Right Homes

You simply can't get your clients into the right house unless you know what to look for. If you've done the Wants and Needs Analysis, dug deeper to get their top five, and know your market, it's time to use that information.

1. Know what type of home your client is looking for (single family, duplex).
2. Know what features and amenities they desire.
3. Know what area they want to live in.
4. Know what their priorities are (close to work, in-home office).
5. Know what their price range is.

If you are missing information from them on finding the perfect home, get those answers. Remember, you will need a signed buyer's agreement to start taking your buyers on home tours. So, if you haven't squared one away yet—now's the time.

When you know exactly *what* they are looking for, and the paperwork is signed, you can start showing them homes that fit their needs.

Looking at homes is an exciting process for buyers. They may come in full of hope, eager to see as many homes as they can. Chances are, they've been looking at properties online already. Ask to see what they've found and try to get them into the ones they like if those homes are still available. But, depending on the market, they could find that their options are not as plentiful as they would hope. Or they may find out that their budget doesn't work with everything they want in the area they want to be in. It's your job to manage their expectations and help them make the best decision. You need a game plan going into the home search, and that starts with knowing the best practices for showing homes.

Best Practices for Showing Homes

A prepared, knowledgeable start to the home search will make it an enjoyable experience for you and your clients. If you are diligent, it will also help you grow your business and establish a solid reputation along the way. Consider these things when showing your clients homes:

Best Practices for Showing Homes

1 **Be knowledgeable of properties and neighborhoods**

2 **Highlight concerns and selling points**

3 **Debrief**

4 **Pick a top three**

5 **Help clients make a great decision**

6 **Be safe**

1 Be Knowledgeable of Properties and Neighborhoods

We want to start by saying the way we talk about neighborhoods matters. The Fair Housing Act (FHA) prohibits agents from steering clients toward or away from neighborhoods based on the seven federally protected classes (and sometimes other state categories as well). And for good reason. Julia Lashay Israel, an agent in Minnesota and Texas, says that having your clients do their own due diligence can solve a lot of these problems. "The benefit in objectively assisting clients is you aren't preventing them from something that might be great," Julia says. "The difficulty is guiding and helping without steering and without imparting your own bias. Help them to do their own work." A good way to think about this is to be a resource, not *the* source.

Promoting Equity in Housing

As agents who are market and area experts, we bring inherent bias to our jobs when we think about location and what is a "good" or "bad" place to live. It's inevitable. But it's crucial that we don't bring this bias into our work when our clients are looking for a home.

Be diligent about following these laws and staying neutral when your clients are looking for something specific. Give them the information you can and help them find answers.

There are a few ways to prevent steering and remain a supportive fiduciary and market expert. Providing your clients with tools for them to discover neighborhoods and areas they feel comfortable in is key.

- Invite them to visit the neighborhoods they are looking at during different times of the day and night.

- Direct them to websites with more information.

If you find yourself in a situation where your clients are asking you directly about a neighborhood, don't be afraid to be direct. For example, if someone asks, "Are there many low-income families in this neighborhood?" say, "Due to Fair Housing, I cannot answer that question." But don't be afraid to use your conversation skills to dig deeper and direct to a topic that you can speak to. "If you're asking because you're concerned about property values, we can discuss the appreciation trends in this area."

Everyone is different, and what people deem appropriate for themselves is different. It's not up to us to determine what is a good or bad place for them to live. Of course, we want our clients to feel safe and taken care of. Fair Housing laws protect people from being discriminated against based on race, religion, sex, country of origin, disability, familial status, and more. Because everyone deserves a home.

Once your clients decide if an area suits their needs, you can then let them know what's available in the community.

If you want to go the extra mile, you can try to preview properties *before* your home tour with clients. This way you know what potential issues will need to be addressed. You can also cut homes that show well online but not in real life. Depending on the speed of the market, you may not have time to view each home. If homes are occupied, the sellers may be averse to having you preview the home. You can still drive by and spot that giant electrical tower next door that was skillfully omitted from the listing photos. They may want to view a home you already know doesn't meet their needs. You still may have to show it to them, but you can better set expectations and guide them in the right direction.

You should also review all comps in the area and know what other houses are for sale and have sold recently. Look up days on market, months of inventory, and list-to-sale prices for the area in question.

Knowing what is happening in the real estate market around your area will give you a high view of what is going on and will help you educate your clients.

Lastly, to show homes smoothly, have any available MLS data available. It will have pricing information and key details of the property you're touring that you can discuss with your buyer. Print them out or send them to buyers beforehand.

It's very possible there will be some disappointment during house-hunting. Offers may not get accepted. A home may go off market. Your client could get house-hunting fatigue if they aren't finding what they're looking for. They might be lost in the clouds, thinking something better will come along, when you know they've already seen their dream home. We will discuss hesitations and how to address them later. But being knowledgeable of properties and neighborhoods will help you establish a solid base to get your clients where they need to be.

2 Highlight Concerns and Selling Points

You'll want to highlight both concerns and selling points of the properties you show your clients. If a house has a glaring issue, or an issue that clients might not notice but *you do*, let them know immediately. You're there as their fiduciary and expert. The same thing goes with selling points. If the home has something that will benefit them for years to come and is exactly what they've been looking for, do not brush over it. By highlighting the concerns and selling points, you show integrity. It helps clients prioritize what they are excited about, what they are willing to work on, and what they will say no to.

3 Debrief

Having a conversation with your buyers about the property they just viewed helps with decision-making. Before the advent of GPS apps, agents often drove their buyers between multiple properties in a day to make the most of their time together. In the car, agents would ask their clients about the pros and cons of the home they just viewed. This custom has changed, and clients now meet their agents at showings in separate cars. But you should still find time to debrief after each showing. After your clients have gone through a property, do a brain dump of their thoughts. This can be outside in the driveway or standing in the kitchen. What did they like? What was missing? What would make this the perfect home? Or, hopefully, "Wow!" They loved it! They want to make an offer! It's always good to remember the basics. As a fiduciary, you need to be on the same page as your clients during the home search. Get details of what's on their mind while they are looking. This will save you time because you can pick future homes that fit their needs better.

4 Pick a Top Three

Clients may need to be reminded of what they love. With buyers, this means having your clients choose their top three homes. This works in a couple different scenarios. If your buyers have searched online and found over a dozen homes they want to see, it's best practice to narrow down the options before viewing. Ask what their top three choices are and go from there. You can take them to more than three homes, but identifying their top three will help them prioritize what they want at the beginning of the home search. If they just can't decide, remind them of the top five wants and needs they landed on for their home search. A quick reminder of their priorities often does the trick.

Another time to ask for a top three is at the end of each showing day. This will keep those top homes top-of-mind. If you view more homes the next day or later that week, ask what their combined top three are out of all the homes they've seen. If they consistently have a top home, point this out to them. They may not even know that they like a home so much until they've compared it against others. It's easy for buyers to get overwhelmed with houses and not remember what all they've seen. If they can keep in mind their top three, it will be easier for them to make a final decision. Suggest revisiting those top three homes a second time. Often, this second walkthrough will provide the clarity they need, even if it's just revising their number one. It's your job to keep them on track and remind them of what they are ultimately looking for in a home.

5 Help Clients Make a Great Decision

No matter what market you're in, a choice must be made. Whether it's to put an offer in or reevaluate your home-search plan, urge your clients to make a great decision at this point in the process.

When your clients can identify their top three homes, they can probably identify their number one as well. While they may not be ready to submit an offer, you should ask them to identify their top home. Have them consider what kind of offer they *might* make. This can help your buyers practice decision-making and see their reality. Depending on the market, educate them on how quickly properties are moving and what kind of offers buyers are submitting. If they aren't finding homes they like, take the time to reassess their wants and needs. Do they need to broaden their search area? Are they able to raise the budget for their down payment? Something needs to *happen* at this point in the process.

6 Be Safe

Your safety is non-negotiable. If you are showing homes alone or have people in your car, make sure you are safe and never in a situation that makes you uncomfortable. If you find yourself feeling uneasy, having an exit plan is crucial. Let's be honest, your clients could be strangers! You have gotten to know them on a certain level, but you never know what could happen during a meeting. Always let someone close to you know where you are and where you're headed.

Do your diligence and make the call. And trust yourself to make decisions if you need to exit a meeting, leave a situation or home, or end a contract. Your comfort should never come at a cost.

Turn House Hunting into Lead Generating

You should always, always, always (did we say always?) be lead generating. If you're not seeing the kind of homes your client wants for sale, go find one! Put in the work to potentially find a homeowner who is thinking of selling that no other agent has contacted. This is a great way to increase business and show your clients how dedicated you are to finding them the right home. You're looking for more people to serve along the way, too.

Practice circle prospecting. If your clients love an area but there are no homes that meet their criteria, use this information to door knock. Ask the neighbors if they or anyone they know in the area is interested in selling. Offer them something like a free market report. You can also send Golden Letters.

Why Buyers Hesitate and How to Facilitate Decision-Making

Even if you've shown your clients the cream of the crop—the tip of the top in terms of homes that fit their wants, needs, and budget—they may still hesitate when it's time to write an offer. These are some of the most common hesitations agents see and the ways to facilitate decision-making:

Buyer's Hesitations and Agent's Solutions

Hesitation #1: Buyers are afraid to commit.

Solution: Revisit their motivation.

Hesitation #2: Buyers mistake wants for needs.

Solution: Provide perspective and calm fears.

Hesitation #3: Buyers want to see more homes.

Solution: Calculate the cost of waiting.

Hesitation #4: Buyers are listening to the wrong people.

Solution: Be their personal cheerleader.

Hesitation #1: Buyers Are Afraid to Commit

Buying a home is a huge deal. It's a big commitment that comes with a lot of responsibility—not to mention it's an expensive purchase. It's common that buyers can get cold feet or feel afraid to make such a big decision. Despite how scary it can be, we know what an amazing investment buying a home is. For first-time buyers, the process presents a lot of new things all at once. People may feel nervous about leaving their old house behind. Wherever their fear is stemming from, it's an agent's job to remind them of the benefits of buying a home.

Solution: Revisit Their Motivation

When people are afraid of what's ahead, remind them why they are looking to make a change. Why were they looking for a home in the first place? Did they need to upsize for a baby or downsize when the kids go to college? Do they want to stop paying rent and build equity? Revisit why they are here and of all the benefits coming their way. At their consultation, did they dream of painting the walls and hanging pictures without fear of losing their rental deposit? Were they excited about building a family and getting more space so they can adopt a pet? Go back to these motivations to keep your clients on track. Things can get scary, but with your help, they can get to a result that will make them extremely happy. Don't let them forget it!

Hesitation #2: Buyers Mistake Wants for Needs

People often get hung up on the little things. Perhaps your buyer was dead set on their home being painted bright red on the outside. But maybe your red-house-must-haver just doesn't understand how easy a fix paint color is. You don't want them to lose out on a great decision based on details that can be fixed.

Solution: Provide Perspective and Calm Fears

Because you have their best interests in mind, listen to your clients' concerns and advise them. Let them know that certain things (like a home's paint color or flooring) can be changed and that you know vendors who can help them. Put things into perspective and remind them of the big picture. Also let them know that you can fight for concessions during the offer period to help them pay for these things.

Hesitation #3: Buyers Want to See More Homes

Sometimes, buyers are reluctant to make a choice because they want to keep seeing homes. As agent Christine Marchesiello explains, "They're afraid that they're going under contract on one house and sure enough, their dream home is just around the corner." However, a good agent knows when to lock down a great opportunity for their buyers. One way to urge action here is to calculate the cost of waiting.

Solution: Calculate the Cost of Waiting

As a market expert, you know the cost of unnecessarily prolonging a home search. Your clients, however, may not. "Data is your friend," Christine says. "People have a harder time arguing with facts when they're concerned. They've heard things in the media and from their friends, and they're worried about making a poor decision. Your job is to hear their concerns, address them, and give them the data they need to move forward confidently."

It's up to you to let them know how fast the market is moving and what steps they need to take. For example, in a sellers' market, a motivated buyer will not wait to put down a competitive offer as soon as possible. If they love a home but take the time to view more just for the sake of looking or having more experiences, by the time they come back ready to submit an offer, the home may be off the market.

There are five "costs" to waiting that you can educate your clients on to help them get clear and confident about their choices:

The Four Costs of Waiting

1. Appreciation

2. Interest rates

3. Lost equity

4. Paying more rent

5. Lost opportunity for life changes

The first four of these costs are financial. Buyers who wait on the sidelines may lose spending power if interest rates rise. They might lose out on building wealth through property that appreciates in value and gives them equity. They could continue to pay rent instead of paying down a mortgage. The final, fifth cost is personal. Some moves are driven by big life changes—a new job or an expanding family. The longer they put off choosing to buy a home, the more they have to deal with whatever uncomfortable situation they may be trying to literally move away from.

House hunting is difficult and overwhelming enough as it is. Knowledge is power. Help counsel your buyers into making a good choice that doesn't cost them in ways they have not considered.

Hesitation #4: Buyers Are Listening to the Wrong People

Home buyers come from many different backgrounds and situations. A lot of buyers rely on or want opinions from people who aren't immediately involved in their transaction. Maybe they received a financial gift to go toward their down payment. They may feel like they need the approval or blessing from the person who gave them the funds. Or they might just struggle to make decisions on their own and tend to call in family members and friends for second and third opinions. It's tempting to seek approval from family, friends, and others who know us.

It's your job to help clients confidently and independently make decisions. Whatever the situation, you can help them see it from a wider perspective.

Solution: Be Their Personal Cheerleader

When your client is making such a big choice, the best thing you can let your client know is that it is exactly that—their choice. Other's opinions may matter to them. But they are the ones signing the papers and taking ownership of the property. Help advocate for them. Offer to video chat with loved ones who may have given them a down payment gift. If they are a young, first-time home buyer, they may want their parent's reassurance that they are making the right decision. Loop these people in when necessary and give them the same market expertise and guidance you give to your buyer. Do your best to get everyone on the same page when looking to make the best decision. If there is too much noise from others, remind your buyer that they are in charge of this decision. They need to trust themselves to do what's best.

Lead with compassion, knowledge, and integrity. By giving them what they need, whether it's help navigating their relationships or a reminder of when to stand firm, you become a true fiduciary.

Even for the most ready, willing, and able buyer, hesitations will probably arise. When you can predict these hesitations and practice navigating them, you will improve the experience for everyone.

Work with Listing Agents

At this point in the transaction, you'll likely be communicating with listing agents on various properties. Although your contact may be brief and sparse, your impression and impact will be lasting. Good relationships with other agents are key to your reputation and a good business experience. You can make yourself memorable in a good way or a bad way—and obviously aim for the good way! Chances are you will work with the agent again in the future. Having a solid working relationship will make other agents be excited about working with you and, in turn, more apt to give you referrals.

The bottom line is, treat everyone professionally and with respect. Like lots of things in life, you tend to get what you give. Establish good practices for communicating, like no phone calls after 7 p.m. unless the situation is dire. Be timely with your responses and be courteous with your words. Many agents miss opportunities from not having consistent contact and good relationships with other agents.

And you won't always just have buyers to work for. Sometimes you'll have sellers to work for, too! In the next chapter, we will discuss how to work with sellers. We will cover advising them on their selling strategy and pricing, creating a solid marketing plan, and maintaining great communication.

It's your job to guide them to an appropriate decision based on facts, not emotions.

CHAPTER 14

Work with Sellers

Congrats. You've landed a coveted listing. Now what?

Thanks to your hard work, the sellers trust you to list and sell their house. The agreement is signed, and their house is in your capable hands. Now comes the next challenge: selling your client's house in a timely fashion and for a great price. Depending on the national and local market, houses may be disappearing faster than free samples at Costco, or they may be staler than a week-old bagel. You need the skills to move a listing in any market, and we're going to show you how.

To win with sellers, you must excel in two critical arenas. First, you must know how to handle sensitive conversations with clients about pricing and condition. Second, you need to create a marketing plan that will help you find a buyer for your listing. When you develop these skills and have the tools you need at your disposal, you can get the job done in any market *and* wow your clients.

Consult and Set Expectations

Sellers always want to know what their house will sell for and how long it will take. The vast majority want to net the most from their sale, but some are less motivated by maximizing sales price. They need to move on a timeline that works for their life goals. Either way, they can only control two highly connected elements of the sales conversation—price and condition. The other factors—location and market conditions—are out of their control. Location is a big deal. It has a huge impact on the price, but that was decided when they bought the home. The market is the market. You can educate them on market conditions and how that will impact their sales experience.

Ultimately, your job isn't to *tell* them what to price their house at. Your job is to *help* them make a great pricing decision. While it's the seller's responsibility to decide on the list price, neither you nor the seller sets the sales price for the house. Only a willing buyer can do that. You will consult with your seller on how their location, the house's condition, and the market will likely impact pricing.

Motivated sellers want to price their house competitively. They want it marketed to as many buyers as possible. And they likely want it sold within a specific timeframe. It's your job to guide them to an appropriate decision based on facts, not emotions.

Most of us have personal connections with our homes. They are where we spend most of our time, where we build relationships, and they are essentially a reflection of who we are. Because of the intimate ties we have to our homes, we can take what is said about them to heart. When that home becomes a property—an asset to sell—it's difficult to make that mindset transition.

If clients don't think rationally, it can be difficult to help them achieve their goals with the sale. Overland Park, Kansas, agent Klarissa Skinner says the transaction is not about your victory as an agent, but about helping your seller make the best decisions. "We can only inform," she says. "We don't need to make things more dramatic than they need to be." Selling a house can feel stressful and difficult when an agent doesn't have their client's best interests at heart. Be an agent who puts their clients first. It may mean having tough but needed talks with your clients. This will ultimately help make the process run smoother.

"I think one of the key jobs of a real estate agent is both to acknowledge emotions and, at the same time, try to take them out of the equation," says Sandy Edry, an agent from New York City. "Stay calm, cool, collected, and fact-based."

There are three areas where you'll have to have some serious (yet sensitive) conversations with your sellers.

Sensitive Seller Conversations

1 Pricing and condition

2 Showings

3 Seller's disclosure

1 Pricing and Condition

The price that a house is listed at, and ultimately sells for, usually tracks with its condition. Obviously, the age and upkeep of the property affects its sale price. If it's not as good as it could be, its price won't be either. Common issues include pet odors, unsightly personalized décor, clutter, outdated finishes, and damage. If you notice these issues, be honest and understanding with your clients. You may need to suggest one of the three D's: deep cleaning, decluttering, or depersonalizing. You should also let them know these things will affect a house's selling price if not addressed.

Detaching stigma and judgment from the circumstances will build trust. Be nonjudgmental in these sensitive conversations. San Antonio, Texas, agent Josue Martin says he does this by practicing empathy. "A lot of times, if you come from a place of curiosity instead of judgment, you can get to the answer much quicker." You are there to help this person sell their house, not evaluate their lifestyle. Explain things for your sellers in terms of the market and buyer interest. The fact is most buyers want a move-in ready, model-like home with as few reminders as possible that someone else has lived there. It's your job to help your clients sell their house for more. Use staging and repairs to bridge the gap between buyer expectations and the listing.

Home Pricing

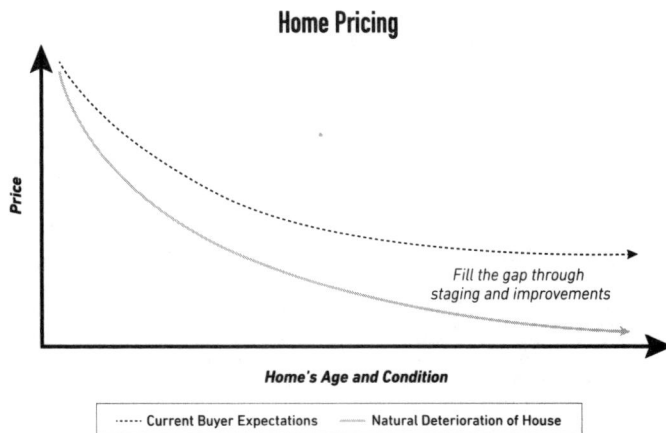

Fill the gap through staging and improvements

| ...... Current Buyer Expectations | —— Natural Deterioration of House |

Figure 45

In the preceding figure, you can see buyers expect prices for older homes to be lower, assuming that conditions deteriorate with age. However, through smart staging and improvements, you can fill the gap and stand out among the crowd. You do this by improving whatever the natural deterioration of the home would have been. Have a roster of vendors available to your clients. From minor to major repairs, list what's the most important. Changing the light fixtures can have a much bigger impact than you think, and it costs hundreds of dollars rather than thousands. Landscaping is another option for a high ROI improvement. Decluttering, deep cleaning, and storage are all things homeowners' might need to help make their house more sellable. You also need to decide how much staging needs to be done.

Even if your seller's house is spotless, there may still be issues finding a buyer willing to pay the price they desire. Pricing is a moving target, and the market will tell you if you got it right or wrong. "Pricing is about positioning in the market," Ty Voyles, an agent from Washington, D.C., says. "It's not about what you think the home is worth, what your client wants to sell the home for, or what anyone else says. It's about what the market shows at a specific point in time and what a ready, willing, and able buyer will pay and what a motivated seller will accept."

The market leans toward buyers, it leans toward sellers, and back again. A market transitioning into a **sellers' market** is good news for sellers. More buyers mean more interest, and you can price accordingly as prices go up. If houses are starting to stay on the market for longer and the market is transitioning into a **buyers' market**, you will want to get ahead of the best pricing to sell and do so urgently. A buyers' market will take more skill to effectively sell the home at a price that feels good to your client.

The market will tell you if the property's price and condition are competitive. If you are getting no showings or offers, you've missed the mark. If buyers are booking showings but you're not getting offers, you still have work to do. You're likely selling the house down the street. Listen to your market and advise the sellers on any changes to pricing strategy. Above all, be communicative and help them prioritize between sales price, timeframe, and other objectives as this target shifts.

A Note on Pricing: The 5 x 5 CMA

Outside of looking at the house's age and condition, you need to do a comparative market analysis (CMA) to effectively price a property. Your seller's competition will be the active houses on the market that most closely resemble it. Buyers will be looking at similar homes in the area. They tend to search neighborhoods for features and amenities within their price range. Once they have narrowed their search, they start picking favorites based on relative value and condition. Your CMA will mimic their process.

Start by selecting the houses most likely to be compared to your client's house. In some newer subdivisions, houses can be remarkably similar and comps are plentiful. Other older or transitioning neighborhoods can present a tougher challenge. Once you've identified at least five solid comps among active listings, look for another five in recently sold or pending. That's the 5 X 5 CMA: Five active, five pending, and five sold comps. The foundation of your suggested price range in the CMA will be the actives. The pendings and solds will tell you whether you should be leaning toward the upper or lower end of the range. If similar properties are selling well below list price, sitting on the market, or seeing price reductions, low end it is. If you see multiple offers and sales prices well above list prices, aim high. The 5 x 5 CMA should supply all the data you need to educate your seller on the best positioning for their house.

If there aren't five of each nearby, you may have to expand your search within a mile and make some adjustments. A comp in a nicer neighborhood across the way can be adjusted down on a price per square foot basis and vice versa. The 5 x 5 CMA helps you understand the "neighborhood normal" and what the minimum expectations are for home shopping in the area. You want to know how your seller's house compares *really*, because the buyers might have just looked at five others down the street. "Learn as much as you can about the market that the listing is in," advises Heather Upton, an agent from Indianapolis, Indiana. "Really study how many days comps are on the market, how many price adjustments it might take, and how many agents make offers so that you can be able to talk intelligently about all of it. You can't spend enough time studying the market you're in or the market you're going to list a property in."

When you do your homework, you'll employ the right things to stand out from the crowd and properly price the house.

2 Showings

How would you feel if you went to a therapy session and your mother decided to sit in on it? Awkward, to say the least. When sellers are present during showings, the vibe is similar. It makes potential buyers uneasy. They won't explore the house fully, ask questions, or express their opinions. Buyers might cut their tour short just to get out and feel at ease again. Advising your sellers to exit the house whenever potential buyers are there is in everyone's best interest.

Try to schedule open houses a few days out and showings back-to-back. This way, they don't have to come in and out of their house multiple times. Showings can be troublesome for sellers with young children or pets. For showings, you sellers will also need to tidy up the place. Children's toys will need to be put away. Dogs or pets may need to be secured. Do whatever you can to make it easier for the sellers and more comfortable for the buyers. This will always help you sell the property.

3 Seller's Disclosure

The **Seller's Disclosure** is a legal document that requires sellers to list previously undisclosed issues with the house's condition. The disclosure is essentially a brain dump of everything the seller knows about the property driven by the state-promulgated form.

The forms vary by state, but things like previous damages or re-pairs, termites, asbestos, liens, and gas or electric appliances may be required to be reported. No new inspections need to be conducted to fill out the Seller's Disclosure, but it does oblige your sellers to be honest about their property. People may feel uncomfortable or ashamed about certain circumstances they need to disclose. Assure them that this is part of the process and that with the proper marketing and pricing, you can still sell their house. It can also help you discover any repairs that may be needed before the house goes on the market.

The Seller's Disclosure allows buyers to make informed decisions. If a buyer feels bamboozled and something comes up later during the inspection period, they might pull out of the transaction. If a house goes back on the market at this point, it unfortunately can create a stigma that something is "wrong" with it. You want to avoid this. Set your clients up for success by walking them through the disclosure, providing the forms, and explaining the process. It's your client's job to fill out the forms. But, depending on state laws, agents have a legal obligation to disclose any material defects they are aware of that the seller omits. Don't get blamed for disclosure deficiencies—add anything you know should be on the disclosure if your client forgets.

Communicate with Your Sellers

You will have sensitive conversations with your sellers throughout your relationship. So, it's important to build a strong foundation for communication. Poor communication is the top reason sellers stop working with their agents or don't use them again after a single transaction. Your communication methods and frequency affect the service you provide.

You set expectations with the seller during the consultation about how and when you'd be in contact. You also shared the best times and ways to contact you when something comes up. This is always a balance of the seller's preferences and your boundaries. If your seller has a strong preference for email over text messages, it makes sense to meet them where they are. You can also set some boundaries around communication outside of work hours. You should not have to interrupt bed and bath time with your toddler to field non-urgent requests.

There are three phases of communication when working a listing. First, there is the communication while you are building a plan to market the home and officially list it. You will likely talk with your clients often at this stage. You will decide together how to prepare the house for sale and then put it on the market. The second phase is when the property is on the market. This is when your communication will likely be less frequent but consistent. A good way to keep in touch with your clients during this phase is to send them a detailed report each Friday. It should include any viewings, repeat showings, and other market data. The third and final phase starts when you get an accepted offer and move under contract. Then your communication will likely ramp up again as you deal with negotiations, paperwork, and readying you clients to move.

Heather Groom, an agent out of Orem, Utah, says she once listed a house for her neighbors who hadn't done a real estate transaction in a while. "Since I knew it had been a while since they had sold a home, I made a point to call them on the phone and check in with them often, almost daily," she says. "It was important for me to always give them a plan of what to expect in the coming week." Setting these expectations of communication and following through will leave your clients ready to work with you again in the future. "At settlement, they said it was their best real estate transaction and they thanked me," Heather says.

Best Practices for Communicating with Sellers

1. Ask sellers how they'd like to communicate (call, email, text, etc.)
2. Agree on the best time of day to connect
3. Provide contact information for all parties
4. Touch base weekly

Now that you've established a communication plan, and how to assist in pricing a house, it's time to build out your multistep marketing plan to attract buyers.

Build a Marketing Plan to Attract Buyers

How people find and purchase homes has changed as the world has shifted to an internet-based society. What used to be advertised by newspaper now largely happens online. Houses for sale included. Different markets need different marketing. But looking at the last decade of statistics can inform your listing plan.

In the last decade, most buyers found their homes through these top five ways: online, real estate agents, through someone they know, open house/yard signs, and through builders. For the purpose of this chapter, let's focus on the first four since builders are not relevant to marketing your seller's property.

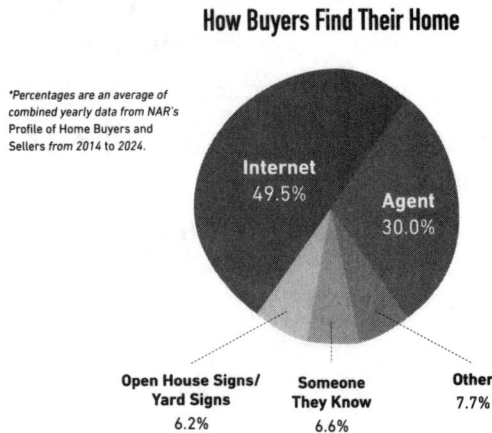

How Buyers Find Their Home

Percentages are an average of combined yearly data from NAR's Profile of Home Buyers and Sellers from 2014 to 2024.

Internet
49.5%

Agent
30.0%

Open House Signs/
Yard Signs
6.2%

Someone
They Know
6.6%

Other
7.7%

Figure 46

By concentrating marketing efforts on these areas, you will essentially connect with just over 90 percent of home buyers.

1. Internet Marketing

Depending on the property, your clients, and the market, you'll want to advertise on specific platforms. Locally, there may be key sites for marketing your listing. You can use national aggregators, niche market sites, blogs, and social media. But two considerations are always necessary when looking for buyers online: the MLS and staging.

Online Listings

Whether you need to show buyers homes before their in-person visits, or you're representing a seller whose listing will attract potential buyers, the **Multiple Listing Service**—or MLS—is an essential part of every real estate agent's marketing toolkit. It can serve you in multiple situations. You may also want to list the property on other online portals.

A listing description highlights the good things about the property and appeals to interested buyers. Does it have an amazing backyard? Is there a basement perfect for an entertainment area? Be descriptive, have fun, and use your market knowledge to paint a picture of the home.

Besides the description, consider these necessities when creating a listing for the MLS:

1. DOCUMENTATION

Each region, brokerage, and market center has its own set of rules and documentation required for an MLS listing. The right documents help answer questions potential buyers and their agents might have. Informative, compliant documentation saves time and shows your professionalism.

2. PHOTOGRAPHS

Each house you market is a representation of you and your brand; each listing should look top tier. Invest in a good, professional photographer to take pictures of a property. These photos will make your MLS listing pop and can be used in other promotions as well. Even lower-priced listings and rentals, not just luxury properties, deserve this effort. High-quality photographs make all the difference. The more, the better!

Great photos and more information will sell your listing faster and for a higher price.

3. SCHEDULE

Just like documents, your showing times can vary from region to region. Depending on your area, these are a couple of things to consider:

1. Does your area have broker and agent tours on specific days?
2. Are you planning on holding an open house?
3. Do you see an increase in interest in homes listed on Thursday or Friday?
4. Are NFL game days a no-traffic day in your area?
5. Are there any big holidays coming up?

The list goes on. That's why you need to know the right schedule for listings in your market and post accordingly.

4. OTHER

Depending on the type of property and market you are in, there may be other things to include in your listing. Floorplans and 3-D tours provide more property details. Drone videos offer wonderful aerial views if a listing has substantial acreage or beautiful landscaping. These things can make an impact if they work for the house and prospective buyers, so get to know your property and what is hot in your market right now.

Staging

NAR's 2023 *Profile of Home Staging* found that 81 percent of buyer's agents said staging helped buyers visualize the property as a future home. The same report says 20 percent of buyer's agents found that staging a home increased offer prices by 1 to 5 percent, compared to similar unstaged homes. The proof is in the production.

The seller may not have an extensive budget for in-house staging and design. Thankfully, technology has created an easy solution. Potential buyers will usually see a property online before visiting it. Investing in a digital or AI stager can have just as big an impact as physical staging. Even if people get to the property and it's bare or needs some work, they will have already seen the home's potential through staged photographs. Opening potential buyers' minds to the possibilities of what *could be* in the home is a great way to get them to act on a property. You sell a house twice: once online and then again in person.

2. Market to Other Agents

Marketing to other agents is a great way to get knowledge of your listing out to potential buyers. This can start with the MLS listing. Send it around to your agent connections. Whether you're a solo agent or on a team, you will work with other agents and should always add their contact information to your database. This way, when you have a new listing, you can let buyer's agents know there is a new home on the market for them to show their clients. Remember, over 30 percent of buyers find their home through an agent. There are two great ways to market to other agents so that your listing can find a buyer.

Pocket Listing

A **pocket listing** is a listing where the seller chooses not to put their house on the MLS. While the MLS will hit the largest number of buyers, it may be in your clients' favor to list their home specifically and exclusively. This mostly takes place with a luxury listing, a client who wants to keep their property and information private, or an estate with specific amenities that appeal to a smaller group.

If you take on a pocket listing, you can market it internally to your brokerage. It's also possible your seller has a buyer in mind. If your client is open to listing on the MLS in the future, but wants to do a pocket listing first, you can use this time to gauge interest and evaluate your pricing strategy. You won't be marketing the listing the way you normally do, so build out a marketing plan that makes sense for a smaller group of people. Include everything you would on an MLS listing but use the right language to engage your specific audience. Make sure to showcase any beautiful staging photos if your client is open to that.

There are rules and regulations when it comes to pocket listings, so educate yourself on what is legal in your market.

Broker Open House/Coming Soon

Listing a property as coming soon or hosting a **broker open house** is another exclusive marketing strategy. But it reaches a broader audience than a pocket listing.

Coming soon properties let you hold a broker open house, where you invite other agents to view the property, hoping they have interested clients. Although you are being exclusive with your invite list by not marketing it to the public, you may actually cast a wide net this way. Agents can have several buyers they are working with and large databases of potential buyers.

While you won't be putting out yard signs and riders, you will need to market the broker open house. Reach out to the agents in your area you think might be interested via phone or email. Include the information for your open house and offer a lunch or desserts for agents to enjoy while they look at your listing. They will want to use this as a networking opportunity (and so should you!), so give them time to relax and talk business after viewing. Ask them to sign in or RSVP to collect contact information if you don't already have them so you can follow up, just like you would at a regular open house.

One thing to note is that different listing platforms and different states have different rules about how long a home can be listed as "coming soon" before it must be made public. Make sure to check yours so that you stay in integrity.

3. Help Your Sellers Find Their Buyer

It's your duty as an agent to educate clients on how to best sell their property. This includes pricing, preparation, and even how they can help market their own property.

Agents often skip over this last part, but that's a mistake! Helping your sellers find their buyer is a great way to potentially make a sale run smoothly and quickly.

Let your clients in on your plan to sell their house and discuss how they can be involved. Provide them with marketing materials, photos, and flyers so they can help spread the word. They can post to their own social media, blogs, or emails, and invite people to any open houses. Chances are they know their neighbors better than you do, so they can spread the word that the house is for sale and when to stop by. Arming your sellers with materials to help them find their buyer is a fantastic play. You are all on the same team anyway, so put them on the court.

4. Market Through Open Houses

Open houses are a simple, effective way to get buyers in the door of the house you're listing. They create excitement and compel interested buyers to put in offers. The more eyes on the property, the better. Having an open house plan for your sellers will let them know you are working hard to get their home sold. They're also a great way to boost your business. We'll talk about open houses in more detail in the next chapter.

Put It All Together

Now that you know how buyers find their homes, you can build a marketing plan for your listing. You will use tactics that match the way home buyers are looking for properties. Remember to ask the seller what's important to them. Is it speed? Price? Low hassle? Privacy? Maybe it's a combination.

Find out what trumps what. When you match your strategy to what your seller values, you become an agent they trust and will want to work with in the future.

A Thirteen-Step Marketing Plan for Listings

This Thirteen-Step Marketing Plan is designed for maximum exposure of a house in the shortest time.

1. Price the house competitively.

2. Advise sellers on how to attract buyers by showing the house in the best possible light.

3. Place "For Sale" signage with riders easily visible to drive-by buyers.

4. Hire a professional photographer.

5. Optimize the online presence by posting the property on local and global MLS systems, and on social media, with plenty of photographs and a description of the property.

6. Market on multiple websites, including your own site, your local office site, and national brokerage site, to attract both local and out-of-town buyers.

7. Create flyers for viewers of the property.

8. Door knock and distribute "just listed" flyers to neighbors, encouraging them to tell family and friends about the house.

9. Target marketing to active real estate agents who specialize in selling houses in the neighborhood.

10. Include the property in company and MLS tours, allowing other agents to see it for themselves.

11. Market and host an open house to promote the property to prospective buyers.

12. Target active buyers and investors in your database who are looking for homes in the price range and area.

13. Provide updates detailing marketing efforts, including comments from prospective buyers and agents who have visited the house.

When you build your marketing plan, you'll customize it to your market and client. Marketing plans will likely be different for every agent depending on their local market trends. A singular approach to marketing a listing may serve you for one or two transactions, but you will need an arsenal of marketing tactics to sustain a listing-based business. Use the thirteen-step plan we showed you as a guide, but don't be afraid to get creative!

With your new knowledge of the best marketing plan and how to best communicate with your clients, you're ready to excel as a listing agent. In the next chapter, you will learn how to carry out one very important step of your marketing plan: the open house.

An open house, *done right,* serves as both a passive and active form of lead generation.

CHAPTER 15

Host an Epic
Open House

The sun has just started to set. You've already swept the kitchen floor of your seller's home. Now, you pick up a large bag filled with used paper cups and napkins that littered the countertop only an hour ago. On your way back from the trash bins, you pluck the "Open House" sign from the curb. "Leave No Trace," you think—the hiker's motto. The sellers are due back in thirty minutes, and you have a few more last-minute fixes to make before they return. You're excited to tell them about the woman who's scheduled a second viewing in a few days. As you gather your things, you check your sign-in sheet and see the names and emails of fifteen new people to follow up with and add to your database. Give yourself a pat on the back! You've just hosted an epic open house.

Not all open houses will run this smoothly. Sometimes we work our tails off and only get a few people through the door. I remember an agent who used to work in my wife Wendy's office. They moved from out of state and didn't know many people in the area, so they chose open houses as their main form of lead generation. They hosted upwards of thirty open houses before they got a single client. They held them over and over, every weekend. They were relentless. As weeks turned to months, they got to know the neighborhoods they were working down to the tiniest detail. As their knowledge and confidence grew, so did their success. It felt like nothing worked until everything did. One day, you're shouting into the void. The next, your pipeline is full to the brim. Over the final quarters of the year, the agent did so much production they won Rookie of the Year in one of the most competitive markets in the country. The point is, don't be hard on yourself if the balloons you bought to decorate your open house sign pop as you try to put them up. Things happen. But when you practice, prepare, and stick to your methods, you'll most likely find a payoff.

Contrary to what you might believe, the most important part of any open house is not the event itself. It's the work around the event that matters most. According to NAR's 2024 *Profile of Home Buyers and Sellers*, only 4 percent of buyers found the home they purchased through an open house or yard sign. But don't let that statistic fool you! Open houses are extremely valuable for both home sellers and the agents hosting them. If the meteorologist on TV says there's a 4 percent chance of rain, you probably won't grab an umbrella as you head out the door. But if you opened a can of soda and someone told you there was a 4 percent chance of it being poisoned, would you drink it? Heck no. Statistics are relative to their opportunity or potential calamity. About one in twenty-five people find their home in an open house. Those are good odds. An open house may not find your sellers a buyer. But it will draw attention to the property, market its availability, and create urgency.

Open houses are also great for lead generation, branding, and learning about your local market. In her first year as an agent, Jenn Baniak-Hollands says about a quarter of her business came from leads she generated at open houses. "Open houses gave me the ability to present myself and my skill set," she says. An open house, done right, serves as both a passive and active form of lead generation. Open houses put you in the path of many potential buyers and sellers today. They allow you to expand your database, practice conversations, and learn what people in your market want. By watching what excites potential buyers—or what amenities the property lacks that make it a miss—you'll gain insight.

The seven-day open house plan we lay out in this chapter is a proven plan created by agent Jen Davis. Her team uses these best practices to help sell hundreds of homes each year. This plan focuses on a week-long timeframe, but don't think this is the only path to success. While some agents prepare much further in advance, others throw together a great open house in just a few days. You'll find what works for you.

One-Week Plan for Hosting an Open House

Day 1	Day 2	Day 3	Day 4	Day 5	Day 6	Day 7
Research	Advertise on the MLS	Invite people!	Advertise on social media channels	Put up directional signs	Block off day	Put invitees and attendees on a follow-up plan
Identify a house to hold open	Create marketing materials	Circle prospect			Require sign in	
Set a date		Partner with vendors			Adapt	
					Pay attention	
					Stay safe	
Select		**Market**			**Host**	**Follow Up**

Figure 47

To help you identify the big-ticket items within your week of work that will make your open house epic, we've divided them into four steps. It starts with selecting a listing that is well positioned to drive traffic. You then will market it much more thoroughly than the average agent would. Hosting it seems like the pinnacle of opportunity, but over time you'll see that most of your business will come from your follow-up plan. That's actually true of almost every lead generation strategy. The fortune, as they say, is in the follow-up.

Four Steps to an Epic Open House

1 **Select a listing**

2 **Market the open house**

3 **Host the open house**

4 **Follow up and win clients**

Let's jump in to making the choice that will define the rest of your week. One of the biggest rookie mistakes out there is selecting the wrong house to hold open. Never worry. We've got you covered. Let's get started!

Day 1: Select a Listing

Open House Plan, Day 1

Day 1	Day 2	Day 3	Day 4	Day 5	Day 6	Day 7
Research Identify a house to hold open Set a date						

Select

Figure 48

On Day 1 of your open house plan, you need to start with a choice: Which home will you select to showcase? Then, you'll need to decide on the best date to do it. This is because you can't start marketing your open house until you have the details! But making these choices isn't always as simple as rolling dice.

As a rookie agent, chances are that you don't yet have any listings of your own. This means you'll need to ask other agents in your brokerage or market center to hold open houses on their behalf. Not only is this a great way to generate leads, but you'll also build connections with other agents at the same time.

After reviewing the listings you could hold open, you'll need to decide which ones might do well as an open house. This isn't a given. For example, a home at the end of a long, unpaved road in the woods likely won't benefit from an open house as much as a home in a busy neighborhood with sidewalks and nearby businesses would. Other types of properties that make for great open houses are recently listed, price improvements, or extreme makeovers. These attributes create a specific draw to a home that can pull in neighbors and passersby—in addition to folks actively seeking a home.

Beyond a home's location, you'll need to do some market research to inform your choice about when to host an open house. Look at other open houses in your area to learn patterns of marketing and attendance. Depending on the area and market, an open house may perform better on certain days. While it's common to hold open houses on weekends, more and more agents are hosting them on weekday evenings. Think about it. If you're a busy parent shuttling kids to swim meets and birthday parties on weekends, dropping by an open house after work on a weekday sounds pretty appealing.

As you research options for the location and time of your open house, you'll also gain knowledge that will help you provide valuable information to attendees. Knowing how to answer their questions or being able to point them in the right direction will set you up as a market expert. Details of the home's history and amenities, neighborhood market information like comps and new listings, and other information about the area will help you put on the best presentation.

As you decide which house to hold open, clear the time with the agent. The listing agent will schedule it with the sellers. Account for the full timeframe you'll be in their home, including preparation, hosting, and clean up. Give yourself plenty of time but be mindful of their schedule. Preferably, they'll be out of the house when it happens. So, make sure they can arrange to be out and about for the duration. Then, plan to follow up with them and confirm the open house the day before and the day of. We hate to think of anyone canceling last minute, but it happens.

Now that you've done your research, made your choice, and confirmed the date with the sellers, you can move on to the real meat of your week: marketing your upcoming open house.

Days 2–5: Market the Open House

If no one knows your open house is happening, how will they attend it? Marketing will take up the most time during your week because it's a critical part of securing a great turnout. With solid marketing, you'll spread awareness about your open. Without it, you could end up standing in an empty home for hours with nothing to show at the end. Those warm cookies you baked to make the house smell great and offer to visitors? You ate them all by yourself. Don't be that agent.

Many agents will do very little marketing, put some directional signs out, and spend a half day sitting in a mostly empty open house. We propose you flip your focus from sitting in the open house to marketing it. Allan Domb, a member of Philadelphia's city council who was a renowned agent before his political career, pioneered this idea. Allan was known as the "Philly Condo King" during his almost forty years in the real estate industry. His open houses were the definition of epic. "Most agents will spend an hour marketing a four-hour open house," he shared with us. "I will invest a minimum of four hours marketing a one-hour open house." Allan knew that the more time you spend marketing, the better your potential for high traffic at your open house. Showing agents and their clients were only allowed in one at a time. That, combined with the small time window for the open house, led to a long line of people at the condo waiting their turn to get in. All those buyers in line created a different kind of energy. People started to assume his listings were extra special to draw so many people. That led to more interest and more offers. He says, "It's more than just extra effort; it's about putting the extra effort where it belongs."

During Days 2–5 of your open house week, you'll spend time generating interest by reaching out to your sphere, creating marketing materials, advertising the open in various channels, and setting up signage around the property. Sound overwhelming? Don't worry. We'll give you the day-by-day breakdown.

Day 2: Create and Place Marketing Materials

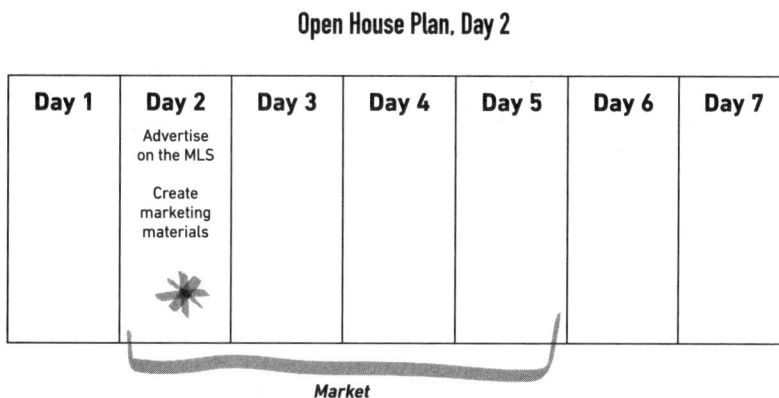

Open House Plan, Day 2

Day 1	Day 2	Day 3	Day 4	Day 5	Day 6	Day 7
	Advertise on the MLS Create marketing materials					

Market

Figure 49

Before you can spread the word about your open house, you'll need to have something for audiences to look at. That means the first thing you need to do on Day 2 of your open house plan is create marketing materials. These will generate awareness of the event into your sphere and beyond.

When creating marketing materials, you need to be consistent, professional, and fun. The advertising should showcase your brand and include information about the listing and event. There are endless creative materials you can use to make your listing stand out and match your specific brand image. For now, focus on non-negotiables. A "For Sale" sign in the front yard is Listing Agent 101. Adding an "Open House this Saturday" sign during the week of the event can further pique the interest of neighbors and local traffic. Create fliers to hand out in the neighborhood closer to the open. You'll also want to post signage with arrows, known as **directionals**, throughout the neighborhood later in the week. There are many national and regional vendors who can supply these. Make sure you order enough to cover all the major entrances to the neighborhood and on any key corners. These signs should include your branding. Even though the listing may not even be your own, all the branded signs create the impression that you are a serious player in that neighborhood.

Although tangible items like fliers, door hangers, and curbside signs will reliably attract foot traffic and neighbors, remember that most people's home search begins online. Your digital strategy should include social media promotion, email blasts, preview videos, and details about the open house on the MLS—and wherever else it is listed online. If it is your listing, we suggest investing in professional photos of the house to really make it pop. If you are holding this open house on behalf of another agent, they may already have high-quality photos ready to go. You can also ask if they have any other marketing materials at the ready, including printed MLS pages, seller's disclosures, brochures for recommended vendors, etc.

Now that you have these materials ready to go—printed out or sitting in a file on your desktop—it's time to spread the word.

Day 3: Invite, Circle Prospect, and Partner Up

Open House Plan, Day 3

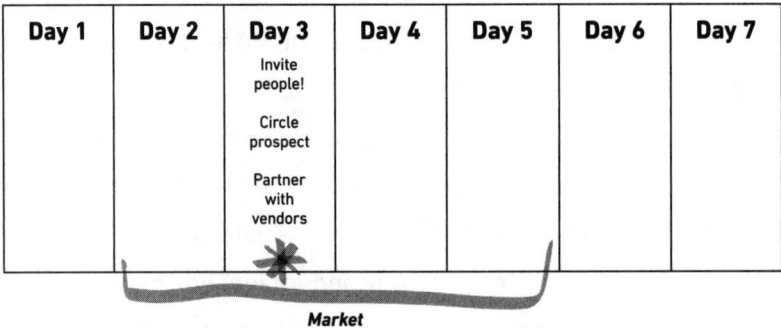

Day 1	Day 2	Day 3	Day 4	Day 5	Day 6	Day 7
		Invite people! Circle prospect Partner with vendors				

Market

Figure 50

On Day 3 of your open house plan, you'll send out invitations for your open house to at least one hundred people. We know that sounds like *a lot*, but you have *a lot* of tools at your disposal.

Open houses will require both kinds of lead generation efforts: marketing, which will reach a wide audience with little contact, and prospecting, which will require direct outreach to potential attendees. One highly efficient manner of direct outreach is circle prospecting. To practice this method, imagine a line reaching out from your listing address in all directions (let's say three to four blocks). That line forms the diameter of a circle. You'll reach out to all neighbors living within that circle by calling or door knocking to tell them about the open house you're holding in five days. ⊗

One universal human truth is that people want to know about other people. "People are curious," Jen says. "They want to know what their neighbors' homes look like and find out what price it's listed for." This is true even if they aren't in the market themselves. Indulge this impulse: Ask them to stop by and view the house. While you're at it, ask them if they, or anyone else they know, is looking to move to the area. Give them a flyer with your contact information and the event's time, date, and address on it. Who knows—you might find a buyer or your next client.

With each open house, you should plan to put your database to work. ⊗ Use phone calls, newsletters, and texts to spread the word. You can use your tags to target a portion of your database that you know is looking at houses in this area or price range. Or maybe you'll message other agents in your database to see if they have clients who might be interested. This is a great way to build rapport, provide service to your fellow agents, and generate attendance.

An amazing trick to boost attendance is to partner with businesses. These include title companies, lenders, home inspectors, or other vendors with whom you have good relationships. This allows you to utilize their databases and networks in addition to your own. You may need to adjust your marketing materials to make them co-branded with your partner business. Then, you can establish a plan for them to share these materials with their audience and write a contract to ensure they follow through. On the day of the open house, have a business representative attend to network and answer attendees' questions. This is a win-win partnership. It brings visibility to both businesses—yours and your partner's—and strengthens your referral network.

Day 4: Advertise on Your Channels

Open House Plan, Day 4

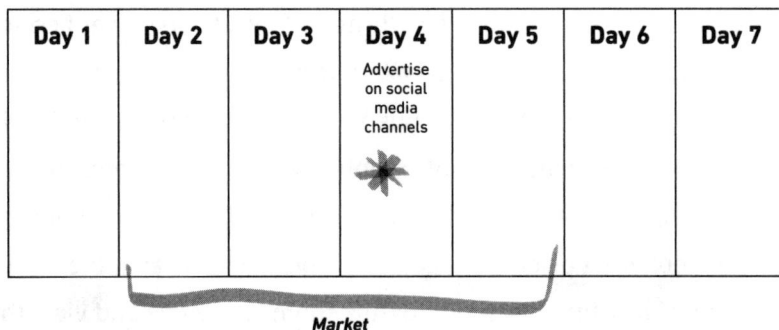

Day 1	Day 2	Day 3	Day 4	Day 5	Day 6	Day 7
			Advertise on social media channels			

Market

Figure 51

On Day 4, it's time to get online and post some of the advertisements you created earlier in the week. We all know attention spans are short in the age of social media. Don't post too early in the week. People might forget about your event. But you want to give folks enough time to fit your open house into their busy schedules. We've found that the middle of the seven-day plan is the sweet spot.

Promote the open house on all platforms where you connect with your database: social media, newsletters, the works. Many agents keep their professional and personal accounts on social media separate, and that's okay. But it is in your best interest to advertise your open house on *all* of your pages, no matter their purpose. This reaches a broader audience and helps establish your professional brand. As a rookie, you might not have the biggest following on your business accounts. Tapping into your personal network is a great way to build a following.

Photos and videos are the best way to attract people from social media. Give them a taste of what they can experience at an open house—without spoiling their appetite for the main course. This could mean putting together a slideshow of professional photos. Highlight some, but not all, of the home's exciting features. Or it could be a video of you announcing details of the open house, with the entryway or another attractive feature of the home in the background. Then, in the caption, promise more information and surprises for people who attend in person. This generates excitement by offering an exclusive benefit. Of course, include important details like the address, time, place, and your contact information in the description.

Day 5: Put Up Directional Signs

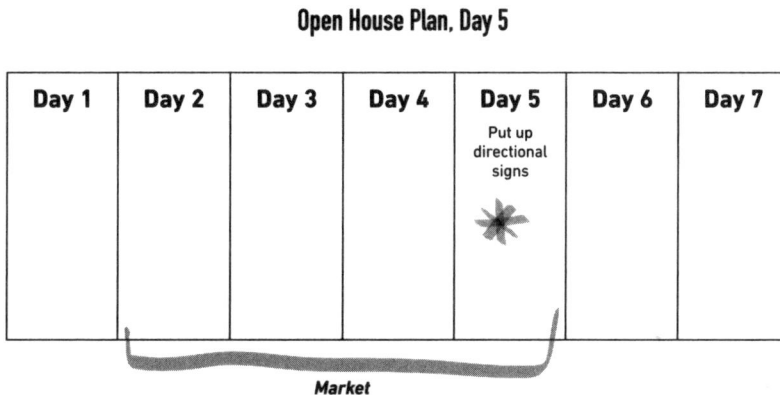

Open House Plan, Day 5

Day 1	Day 2	Day 3	Day 4	Day 5	Day 6	Day 7
				Put up directional signs		

Market

Figure 52

The day before showtime, go ahead and place the directional signs you ordered on Day 2. This helps advertise to local traffic, as well as avoids any confusion for people who drive in from other areas. You should be aware that different neighborhoods have different signage restrictions. If the neighborhood has an HOA, check with them to ask about any restrictions and see how early you can set out signs. "The signage should go out at the earliest time your area will allow," Jen shares. "And we're not going to put just one sign out. We're going to learn the routes to the house and put as many signs as possible, driving people by that home."

Agents place anywhere from five to fifty directional signs depending on whether the home is on a main road or tucked into a suburban cul-de-sac. In rural areas where houses are more spread out, even more signs may be necessary to attract attention. When you think you have enough, add two more! It's better to have too many signs than too few visitors because no one can find the open house.

Branding information or pictures of your face on these signs can help build recognition. But remember their main purpose is to effectively direct people to the open house. Don't overdo the branding at the expense of clarity.

You may also want to add something snazzy to jazz up the "Open House" sign in the front yard and denote the main attraction. A lot of agents choose to place balloons on the mailbox or the sign itself. "Balloons are like catnip for adults," Erin Holloway, an agent from Franklin, Tennessee, laughs. "They are must-have and draw people in." If you agree, stop at a party supply store to pick up unfilled balloons. Plan to arrive early the next morning to fill them. This way, you won't end up with a horde of balloons in the backseat of your car obstructing your rear-view mirror. That's dangerous and should be avoided.

Day 6: Host the Open House

Open House Plan, Day 6

Day 1	Day 2	Day 3	Day 4	Day 5	Day 6	Day 7
					Block off day	
					Require sign in	
					Adapt	
					Pay attention	
					Stay safe	

Host

Figure 53

At this point, you've done your due diligence to prepare for the open house. Now it's time to watch the dominoes fall into place! You should be excited to show off your hard work. But don't forget that it's game day, which means you must put on your game face. Try not to have awkward energy. You don't want people to have time to question what they should do. Greet everyone and don't leave guests wondering if you'll offer a tour or let the open house be a free-for-all.

Treat everyone that comes in like a current or future client. Give them your attention, time, and respect. Above all, be yourself, act professional, and enjoy your time meeting people and building new connections. Mooresville, North Carolina, agent Kent Temple says that when he first started in real estate, holding open houses was the best and quickest way to add people to his database and get the appointments he needed to reach his goals. "To this day, no matter what market we are in, open houses are one of my team's top five sources of lead generation," he says. Here are a few best practices to help you be like Kent and get the most out of this epic event.

Block Off the Day

Such a big event will require your full attention, so block off your schedule for the entire day. Arrive early to ensure everything is set up and your materials are in order. You should also plan for time after the event in case your lead generation pays off and you meet people who want to look at other houses in the area. Leaving your day open leaves room for any opportunities that may walk through the door.

Require Signing in

As you set up, place your sign-in sheet or tablet on the counter or kitchen table alongside printed MLS listings and other information.

"Some agents get nervous about asking for information," Jen says. We get it, it can feel weird to ask strangers to provide personal details. But the thing is, you can use an assumptive close (remember, from your conversation frameworks?) and simply tell them to sign in. Your sign-in sheet is *crucial* for capturing leads, consent, and following up ⊗. Lead generation isn't the only reason you should require that guests sign in—it's for your own safety. If anything happens during the event, guests' information can be vital. So don't make it optional.

Some agents recommend that their seller require a sign-in for the security of their belongings. That way they can honestly tell anyone who attends that the seller has requested a record of everyone touring their home. Direct, reasonable, and highly effective. On that note, you should recommend that the sellers secure any jewelry, guns, or prescription drugs before the open house. Rarely, items do go missing, and those are the most likely targets.

Along with names, require one piece of contact information, whether that's a phone number or email address. Also include a "yes" or "no" box for whether they are already represented by an agent. People are more likely to fill out this information and be honest about it if it's provided in a simple layout. If someone is still hesitant to fill it out, let them know they can add a "do not follow up" note so they won't hear from you after.

Agents have different thoughts on the merits of physical versus digital sign-in sheets. A physical sheet helps deter fake names and information. But it's easier to input and be "done" with a digital form. A digital sign-in option helps decipher bad handwriting and is easy to transfer to your CRM and obtain consent for follow-up calls and texts. Whatever you choose, gathering the information itself is what's important. Without it, you won't be able to implement your follow-up plan, add to your database, and capitalize on potential business the open house will bring you.

One tip is to place the sign-in sheet in the kitchen next to any food or refreshments instead of in the entryway. If people are stopping to sign in near the door, you may cause a traffic jam that could turn people away from the event. A bonus tip from agent Erin Holloway is that she has noticed people tend to prefer individually wrapped treats instead of platters. Pick your party favors as you will—either way, we're believers that if a snack is "fun sized," the calories don't count.

Pay Attention to Attendees' Needs

As you meet people throughout the event, pay attention to their needs. Ask questions. Be curious. Take notes on the feedback they give you about the home, look for ways that you can be of service. Maybe a visitor mentions that they love the house, but it's out of their price range. First, ask if they have an agent. Then, if they don't, ask if they are interested in meeting with you after the open house to look at other homes that fit their criteria. This can lead to a signed buyer's agreement and a client! If they're already represented, ask for their agent's contact information so you can let them know you have some other houses for their clients to look at. You might secure a buyer for another seller you're representing. If you pay attention and look for ways to help others, the opportunities are endless.

Create a Safe Environment

Unless you have a vendor partnership for your open house, you'll likely be running it alone. To help you avoid an uncomfortable or unsafe situation that could arise from interactions with strangers, follow this safety checklist:

Open House Safety Toolkit

- **Tell someone what you are doing.** Let a co-worker, friend, or family member know the address of the open and the times you will be there.

- **Have a means of communication.** Keep your phone on you at all times. Check in periodically with people to update them or how the event is going and how many people are there.

- **Keep your belongings in the car.** Carry only your phone and business materials.

- **Require sign-ins.** Signing in isn't just for your database, it's a safety precaution, too. Have every person that comes through the door sign in and fill out their information.

- **Greet all guests and do a gut check.** If a visitor feels off or you feel uncomfortable, exit the home and call someone you know.

- **Turn the lights on.** Make sure the home is well-lit if you are doing an evening event.

Meet the neighbors. Introduce yourself to the neighbors (good for business, too!) and let them know you'll be in the house.

Stay aware. Always know your exits and have a plan for getting out of a situation. Don't go into basements or attics with anyone alone.

Park in a safe spot. Leave your vehicle near the house and in a place where you can see behind it and under it at all times.

Have someone meet you to close down. Ask a co-worker, friend, or family member to meet you at the end of the open to close down. Walk to your cars together.

Figure 54

This list isn't here to frighten you. The vast majority of people you meet at an open house will be friendly and harmless. But please play it safe when you're in a new environment by yourself. You are worth more than any transaction.

Day 7: Follow Up and Win Clients

Open House Plan, Day 7

Day 1	Day 2	Day 3	Day 4	Day 5	Day 6	Day 7
						Put invitees and attendees on a follow-up plan

Follow Up

Figure 55

Your open house may be the "main event," but the truth is that you've saved the best for last. In fact, agents rarely find a buyer or new client on the day of the open house. Most clients are won during follow up. An open house represents hours of your hard work, so don't let that effort go to waste by not setting visitors up on a follow-up plan. "One of the things I've seen when people forget to follow up is that people will get really excited about selling ... and then list with someone else," Jen says. Your open house plan isn't complete if you don't plan for follow-up.

Follow up begins the day after the open house—Day 7. You'll have reached one of two outcomes: the sellers have received offers on their house and are on the road to going under contract, or not. If you held the open for another listing agent, let them know the outcome, including any prospective leads or feedback from attendees.

Whether the listing sold or didn't, "Either way, we're going to call the same neighborhood again," Jen says. 🌀 "We'll let them know we had this many people go through the open house, and we had this many offers. We'll tell them whether we accepted an offer or not."

People are curious, remember? When you circle prospected, you may have piqued a neighbor's interest in selling their own home. Don't let their excitement fizzle out. Reach back out to them and tell them how your open house was received by prospective buyers. Ask again if they know any other neighbors who are interested in selling, or if they might be. After all, you just told them how popular a house in their neighborhood was! If they say yes, imagine Jen giving you a thumbs up and saying, "That's awesome. Set an appointment." But if they don't seem interested in doing business now, collect their email address and ask if they want to receive your regular market reports. You can set them up on a follow-up plan that will keep them engaged. We're pretty sure Jen would give you a thumbs up for adding to your database, too. (Spoiler: We asked, and she totally would.)

Let everyone you invited know that you either appreciated them for coming by or that you missed their presence. People may want to buy a home now, or they may be comfortable where they are. Either way, you can put them on a plan in your database with information that is relevant to their stage in life. If you provide value, you'll be top-of-mind when they decide to use your fiduciary services.

The title of this chapter may be "Host an Epic Open House," but the key to obtaining business happens before and after the day of the event. Once you've mastered these events, you'll be on the road to achieving a closing. But, before you get there, you'll also have to learn the ins and outs of negotiations in the next chapter.

CHAPTER 16

Make, Receive, and Negotiate Offers

Your expertise as an agent will truly be on display during the offer process. This is where it all comes together—your market knowledge, your negotiation and communication skills, and your fiduciary mindset. Although they follow a familiar process, every transaction is different. Comps may be hard to identify. A buyer may get cold feet. A seller may get unnecessarily attached to an unlikely outcome. The other party's agent may not be very cooperative. You name it and it can happen. To navigate to closing, you'll focus on consulting with your client, communicating clearly with all parties, and collaborating with the other side's agent whenever needed to ensure a great outcome for all. The outcome both sides want is an accepted contract for the sale that checks off as many needs and wants as possible.

To help you navigate making, receiving, and negotiating offers, we will look at the transaction from both the buyer's and the seller's perspective. We've divided the process into four parts. First, we'll examine what the offer process on both sides looks like, so you know points of communication and guidance. Second, you'll learn how buyers' agents present and submit offers to sellers. Third, we'll explore how listing agents receive and respond to offers. Finally, we will talk negotiating for both buyer and listing agents.

The Offer Process

The offer process is rarely linear. More often, it's a path that can loop back on itself. As offers are countered or rejected, the process may jump back to the beginning and start again. Here's what that might look like:

The Offer Process

Figure 56

Almost always, the process begins when the buyer's agent submits an offer based on their client's wants, needs, market information, and other relevant factors. On rare occasions, sellers can write an offer to a buyer who is dragging their feet or in a stalled negotiation. In that case, the buyer would still need to sign it and send it to kick off the process. Either way, once the listing agent has an offer in hand, it's decision time. The seller can now choose to counter the offer, accept it, or reject it.

The next steps depend on this response. If the seller counters, the negotiation has begun. If the seller accepts the offer, it goes into the contract-to-close phase. Even if your offer is rejected, don't always take that as a hard "no." The buyer's agent can reach out to their counterpart to find out what's needed to get the seller's consideration. Depending on the answer, the buyer can move on or submit a brand-new offer based on this new information. Dizzy yet? Like we said, it's not often a linear process.

Manage Emotions and Expectations

Throughout the offer process, you'll wear many hats. You'll also have to manage your client's emotions at each step. This stage of the transaction can be emotionally charged, no matter which side of it you're on. Rejection, competitiveness, loss, and disappointment may arise as offers get rejected and fall through. Sometimes, clients will be riding a high as a transaction moves along and things appear to be going well. Then, out of nowhere, negotiations may fall apart for any number of reasons. If an offer doesn't work out in the end, your clients might feel gutted. Help them process their emotions when things don't go as planned. You might be thinking, "But I'm not a licensed therapist." While true, your clients still need you to help them understand the process, stay optimistic, and develop a solid plan to move forward.

Here's a tip from Austin, Texas, agent Jenn Lewis: Try not to use ownership words like "my" when referring to your client and instead call them "the" client. "When we tie ourselves too tightly to the outcome, we get ourselves in trouble," Jenn says. "We stop being able to see clearly so that we can get through the negotiation in a very logical manner, while also understanding the emotions that are in it without using emotion." Remaining level-headed is key. Communicate with your client about what you are doing and why you are suggesting certain decisions. This will calm them down when tensions are high. Your job is to help your clients navigate these emotions and take reasonable, fact-based action. Besides serving as a "therapist," you'll also manage logistical responsibilities, like writing up, delivering, and receiving offers. Throughout, you'll serve as your client's representative, advocating for their preferred outcome in negotiations.

When clients look back on their experience of working with an agent, they likely won't remember the details of the offer you managed to secure them. Instead, they'll remember the way they felt during the (often stressful) stage of making, receiving, and negotiating offers. Remind them of their motivation and keep them on track whether you're coasting along or zigzagging on the proverbial cliffs of the offer process.

Buyer's Side: Write and Submit Offers

After you've helped your client reach the decision to make an offer on a home, you'll need to write an offer, and present it to your clients before submitting it to the listing agent.

The Buyer Side of the Offer Process

Figure 57

Sometimes, you may have multiple offers out at once.

In a **sellers' market**, having multiple offers in play at once happens because you're "competing" against a huge pool of buyers, and houses seem to go under contract in the blink of an eye. (You'll have to cast lots of lines if you want to catch a fish).

In a **buyers' market**, you might submit multiple offers if your client is an investor, wants to shop for "deals," or is time motivated and needs to increase their chances of closing on a home as soon as possible.

Whether you plan to have multiple offers out or just one, the process is easier when you are prepared.

Prepare

You can increase the chances of an accepted offer with a bit of research. Contact listing agents directly to dig deeper into their sellers' wants and needs. You can ask questions like, "Outside of price, what's the most important thing for your seller to see in this offer?" You should also ask how they would like to receive the documents. The listing agent may want offers sent to a specific email, by a deadline, or with a specific closing agency. Verify that you are doing things right and meeting the other side's requests. Show them you are proactive and professional.

You also have your own details to manage. You'll need to round up your buyer's pre-approval letter and review the listing's details and tax records, among other tasks.

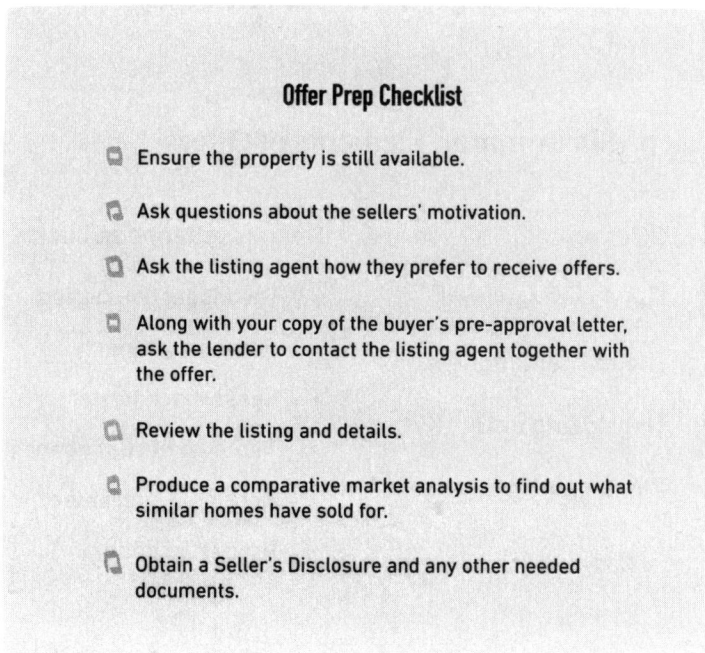

Offer Prep Checklist

- Ensure the property is still available.
- Ask questions about the sellers' motivation.
- Ask the listing agent how they prefer to receive offers.
- Along with your copy of the buyer's pre-approval letter, ask the lender to contact the listing agent together with the offer.
- Review the listing and details.
- Produce a comparative market analysis to find out what similar homes have sold for.
- Obtain a Seller's Disclosure and any other needed documents.

Figure 58

Details matter. I remember a story of a buyer who wanted to purchase a home in a specific school district. Their agent found one, they made an offer, and it was accepted. Only later they discovered that they were in the wrong district! You see, homes on one side of the street were assigned to the desired school district and the other side of the street were assigned to a different school. The listing agent had misread the data, and as a result, the MLS information was incorrect. Even though they reasonably assumed the MLS data was correct, the buyer's agent and their broker got sued. Don't worry, they worked it out and got the buyers into the right district at no additional cost. Still, if ever there is a time to dot your proverbial i's, it's when you're preparing your offer.

Write the Offer

When you feel prepared, it's time to write the offer. While rules and regulations differ from state to state, all offers contain six common elements.

Six Common Elements of Offers

1 Offer price

2 The down payment

3 The earnest money

4 The closing date

5 Financing

6 The miscellaneous bucket

- The inspection period
- Personal property
- Lease-back terms
- Removal of contingencies
- Appraisal guarantee
- Property condition

The highest-priced offer doesn't always win—the strongest one does. In a pie baking contest, the pie made with the most expensive ingredients won't always win.

The one with carefully measured ingredients or topped with Meemaw's blackberry sauce will. That's why the sixth category, the miscellaneous bucket, is where you have power to make the offer stand out.

The specifics of items in the miscellaneous bucket may differ from transaction to transaction. It's an opportunity to customize and curate the perfect offer based on everything you've heard from the seller. Portland, Oregon, agent Sarita Dua says, "Think of all these items as levers or buttons you get to push or pull based on what you know about the seller and how far they are willing to go." If you work with a buyer who isn't in a rush to move and the sellers need more time to get out of the house, consider adding a lease-back clause to the offer. That's a convenience more money can't buy.

When you show your clients that you understand what they are willing to work with, you can then share creative ways to make their offer shine. Here is a seven-part checklist to make sure you're hitting all the key notes when writing up an offer.

1. Property Information

All basic information—including the home's legal address, the name(s) of the buyer and anyone else who will be on the title, and the sellers' names—needs to be written in the offer. Make sure it's all accurate and spelled right!

2. Conditions and Contingencies

The successful closing of a contract hinges on several terms, conditions, and **contingencies** that will need to be met. This list must cover everything that could go wrong with the transaction. It will give your clients the opportunity to exit a contract if something goes awry. Standard items include a contingency based on inspection findings or loan approvals. Other common contingencies include assurance of a clear title, appropriate appraisal valuation, or the sale of the buyer's current home. Accounting for all scenarios will save your buyer any grief in the future if they uncover concerning information. It enables them to back out without consequence or penalties.

3. Sales Price, Terms, and Financing

All financing items should be covered in the offer or financing **addendum**. This includes the offer price, the down payment, earnest money, closing costs, lender information, and the specifics of how each piece of financing needs to be paid (when, to whom, and in what format).

Besides offer price, other financial aspects can be adjusted to make your offer more appealing. For example, the amount of earnest money—in other words, "good faith" money. If the buyer backs out for reasons beyond the scope of the contract, or if they do so after the inspection period, the seller gets to keep the earnest money. It's a way to put some skin in the game, so to speak. The number could be large or small; it depends on the area and the market.

During a sellers' market, a buyer may be more inclined to put down more earnest money to show how motivated they are to get to close.

Remember, if the buyer backs out for a reason outlined by the contract's contingencies, their earnest money can be returned. The earnest money protects the seller from everything else, including a bad case of cold feet.

4. Conveyances

When an offer is accepted and financing is confirmed, there will be an official **conveyance**, or transfer, of the property between owners. This is usually done through a title company or real estate attorney and needs to be notarized. The title company and any fees should be included in the offer. Also include all appliances, structures, warranties, etc. that your buyer wants to convey along with the property. Usually, items like stoves and built-in microwaves convey, but refrigerators do not. If in doubt, don't assume, ask the seller.

5. Due Diligence/Inspection Period

After an offer is accepted and the house goes under contract, the transaction will enter a phase of **due diligence**. During this period, the buyer will need to hire and schedule an inspection, review the findings, and then potentially adjust their offer accordingly. The timeframe and dates of the due diligence period should be clearly written out in the offer. Abiding by this period is crucial to ensure your clients can back out of the contract without losing their earnest money.

6. Buyer Concessions

Depending on the Seller's Disclosure and the inspection, the property may need to have repairs before buyers inhabit it. Some sellers may refuse any repairs and only sell the home as-is, depending on the market. Others may make repairs themselves prior to the sale. After the inspection, buyers may ask for a repair allowance to put toward any necessary fixes, or they may want a lower price on the home. This will depend on negotiations, but is something you should write into the contract depending on your clients' wants and needs. Buyers can also request concessions for other reasons, like paying their agent.

7. Closing Date and Possession Date

Solidifying the closing date gives buyers, and the other side of the transaction, something solid to look forward to. Most **closing dates** occur thirty days after the contract is signed. Be sure to distinguish between this date and the **possession date**, when your clients actually get the keys. Often, these two dates are the same. But if you are working with a lease-back agreement or are offering more time for the seller to move out, those dates would be different.

After you consider what the sellers want and write the best offer, discuss the offer with your buyers. Be sure that your buyer understands the contract. Go over the offer and be transparent about items in the offer that make it stronger or weaker. Explain timelines and set expectations for the inspection periods, funding, and potential negotiations.

Double check you haven't left any items out. Some things in the offer may be met with a counter-offer, and sellers will likely be more willing to negotiate down than up.

The Problem with Buyer "Love Letters"

For a long time, buyers wrote "love letters" to sellers. They hoped to tug at their heart strings and get their purchase offer accepted. These letters included introductions to the buyers, personal information, and feelings about the property. Often, a picture (think a family of four, a black lab, etc.) accompanied a love letter. The idea was to add a little human connection that could nudge the seller toward accepting an offer in a multiple offer scenario or if the offer was lower than asking price. The problem with love letters, though, is that they can easily violate the Fair Housing Act. Things like race, sex, disability, and religion are protected classes. By disclosing this information to the seller, especially through a photo, the seller may violate the law if they choose to sell or not sell based on any of these protections. The buyer wouldn't be in the wrong by disclosing personal information. But these protected factors should not play into the seller's decision-making. Tell your clients that by opting out of sending a love letter, they are doing their part to promote equality in housing.

Submit the Offer

Once you've written the offer and discussed it with the buyers, you will present it to the listing agent to go over with their sellers.

Execution Hurdles for Offers

1. **Check all your documents:** Check, recheck, and check again to make sure you have every document you need. Make sure they are logically ordered and labeled clearly.

2. **Follow state laws:** Every state and region has different laws and requirements when it comes to submitting offers. Make sure you are privy to all the rules. If you can, have someone check your work.

3. **Email a summary:** Along with the offer, you can email a summary of highlights, so the other agent has them ready to give to their client. This shows you will be a serious and helpful to the listing agent.

4. **Notify the listing agent:** Using the listing agent's preferred method and timing of communication, let them know you are submitting the offer. This proactive move helps establish your communicative reputation.

5. **Notify the lender:** It's a good idea to have the lender reach out to the listing agent directly with a pre-approval letter so the seller knows the offer is legitimate. You should at least give the listing agent the pre-approval letter yourself and notify the lender that you are officially submitting the offer.

6. **Consult with your buyer:** Tell your clients the offer was submitted and fill them in on next steps. This should include when you should hear back about the offer, what negotiations might look like, and how you will help them through it all. Let them know what will happen if the offer gets accepted and if it gets rejected. Expectation setting is key.

Even if an offer seems perfect, a seller may still reject it for any number of reasons with little or no explanation. Because you can't predict how an offer will be received, don't make any promises about the outcome to your client. Instead, set yourself up as an expert so that they trust your advice and you can move quickly to submit. When your clients know what's going on and when they're going to hear from you, you can meet and exceed their expectations. If they're left in the dark, anxiety and mistrust may creep in. Perform your duties as a fiduciary for every buyer you represent and proactively keep them in the loop.

Seller's Side: Review, Present, and Respond to Offers

Now that the offer has been submitted, let's turn our attention to the other side: reviewing, presenting, and responding to offers as a listing agent. Even if you are primarily working with buyers at the beginning of your career, it's good to know what's happening when the offer is out of your hands. Seeing the world from the eyes of a great listing agent will also help you make better offers.

The Seller Side of the Offer Process

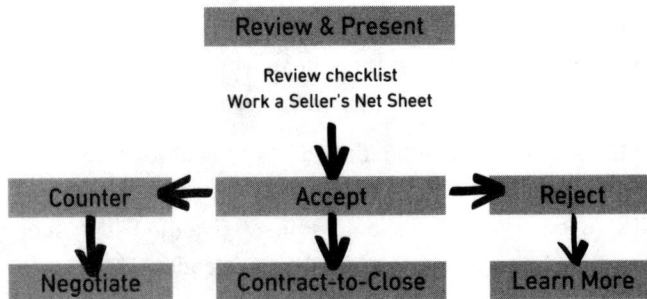

Figure 59

Much like on the buyer side, this stage of the offer process can be highly emotional. Receiving offers can be disappointing, or perhaps a reality check that the sale of a beloved home is really happening. Be ready for a deep conversation about whatever offers you receive. If you are prepared, you'll help the seller see through their emotions, walk through their options, and determine the best way to a win-win.

Review and Present the Offer

Review an offer so that you understand it and can accurately present it to your seller. Be aware of your market, in case you need to respond promptly. And encourage your seller to move forward, in whatever way they decide. Here's a handy checklist to reference.

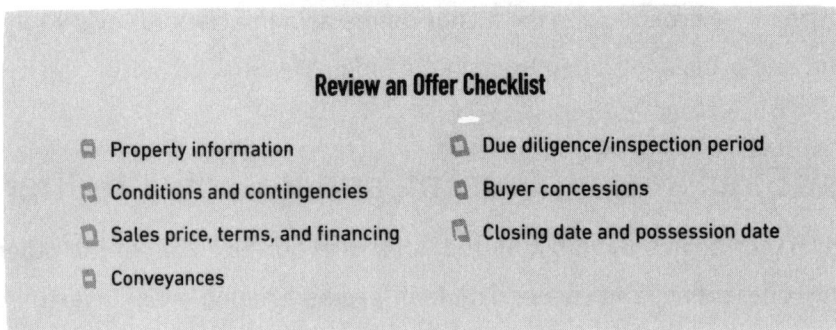

Review an Offer Checklist

- Property information
- Conditions and contingencies
- Sales price, terms, and financing
- Conveyances
- Due diligence/inspection period
- Buyer concessions
- Closing date and possession date

Figure 60

It's a best practice to create a Seller's Net Sheet. This document lists the fees and costs subtracted from the amount offered, so the seller can see how much money they will walk away from the transaction with. These costs include mortgage payoffs, liens, taxes owed, requested buyer closing costs or concessions, home warranties, seller closing costs, agent fees, locale-imposed fees, and anything else related to the sale. This document helps your clients make informed decisions and creates a baseline for a win-win later in the process. The best agents work one up for each serious offer. Here's an example of what one looks like:

Seller's Net Sheet

Sales price	....
Existing costs (subtract from sales price)	
Loan payoffs	....
Property tax (prorated)	....
HOA dues (prorated)	....
Misc. late fees	....
Estimated expenses (subtract from sales price)	
Title fees	....
Escrow fees	....
Buyer concessions	....
Commission	....
Service fees	....
Closing costs	....
Net Proceeds	....

Figure 61

After you analyze the offer, discuss it with your seller. You know your clients and can anticipate how they will respond, so determine whether it's best to meet in person or discuss over a phone call or on Zoom. You should have reviewed the offer process during your seller consultation and agreement. Now, you can get to the specifics of the offer at hand.

Make sure the tone of your conversation doesn't get negative. Never criticize the buyer, the buyer's agent, or the offer. The offer might not always be what you want, but every offer is an opportunity for education. Make sure your clients are focused on the terms of the offer, not the people submitting it. Discussing offers from an objective viewpoint will facilitate the best decision-making. Provide your seller with context and discuss the details of the offer and how it pertains to their situation. Things to point out include days on market, number of showings, and past offers. Answer any questions and remind them that you have their best interests at heart. Whatever decision they come to is their own, and you are there to support them.

Respond to the Offer

There are three options when it comes to responding to an offer: counter, accept, or reject. Be prepared for any of these responses and the courses of action they trigger.

If your clients like portions of the offer but are uncomfortable with some aspects, they may choose to counter. It's important that your clients know a counter-offer is a rejection of an initial offer. You've effectively said "no" to the buyers. The buyer may reject your client's counter and walk away. You need to discuss what your clients feel is a reasonable counter and give guidance. Depending on the market, it may be in your client's best interest to accept the offer even if it falls slightly short of what they are expecting. Or, if the market is in their favor, encourage them to counter an offer you know is better. Make sure they know the risks involved in this type of decision. Go over every option with them and weigh the outcomes. Remind them of their goal and support them as they navigate this choice.

If the offer is reasonable and your clients feel comfortable with it, they will accept the offer. Remind them that if they accept the offer, they are under contract to that buyer—and that buyer alone. While buyers can choose to back out during the inspection period, sellers don't have the same option. Negotiations can continue through the inspection period, but essentially their property is sold based on the original offer they've accepted. Once an offer is accepted, your clients will likely feel excited and anxious to get the transaction closed. Prepare them for any bumps and assure them that you will be with them for every step. Create a timeline of what happens next and let them know when you'll be in communication.

If your clients feel an offer is unreasonable, they might choose to reject it entirely. Instead of countering, they may invite the buyer to submit a completely new offer. Or they may decide it's not worth their time. Remember, you can only tell other parties what your seller has instructed you to disclose. If they reject an offer but are happy to tell the other party what terms would be accepted, you can talk to the buyer's agent about it. But you can't tell the buyer's agent any information unless your seller gives you permission. Depending on how they decide to move forward with an offer rejection, you will need to take different actions.

Multiple Offer Scenarios

Your client may find themselves receiving multiple offers. Analyze all of them. It's a legal requirement for you to present your clients with all offers submitted. Then, your seller can decide which offer appeals to them the most. They can choose to accept the best offer or ask you to consult with the buyer's agent for adjustment. For example, if your seller likes the price and terms of one offer, but the closing date is too soon for their comfort, you can ask the buyer's agent if their client would accept a later closing date.

Your seller can also decide to put out a call for the highest and best offers. There are general parameters for how to put out this call. Make sure you are following the rules and regulations for your market and broker.

In a multiple offer scenario, your client may depend on you to help them make the best decision. Educate them on their options and what each decision would mean for them.

Buyers and Sellers Negotiate Offers

Negotiating will play a big role in your real estate career. If an initial offer was not accepted and a counter-offer was made, you're officially in the negotiating stage. And while it's certain that you will need to practice negotiating as an agent, people have mixed feelings about the whole idea. Some people jump at the opportunity to exercise their skills as a master negotiator. Others shudder at the thought. But no matter how you feel about negotiating, one thing is true: It's not easy. There is even an entire department at Harvard, called the Harvard Negotiation Project, dedicated to finding effective means to reach amicable agreements.

The department's solution lies in something called "principled negotiation." In Roger Fisher and William Ury's book *Getting to Yes: Negotiating Agreement Without Giving In*, they suggest looking for "mutual gains whenever possible, and that where your interests conflict, you should insist that the result be based on some fair standards independent of the will of either side." We couldn't agree more, and this is where you can help every negotiation reach a win-win conclusion. Sometimes, that means moving on from a transaction. Other times, it means finding the middle ground where both parties feel good and decide to commit to a sale.

Negotiation is only successful if it's rooted in integrity and communication. Those things are what breed a win-win result. With this in mind, you need to understand the negotiation process and how to approach it.

The Negotiation Process

The most common points of negotiation fall into two categories: price and terms. **Pricing** is about the cost of the property. **Terms** can either be financial, time-based, or both, and can include things like costs, closing dates, and repairs. Each transaction is unique; be prepared for many negotiation points.

You will negotiate with both your clients and the agent on the other side of the transaction. As a listing agent, if your seller wants to counter an offer, you'll need to discuss what they would be comfortable accepting and therefore what to propose in a counter. As a buyer's agent, when an offer is rejected or countered, you need to discuss the same things when writing your counter or new offer. Then, you will present these offers to the agent on the other side and negotiate with that agent on your clients' behalf.

Communicate to Negotiate

Every time you enter negotiations, it's important that both parties know a rejection is happening, but the conversation is continuing. That's why the way you communicate is so central to negotiating. Try to be an active listener and understand what the other party is saying.

Negotiations happen because a seller has seen something in the offer the buyer is submitting and thinks, "I can do better." A win-win transaction doesn't necessarily mean it's it perfectly balanced. One side may be getting a bigger win than the other. Yet when both sides get a win, everyone walks away from the closing table with something that matters to them. Working to get the best win-win for your client is imperative to a successful transaction.

If you're a listing agent, get clear with your clients about why you are countering. What exactly did they feel was missing from the original offer? What would they add or take away from that offer to make it a win? If you're the buyer's agent, make sure you're clear on what you are authorized to concede in the original offer, if anything. Spell out and give the material verbatim to your clients. When you think you've found the win, go over it in detail with your clients before speaking to the other agent.

After you're clear with your clients, talk with the other agent before you put anything into writing. This primes you for better reception and avoids any blindsides. "When negotiating with other agents, you should typically avoid burning bridges because you never know when you may run into that particular agent again," agent Alison Simon says. "You never want to become that agent that people don't want to work with because that'll never serve your client well and it won't serve you well."

Getting on good terms and being communicative will help build trust and good rapport for a transaction to go through. And when you know what you're dealing with on the other side, you can make your offer and contract even sweeter.

And, like anything else, know when it's okay to walk away. If the other side doesn't want to budge and you know it's not moving in a direction that benefits your clients, talk your clients through their options. Be there for their disappointment and assure them that brighter options are on the horizon.

A Win-Win for Everyone

Making, receiving, and negotiating offers is an exciting part of a real estate transaction. It's also an emotional one. But when you understand the process, communicate with your clients, and use skills to negotiate on their behalf, managing emotions becomes easier and win-win situations enter the realm of possibility. Now, it's time to talk about what to do when an offer is accepted. It's time for contract-to-close.

CHAPTER 17

Navigate Contract-to-Close

Can you see it? The light at the end of the tunnel? It's there! You've made it through the offer and negotiation process. Some would call that the toughest part of the transaction. But, just as capturing a lead doesn't guarantee they will become a client, an accepted offer doesn't automatically mean a closed transaction. There are several steps in the contract-to-close period where a transaction can falter. This is especially true if you are unprepared, disorganized, and haven't set the right expectations with your client.

To help you reap the rewards of all that you've sown, let's walk through best practices for the contract-to-close period. Many agents hire a transaction coordinator to handle this portion of the process so they can focus on helping their next client. Some agents choose to be directly involved from start to finish. This chapter will prepare you to work with a contract-to-close specialist or to DIY the closing process. We'll focus on the latter, since it requires a deeper understanding.

Also, the contract-to-close can vary significantly from state to state due to laws, regulations, and local customs. Some states require an attorney to oversee the closings, while others use title companies or escrow agents. As such, timelines and costs can be very different. We've done our best to cover the process from 30,000 feet here. Our goal is to familiarize you with the process and where you deliver value.

Contract-to-close duties include maintaining solid lines of communication, meeting deadlines, and avoiding risks. You must do this in all four stages of the contract-to-close period: writing and signing the contract, the inspection period, the appraisal-to-close-period, and the closing. You also have to inspire confidence and remain a steadfast partner to your client, the other side's agent, and your vendors. Sound like a lot? It is. But with a clear head, good communication, and a professional attitude, you can handle it.

Be Proactive with Communication

Great communication is essential to ensuring your closing goes smoothly. Ask yourself: How many different people are involved in closing a transaction? The answer will vary by region, but generally, it's several. Below is a list of some potential parties besides the buyer, seller, and yourself.

Parties Involved in a Real Estate Transaction

1 Other party's agent

2 Title company/attorney/ escrow agent

3 Inspector(s)

4 Lender

5 Appraiser

6 Insurance agents

7 Property managers

8 Tenants

9 Movers

10 Contractors

11 Family members

As the real estate agent, it's up to you and the other party's agent to coordinate everyone and their tasks across the finish line. You need to know who to contact and when, as well as make sure that every person has the information they need to move forward. This is a lot of juggling, but we believe in you. Set expectations and follow through on your commitments. Build trust. Communicate with everyone involved positively and in a timely manner.

Keep in mind that your relationships with the larger transaction team affect how quickly and pleasantly things get done. Don't be shortsighted. Even if a vendor is patently unpleasant to work with, you can still choose to maintain your professionalism. They may not be your cup of tea, but if they are good at their job, you may find yourself working with them again and again. Take the high road and look to the future.

Follow Timelines and Meet Deadlines

The purchase and sale of property is ultimately a legal process. There are several deadlines that must be met in order for the property to close and for you to get paid. Missed deadlines are a common reason transactions fail. If there is a mistake you must make as a rookie, *don't let it be this one.* The good news is that it's easily avoidable. To help get to closing and meet every deadline, you need to sufficiently plan and manage your timelines and duties.

Letting a transaction fall apart because of a missed inspection or wrongly filled out form screams amateur hour. These details matter! Dave Knight, an agent from Los Angeles, California, refers to navigating the contract-to-close period as "proactive prevention." He advises agents to "eliminate the snares before they exist." Have systems and checklists for keeping yourself, partners, and clients aligned. During the contract-to-close phase more than any other, your reputation (not just the transaction) is on the line.

Four Stages of Closing the Transaction

As both a buyer's agent and listing agent, you can set yourself up for success during the contract-to-close period by creating a timeline. Follow along for the various check-in points with your client. As Dave says, "Keep lines of communication open with clients. Ask, 'Do you want to be updated every day? Every other day? Text or phone?'" This will help you avoid missing deadlines and keep your client from being in the dark during this emotional time.

The contract timeline starts when a contract is executed. It then enters the inspection period, followed by the appraisal, and finally goes to closing, as illustrated in the following figure.

Contract Timeline

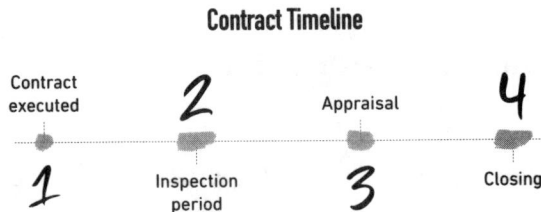

Figure 62

Each of these stages has a buyer's side and a seller's side with different tasks to complete. Odds are you're working with buyers at this stage in your career, but we are going to address both sides. It will help you grow as an agent to know what the other side's agent is doing and what their duties are as well.

Stage One: Executing the Contract

Knowing your contract timelines, deadlines, and guidelines is essential to being a real estate agent. (You might as well be an actor you have so many lines!) In the last chapter, we covered how to get both parties to come to an agreement about the terms of the sale. Here, you'll learn about the executed contract as a legal document and how it will guide the transaction to closing.

Throughout the four stages, the buyer and seller and their agents have lots of things to do and deadlines to meet. Once the offer terms are in the contract, and it's signed by both the buyer and seller, you have an "executed contract." You then enter the inspection period.

You will need to know your area's rules and regulations. This includes how a contract is filled out, what information is needed, and how it needs to be submitted. Nashville, Tennessee-area, agent Lauren Garner says the best way to prepare is to familiarize yourself with the contract. "When you know the contract, you sound more knowledgeable to your client," Lauren says. "You're able to see around corners and set the correct expectations." Adhering to your area's contract guidelines is vital to providing thorough service, making sure your buyer or seller is comfortable, and getting paid on time. Your brokerage will hopefully teach you best practices and support you when you're first starting out. This is a great time to ask more seasoned agents to show you the ropes. Rules and regulations change often, so set reminders to make sure you're up to date.

Contracts should include sales price, financing (or cash), where earnest money should go, and deadlines for all funds and contingencies.

Financing Areas of Focus

For a Buyer's Agent:

1. Communicate with your buyer about the earnest money deposit amount, deadlines, and how they can pay.

2. Advise them to avoid large purchases or opening new credit cards.

3. Remember to keep the lender in the loop.

4. Notify the escrow company and introduce them to the buyer and lender and give them a copy of the contract.

For a Listing Agent:

1. Once the contract is in place and the earnest money has been paid by the buyer, the listing agent should change the listing in the MLS to "Pending."

Whether you are representing the buyer or the seller, make note of the items that will be conveyed. The seller will need to be reminded before moving to leave them behind. If you're on the buyer side, you'll want to make sure they were left behind during the final walkthrough.

Conveyances Areas of Focus

For a Buyer's Agent:

Talk with your buyer to clarify what items they want conveyed. Know what you need to fight for and what can be let go.

For a Listing Agent:

Understand what your client is willing to do when it comes to conveyances. Know their true motivations for selling and where they draw the line.

The closing date will be written out. This date is when the transaction ends and the property transfers from one owner to the other. The time between going under contract and closing will vary by transaction.

As far as costs, both parties have a portion to cover. Depending on your buyer's or listing agreement, there are commissions or fees to be paid at closing. There are also title insurance fees, escrow fees, attorney fees, HOA fees, property taxes, lender fees, and more, depending on the transaction. Prepare your client for their closing costs and how they will pay or be paid—either out of pocket or from the sale proceeds. You need to know the details and communicate the way funds will be exchanged so there are no unpleasant surprises.

Closing Dates and Costs Areas of Focus

For a Buyer's Agent:

1. Remind your buyer of the closing date and how much they can expect to pay in closing costs. Tell them how this should be paid.

2. Continue to work with the lender, the title company, and your buyer. Remind everyone of contract deadlines. Make sure your buyer has all materials and funds ready to send to the appropriate parties.

For a Listing Agent:

1. Prepare your seller for the amount that they can expect to pay in closing costs by preparing a Seller's Net Sheet.

2. Solidify a closing date your client is comfortable with and help them if they need assistance with their move and they currently occupy the property.

Contingencies and termination conditions are laid out in a contract so that both parties have safeguards. They basically say, "If this happens, then this can happen." Contingencies include lending, the inspection, the appraisal, titles, insurance, and miscellaneous factors that apply to the transaction. Contingencies and termination conditions allow either party to back out or renegotiate without incident if major issues pop up. Protecting your client from potential disaster is your job, so make sure the needed contingencies are in place.

Take all the important dates and create a timeline of the transaction for your seller or buyer. Inspection and financing are two of the most important hurdles to clear. Buyers' agents will want to communicate with their clients early to prepare them for the inspection period. Refer them to an inspector if they need one, and get it scheduled well in advance. For items that haven't been scheduled—inspections, appraisals, final walk-through, etc.—just plot them in chronological order and update your clients when the timing is finalized.

Stage Two: The Inspection Period

The inspection period, or due diligence period, is the time after the contract has been accepted before a buyer can back out of the transaction without losing their earnest money. The length of the inspection period is commonly negotiated in the contract, but often, it will be a tight turnaround. The due diligence period is when the contract is vulnerable. Advocate for your client and help them complete their tasks. For both buyer's agents and listing agents, share the following inspection timelines with your clients.

The Buyer's Side of Inspection

Once an inspection period is set in the contract, all parties should be on the same page to get the proper activities and documentation done on time. Knowing your deadlines and establishing your timelines is the crux of this portion of the transaction. Here's what a timeline can look like for the buyer's side:

Buyer's Inspection Timeline

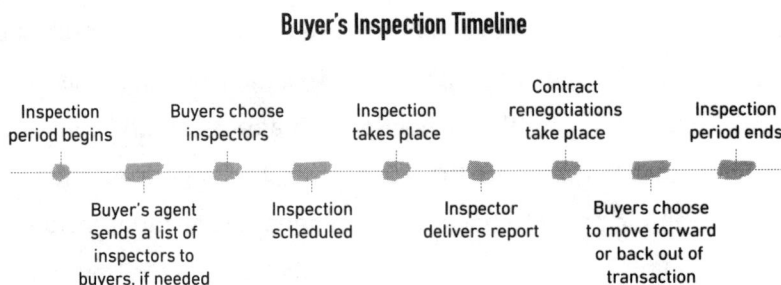

| Inspection period begins | Buyers choose inspectors | Inspection takes place | Contract renegotiations take place | Inspection period ends |

| Buyer's agent sends a list of inspectors to buyers, if needed | Inspection scheduled | Inspector delivers report | Buyers choose to move forward or back out of transaction |

Figure 63

As a buyer's agent, first you will send a list of inspectors for your client to choose from. Typically, a buyer will pay out of pocket for the inspection, so remind them of the cost and how this will be paid. Once they choose an inspector, have them schedule the inspection—the sooner the better—and let the listing agent know the date. Also, ask your clients if they'd like to attend. Inspections are often lengthy, so they may just want to go over the report with you and the inspector after it's done.

For first-time buyers, an inspection report can be daunting. Prepare them for the process. Even for new construction, the list of flagged items can seem endless. Remind your clients that big-ticket items and safety issues—like problems with the foundation, roof, electrical, and plumbing—are what they should look out for. Normal signs of wear and tear are often not in need of an immediate or costly fix.

RE-ENTERING NEGOTIATIONS

Whether you and your clients attend the inspection or not, go over the report in detail. A good inspector will walk you through the report and highlight major issues. Depending on what the report finds, you may re-enter negotiations. Help your clients understand the cost of fixing any issues and advise them on any recommended amendments to the contract. If something major needs fixing, you can ask the seller to reduce the sales price to cover the repair. The seller may choose to have it fixed before closing instead. These fixes may change the closing or move-in date. If a problem arises that makes your client uneasy about the purchase, share their options. If there's a contingency on the earnest money in the case of major repairs needed, your clients may be able to back out of the contract with no loss. Other times, there may be smaller things the buyer wants done before the move in.

Your job is to help your clients find what works for them and help them make the best choice for their future. Your gut should guide you. Would you buy this house yourself given the inspection report? Do you know your client has the funds needed to make any major repairs? Are they seeing things clearly under pressure? This is when you can provide perspective. Older homes will have lots of little problems. Even new builds can include a laundry list of potential small repairs. (Builders will often fix them.) Help your client separate the cosmetic from the structural, the annoyances from the real deal-breakers.

Once you've discussed, let the listing agent know the buyer's response. You can negotiate any changes to the contract in the response, including repairs, conveyances, closing dates, and other amendments. If the seller agrees to the new terms, you can move forward with the contract past the due diligence period. If the seller is unwilling to make changes, talk to your client about their wants and needs. Is this still a transaction they want to move forward with? Although you'll negotiate to get the best for your buyer, things may not always work out. Do what you can to make it a win-win transaction, but know when it's best for your client to walk away.

The Seller's Side of Inspection

As a listing agent, you need to be on top of dates and timelines for the seller. Once the buyer's agent has arranged an inspection, let your sellers know in case they are still occupying the house. They'll need to make sure everything is accessible for the inspector. The timeline below shows what this process looks like.

Seller's Inspection Timeline

Figure 64

Once the inspection is done, the buyer's agent will let you know if they have any concerns or are requesting repairs. If the inspection report says the HVAC system needs replacing, see if your sellers have a warranty they could use to replace it before moving. If your clients aren't willing to make any major changes, ask if they could do smaller things the buyers have asked for instead. Maybe they can offer cash back at closing for the buyers to take care of the repairs after closing. Both you and the buyer's agent are working to get your clients the best outcome. Hopefully there is a middle ground and both parties are motivated to get to the close. Walk your clients through their options and refer them to any vendors if repairs are necessary and in the cards.

Keep in contact with the buyer's agent. If the contract is amended, make sure the new details are precisely what you agreed to. Everything needs to be good to go by the end of the inspection period. Let your sellers know that until the period ends, the buyer can choose to back out for any reason. Managing emotions is a key part of your job. Like the old saying goes, prepare for the worst and hope for the best. Once the due diligence period is over and the contract is solidified, let your clients know that the buyers still could back out. Because you've secured earnest money, the buyer should be motivated to close the transaction. That doesn't mean something can't come up to change their minds. The buyer could choose to void the contract and lose their earnest money (with a common caveat being the appraisal).

Stage Three: Appraisal-to-Close

Once the due diligence period is over, a few things remain before the close. For a buyer's agent, your client's lender will have scheduled an appraisal, and you'll do a final walkthrough with your clients. For a listing agent, this means telling your clients the options based on the appraisal outcome and preparing them to move out by the closing date if they still occupy the home.

Appraisal-to-Close Timeline

Figure 65

The Appraisal Process

After the inspection period ends, the buyer's lender will order the appraisal. This is a market analysis comparing the property to similar homes that have sold in the area. It gauges the home's worth so that the lender knows the loan is a secure investment. This process involves both the buyer and the seller, and depending on the outcome, each side will choose how to move forward.

THE BUYER'S SIDE OF APPRAISAL

Appraisals can be ordered by a buyer or a seller. But typically, if there is a mortgage involved, the buyer's lender will request the appraisal that will then be authorized by the buyer. The appraisal process can take time, so be sure to set it soon after the inspection. Also, remind your buyer that the appraisal is typically an expense they will cover. If your buyers are paying cash, no appraisal is needed, but sometimes a buyer will want to do one for peace of mind.

Once the appraisal is complete, you will be notified. If the appraisal comes in at the value of the mortgage, the transaction can move through to closing. However, if the appraisal comes in lower or higher than the cost of the loan, more action will need to be taken. According to a 2017 Fannie Mae report, only 8 percent of homes come in with a lower appraisal. But we want you to be prepared in case you are not in the 92 percent.

If an appraisal comes in low, you have a few options. The state of the market will likely dictate which to choose. If an appraisal comes in lower than the purchase price, the buyer will have to cover the difference or the seller will need to lower the sales price.

Before you walk away from the transaction, first see if you qualify for a second appraisal. Check with your buyer's lender. Usually, you'll have to show that the first appraisal wasn't done correctly or missed something. Your buyer can also choose to make up the extra cost out of pocket, especially if you're working in a sellers' market. If your client has found their dream home and has the cash, go for it. If the contract has an appraisal contingency and the buyer doesn't have the extra funds, the buyer can back out of the sale and regain their earnest money. While backing out can feel disappointing, reassure your buyer that it's best not to purchase an asset for an amount higher than it's worth.

In some cases, the appraisal may come in higher than the purchase price. This is great news for a buyer. When the sale goes through, they get instant equity! However, some stipulations may make the purchase vulnerable if this happens. It's possible the seller added a provision to the contract. They could argue for a contract that states that if an appraisal comes in high, they can visit a previously presented backup offer. If the buyer then chooses not to meet the backup offer, the seller could back out of the sale.

At this point, when the appraisal has been reviewed, both parties are motivated to move through to closing. If you are negotiating with the listing agent on purchase price, keep this in mind. Keep your client involved and up-to-date on their options as you move forward.

THE SELLER'S SIDE OF APPRAISAL

Although the buyer's lender manages the appraisal, a listing agent must prepare their sellers for the process and its outcome. If you're a listing agent and the appraisal comes in at cost, you can celebrate! It's time to move to close. But in real estate, you never know what could derail a transaction. It may be in your client's best interest to write in an appraisal provision to the contract (if your state allows them) in case an appraisal comes in higher than the purchase price. If the appraisal comes in lower, your sellers have options, and you'll need to walk them through making the best choice for their situation. One thing to note here is that the first and best way to avoid a potential low appraisal is to do your due diligence when listing the property. Review all comps thoroughly and encourage your sellers to list their house at an appropriate price. Having a good listing price up front can be proactive prevention.

When prepping for the appraisal, ask your clients to ready their home inside and out so that it looks its absolute best. Then, have them make a list of any recent improvements or fixes with the appropriate documentation. Preparing for the appraiser smooths the process and ensures things don't get missed.

Like the buyer's agent, if an appraisal comes in low, a listing agent can advocate for a second appraisal if there are discrepancies or mistakes in the report. If a second appraisal is granted and comes back below purchase price again, the buyer side will most likely negotiate for a lower price. Your seller can choose to meet these asks or move forward without selling. It's a tough place to be in, and they'll need you more than ever.

If an appraisal comes in above asking price, you've also got options. If you've stipulated in the contract that your client can go to a previous backup offer, they may choose to do so. Then the buyer can decide whether they'd like to meet or exceed the backup offer. Do your best to help everyone arrive at a win-win solution while keeping your client's interests top-of-mind.

Moving Out and Final Walkthrough

Once the appraisal is conducted and both sides approve, the transaction will move to the close. Before the closing date, the buyer's agent will coordinate a final walkthrough with their client to make sure everything is as it should be. The listing agent will work with the seller to vacate the property in time and complete any tasks outlined in the contract and amendments.

THE BUYER'S SIDE OF MOVING OUT AND FINAL WALKTHROUGH

A final walkthrough is usually scheduled the day before closing. It's a good idea to keep a checklist of all the things that you've negotiated for the seller to do and any conveyances that should still be there. In the hustle of moving out, it's not uncommon for sellers to forget to clear out a hallway closet that's full of wrapping paper or cleaning supplies. Make notes of things that still need to be completed. If the seller made repairs, make sure you get receipts. After the walkthrough, let the listing agent know if anything needs to be done before signing. Remind your clients they might not get their keys at signing, and will probably receive them a few hours later, after the funds go through. Decide with them whether or not you'll attend the signing and make a plan to celebrate!

THE SELLER'S SIDE OF MOVING OUT AND FINAL WALKTHROUGH

Make sure the seller's home is ready and that your clients are prepared to move. Go over the contract so the sellers know all the repairs and fixes they need to make and what, if anything, they need to leave behind. Give them your list of vendors so they can easily make the changes needed for the sale to go through. Doing this in a timely manner will ensure a smooth closing. Ask them to save receipts for the buyers. Advise them to hire a cleaning crew if necessary. If your clients have moved out and are no longer nearby, you'll be the contact for any post-walkthrough tasks at the house. Be prepared for any last-minute services the property may need, like cleaning junk out of the garage.

Moving is stressful for both parties, so be on hand to help with any problems. Keep your clients on track with timelines and assistance. Cheer them on throughout these final days as they get to the signing table.

Stage Four: The Close

Heeeere's closing! When it comes time to close, how you interact with your clients is largely up to you. What's most important is that you prepare them for the day and everything that comes with it. Set expectations and stay in contact with them until after closing (and far beyond!).

Closing Timeline

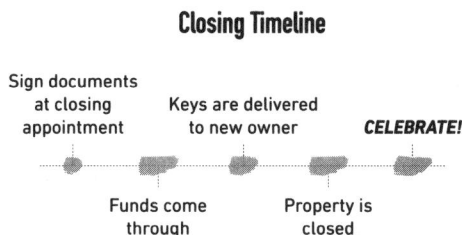

Sign documents at closing appointment

Keys are delivered to new owner

CELEBRATE!

Funds come through

Property is closed

Figure 66

Closing as a Buyer's Agent

You've already coordinated the signing with your clients and the title company or closing attorney. By setting up a tight timeline and keeping all parties informed, the lender will know the closing date and time and will have the documents ready. They will be prepared to come through with funding after the signing.

Whether you attend the closing is up to you. As a new agent, however, we highly recommend you do. It shows that you support clients to the end. A transaction isn't done until the contract is signed. Having you by their side shows them how much you care, especially if you are working with first-time buyers. Also, it's a wonderful opportunity to get a picture after closing. This is a great keepsake for your clients— and it makes for great marketing material.

Closing as a Listing Agent

Your main duty during closing is to make sure your clients can sign the contract wherever they may be. You may have to get a mobile notary to come to them if they've relocated out of state. Make sure to schedule these things beforehand to prevent any hiccups on signing day. It's also a good idea to have your sellers package up all the keys (front door, back door, mailbox, shed, etc.), garage door openers, warranties, appliance information, and anything else the buyers will need.

After the signing, for the transaction to be truly done, the funds must come through from the lender. This might not happen immediately, so let your clients know there might be a short wait. Once the funding comes through, the buyers can get the keys to their new home and start moving in. Your sellers can celebrate their successful sale! You can do your happy dance for a job well done.

Celebrate Good Times, Come on!

A good rule of thumb for any agent, but especially a new agent, is to celebrate a client's closing. You can mark the occasion with a gift or something memorable for the buyer or seller. Whatever you decide to do, making it personal will go a long way. Agent Caroline Huo says more expensive gifts don't necessarily go further for her clients. One of the most memorable gifts she's given is priceless. An elderly, widowed client who was selling her home to downsize had a lemon tree in the backyard. The woman and her husband had transplanted it to each property they lived in over the years. Caroline took a clipping from the tree, propagated it in a planter, and gave it to her client so she could keep a cherished piece of home with her at her assisted living facility. "Luxury is not a price point," Caroline says. "It's the experience of feeling seen, heard, and special." You don't need to spend lots of money to make an impression on your clients. You've gotten to know them. Doing something meaningful will help them remember you for years to come.

Gift-giving might not be your love language. In this case, consider an event or a dinner with your clients to celebrate. Cincinnati, Ohio, agent Flor de Maria McNally offers to throw her clients an all-expenses-paid housewarming party in their new home. The point of the event is to cultivate relations, with the added benefit of expanding her database. A true win-win.

Whatever you decide to do, your clients should feel celebrated at the end of their journey. Being a part of that celebration solidifies your relationship and continues to put you in good graces for a lifetime.

Troubleshooting

When you're approaching closing, practice proactive prevention. Learn which parts of a transaction are most vulnerable and prepare. It's usually during the lender approval process, the inspection period, after the appraisal, and during any renegotiations of the contract. Set expectations with your clients about the process and associated costs early on. Then, communicate with them throughout the contract timeline so you are on the same page. Also, maintain a good relationship with the other agent and all parties involved. When everyone feels respected, everyone has a good time.

You never know what could go awry. Knowing what to do when "stuff" hits the fan will earn your clients' respect, no matter how things turn out. You'll get better at this with practice, and the best way to practice is to start.

Post-Closing Fiduciary Duties

The best agents know that a business grows between home sales. Now that one transaction is done, you have a database to tend to. Update your new "past clients" and keep in touch with them after closing through a follow-up plan. Remembering their "home-a-versaries" and offering information regularly will keep you top-of-mind and build your reputation as an agent that people like and trust.

"It's important that I maintain a relationship post-closing with my clients, because real estate is not a transactional business, it is a relationship business," says agent Chris Hall. "Once we've closed, we have consistent check-ins to ultimately to ensure not only that this home is right for my clients, but also that this investment is right.

"Our goal is not to just do this one transaction with you. We want to be there when you decide to buy that next investment property. We want to be there when you decide to move up. We want to be there for your friends and family. And we do that by maintaining a relationship post-closing."

In the next chapter, we will talk about how you can put all the skills and tools you've learned from your rookie journey together to create a career without limits.

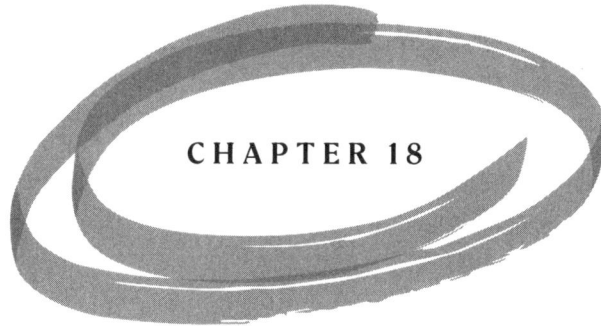

CHAPTER 18

Put It All Together

Steven Pressfield wrote about "shadow careers" in *Turning Pro*. The idea is that we all have a true calling in life that we should embrace. Many will walk right up to their calling but never cross the threshold. They're terrified at the idea of trying and failing at the one thing they should do. They pursue a shadow career instead. This shadow career looks a lot like their true calling, but there is no real risk involved. They're not really trying. If they haven't really tried, they can't really fail. Pressfield uses the example of a wanna-be rockstar living the rockstar life (staying up all night partying) but never writing any music. Pressfield himself spent twenty-seven years living the shadow career of a writer. He worked as a copywriter, a migrant worker, a screen writer, a truck driver... until finally he *committed* to do the real work of being an author. His first book? Maybe you've heard of *The Legend of Bagger Vance*?

Don't let that be you. Many a new agent has launched a shadow career. They spend their days doing career-adjacent activities. They design and order custom business cards. They hit Wayfair and Design Within Reach to build out the perfect home office. Lest I forget, the time invested getting the perfect business name with an available dotcom and social handles. With the brand name ready, they design, build and refine the ultimate website. They go to networking events but gravitate to people they already know. If they really want to create the ultimate shadow career, they preorder cutting boards and insulated cups as future closing gifts with their painstakingly designed logo. The list goes on.

Like Yoda infamously says, "Do or do not, there is no try." Do not let the fact that you're new to real estate give you the excuse of only "trying" and not making the commitment to yourself, your business, and your future that you need to. Remember, you'll thank yourself later for how strongly you commit now.

The real work of launching your career is in these pages. We've covered everything from mindset to markets, role play to lead generation, holding open houses to building habits for success. We've walked through the fundamentals of creating and nurturing your database. You know how to set an appointment and convert it! Finally, we covered working with buyers and sellers from signed agreement to closing day. Focus on the fundamentals and your career will take hold.

Fear gets in the way of a lot in our lives. It can make us miss once-in-a-lifetime opportunities. It keeps us from thinking big and reaching our highest potential. It can repel us from taking a leap of faith and embarking on our dream career. Our true calling. We encourage you to break past that fear and do what you were meant to do. You have all the tools at your disposal to launch a limitless real estate business. The main thing you need to do now is show up and do the work. You'd be amazed how an ounce of productive action can make those fears fade away!

Your Big Why, Revisited

In Chapter 2, we talked about how finding your Big Why will help you build a foundation for a success mindset throughout your career. Your Big Why is your drive and motivation for doing what you do. It will help you get through the hard days and make your wins extra sweet. You're working for a reason that is BIG. It keeps you grounded, focused, and on the path to achieving your dreams.

After reading this far, you still may not know your Big Why. You may have a lot of little whys lined up in your head. That's a good start! We know you picked this book up because you have big aspirations to become a successful real estate agent. So, your Big Why is in you somewhere. You just need to find it.

Take the time to think about why you want to be a real estate agent. Is it to spend more time with your family because your supposed-to-be nine to five is really a five to nine? Is it to unlock the earning potential that will finally bring you financial freedom. Now is the time to dig deep and get to the purpose of your path here. Because when you discover your Big Why, it will make showing up every day and being consistent on the job much easier. And that consistency is what breeds success.

Show Up and Get into Action

The key to being good at anything is showing up and doing the work. Even if you have all the skills and all the knowledge, you can't make any progress if you aren't acting. Now that you know about lead generating, building a database, holding open houses, negotiating, and everything in between, it's time to lace up your metaphoric running shoes, cross the starting line, and set your pace on the track.

The Three Areas of Focus to Get Into Action

1 Be consistent

2 Maintain your database

3 Lock in and be accountable

1 Be Consistent

You may feel ready to burst onto the real estate scene full steam ahead. Or you may feel hesitant about getting started. We don't want you to get burnt out before you hit your stride, and we don't want you to worry too much about what comes next. Instead, we want you to focus on showing up and doing things every day, consistently.

Remember in Chapter 12, when I wrote about the merry-go-round? It takes some effort to get spinning, but once going, it's almost effortless to keep the momentum. The key here is consistency. No matter how big or small a push is, the point is that you're pushing every day. When you build in purposeful habits to your daily, weekly, monthly, quarterly, and annual routine, you will consistently make progress. You're "pushing" every day. That's why forming these habits early in your career will set you up for success. And one of the biggest habits to focus on, whether you're a rookie or a veteran, is doing your lead generation.

If there's one single thing you do every day, lead generate!

When you show up and do your lead gen day after day, momentum will build. There's no doubt about it. You will find people to add to your database, get people to sign agreements with you, and set your pipeline in motion. Get your lead generation done early in the day and move forward. Velocity will build and your business will take off. Soon, you'll have repeat and referral clients coming to you for your services. All because you showed up and did the work over and over. Use the skills you've learned and be confident in the fact you're building a business you can be proud of, little by little.

2 Maintain Your Database

We included multiple chapters on the database. That's because after all your hard work lead generating, you want to be able to reap your rewards. You do this by cultivating your database, tending to it, and automating systems within it. With no way to organize your contacts or stay in consistent and purposeful communication with them, you're banking on luck to propel your business. We want it to be a sure thing.

We interviewed over 200 successful agents for this book. In their suggestions for how new agents can build a great business, keeping up with your database was one of the non-negotiables. Now that you know how to build and manage your database, we urge you to stay on top of it. Your database will fuel your career as an agent. It will do a lot of the hard work for you if you treat it the right way. This means consistently adding to it and connecting with the people inside of it so that you stay top-of-mind. For all of the habits and consistency you implement during your journey, make sure keeping up with your database stays at the top of the list.

3 Lock In and Be Accountable

Your Big Why will help you understand your purpose for being in the real estate business. It will help you create a vision for how you want to operate and meet your goals. The final piece to the puzzle is all about locking into that vision and holding yourself accountable to achieving what you set out to do.

This brings to mind a poem by Charles Osgood about responsibility. To paraphrase, there are four people named Everybody, Somebody, Anybody, and Nobody. An important job needed to be done. Everybody was asked to do it. Everybody was sure Somebody would do it. Anybody could have done it, but Nobody did it. Somebody got mad because it was Everybody's job. Everybody thought Anybody could do it, but Nobody realized that Everybody couldn't do it. The job didn't get done, and Everybody blamed Somebody when Nobody did what Anybody could have.

We think this poem is also about accountability. No one knew their job or held themselves or each other accountable for taking action and getting it done. When you know what you need to do, it's important that you follow through. As an agent, you set your own hours and goals, and the only person who is responsible for doing these things and ensuring your success is you. It's hard to always stay accountable to yourself. That's why we recommend investing in a coach or finding an account-ability partner to help you stay on track and not lose focus. It may not seem like a big deal if you don't meet all your outreach goals one week. But if that happens the next week, too, you can quickly build momentum in the wrong direction.

Researchers sometimes refer to this as the "what the heck" effect. You're doing great with your diet. You decide to cheat and have an iced caramel coffee on the way to the office. You avoid looking at the calories on the menu, as if that will prevent them from being ingested. A little while later, an agent brings donuts to the training room. What the heck, you think. You already cheated a little... You see (and maybe have expe-rienced) how this can snowball. A great accountability partner will help you avoid serial slips and get you back on the program.

You have a vision and a purpose for being an agent. Now you need to make sure you follow through in your actions. Make accountability a part of your business plan. Like we said before, consistent action, no matter how small, will get you to your goals. Having someone who checks in with you and asks you why you did or didn't hit your marks for the week will help you put things in perspective and make necessary changes.

Lock in to being the best you can be. You owe it to yourself to see just how far you can go.

Launch

We wouldn't tell you that you could achieve your wildest dreams in real estate if we didn't know it was the truth.

In May of 1954, Roger Bannister was the first person to break the four-minute mile. In his book *3:59.4: The Quest to Break the 4 Minute Mile*, John Bryant says that runners had been trying to beat this mark since 1886. He writes, "For years milers had been striving against the clock, but the elusive four minutes had always beaten them. It had become as much a psychological barrier as a physical one." When Bannister finally ran his 3:59.4 mile, it created a domino effect. After decades of no one breaking four minutes, suddenly lots of runners were doing it. Forty-six days after Bannister broke the record, an Australian runner broke Bannister's record. A year later, three runners ran an under-four-minute-mile in a single race. Since then, thousands have gone on to do the same. This is a story we shared early in *The Millionaire Real Estate Agent* for the same reason. You need to believe not only that it's possible, but also that it's possible *for you*.

There are also thousands of successful real estate agents who have come before you. They have mastered the basics of what we laid out in this book and blazed trails for you to follow. They put proven models and systems into action first and added their own creativity to it once they nailed them. You don't have to go in blind or think anything is impossible. You know it's possible. With the right tools and dedication, you can break any barrier you thought was in your way.

We encourage you to use this book as a guide. Reference the chapters you need when you need them. Feel confident moving into this next stage of life, ready to take on buyers and listings and knock it out of the park. You can finally come into your true calling and launch a limitless real estate career that lasts.

You have **all the tools at your disposal** to *launch a* **limitless real estate business.**

Appendix

Example A: A Full Economic Model Calculation

	$75,000	Net Income (50%)
+	$30,000	Operating Expenses (20%)
+	$45,000	Cost of Sale (30%)

	$150,000	**Total GCI**
÷	$10,000	Average Commission/Fee Amount

15 **Total Units Sold**

	15	Total Units Sold
÷	75%	Closing Conversion Rate

	20	**Total Agreements Needed**
÷	75%	Appointment Conversion Rate

	27	*Total Appointments Needed*

Example B: A Full Economic Model Calculation

	$180,000	Net Income (60%)
+	$45,000	Operating Expenses (15%)
+	$75,000	Cost of Sale (25%)

	$300,000	**Total GCI**
÷	$8,000	Average Commission/Fee Amount

(37.5) **Total Units Sold**

(38)	Total Units Sold
÷ 60%	Closing Conversion Rate

63	**Total Agreements Needed**
÷ 80%	Appointment Conversion Rate

79	***Total Appointments Needed***

Example C: A Full Economic Model Calculation

    $100,000   Net Income (30%)
+ $66,667   Operating Expenses (20%)
+ $166,666   Cost of Sale (50%)

    $333,333   **Total GCI**
÷ $14,000   Average Commission/Fee Amount

---

    24   **Total Units Sold**

    24   Total Units Sold
÷   70%   Closing Conversion Rate

---

   34   **Total Agreements Needed**
÷   70%   Appointment Conversion Rate

---

   49   *Total Appointments Needed*

Details matter.

Index

P

of sellers, 183
of warm leads, 63
Turner, Danielle, 116
12 Direct touch plan, 100

U

unbundling commissions, 191
UVP (unique value proposition), 20–22, 73, 124, 185

V

value
  for clients, 31
  and conversion rates, 31
  creation, 6
  home prices, 48–49, 178
  market knowledge as, 38, 47–48
  offered to cold leads, 112–113
  of open houses, 232
  of teams, 29–30
  UVP, 20–22, 73, 124, 185
  of your services, 19, 164–165
Van Wickler, Will, 4
virtual assistants, 96–97
Voyles, Ty, 217

W

walkthroughs, 188, 189–190, 280–281
Wants and Needs Analysis, 163, 164, 196–197, 199, 208
warm leads, 63, 175
weekly schedule, 136–137
Weinberg, Mark, 11
"why," your, 16–17, 18, 141, 286–287
Williams, Troy, 51
willingness, buyer/seller, 150

win-win transactions, 14, 199, 264, 266, 283
work/life balance, 143
writing offers, 254–258

Y

yearly review/scheduling, 140–141
Young, Alex, 121

Z

Zarghami, David and Toni, 12

Acknowledgments

This book was born in a brainstorming session in 2015. We were updating our research for *The Millionaire Real Estate Agent* and creating new interview questionnaires. I wondered aloud, "What did they do in their first year that other agents do not?" The original working title was *MREA: Year One*. Over the past decade, we kept asking top agents that question and many more. Eventually, the concept evolved and *Rookie Real Estate Agent* came into focus.

Many talented individuals enriched this manuscript with their expertise and craft along the way. We would like to thank them for their contributions and assistance.

Kathryn Cardin shined as the lead writer on our writing and research team. Working from our outlines, she conducted countless interviews, drafted multiple versions of the manuscript, and circled back at the end to help edit. AprilJo Murphy directed the project from outline to print-ready files. She served as lead editor, pitched in drafting several chapters, collaborated on large revisions, and talked me off the proverbial ledge on more than one occasion. Without the creative duo of Kathryn and April, this book would not exist. Morgan O'Hanlon helped us iron out the lead generation and database chapters. Allison Tsakiris provided keen insight in the writing room. Our research has been aided by interviews performed by Vickie Lukachik, Garrett Lenderman, Madelaine Davis, and Jake Dromgroole. Special thanks to economists and researchers Ruben Gonzalez and Isaiah Tabach. Emily Frierson, Nicole Hazari, LuAnn Glowacz, and Wes Crowley helped us polish up the prose and double-check some facts. Ashley Calhoun may have joined our team toward the end of the writing process, but her contributions from review to operations were notable. Carly Fox supported us throughout with strategic insights, good humor, and no shortage of calendar Tetris.

Our gratitude goes to Cindy Curtis-Rivera for an eye-catching book design. Kudos also to Owen Gibbs and Adam Dudd for their artistic review and design assistance.

A good book is a collection of ideas that have been stress-tested. We are lucky to have been able to collect feedback from some of the smartest real estate minds in the world, including my long-time writing partner Gary Keller. Other stellar reviewers include: Jason Abrams, Robert Bell, Donnie Brookman, Kelly Cote, Mona Covey, Julia Lashay Israel, Molly de Mattos, Marc King, Jenn Lewis, Meredith Maples, Jeanne Osness, Sajag Patel, Natalie Risen, Sarah Stotz, and Avery Thomas. Special thanks to Ian Raney and Jay Yurkiw for their legal reviews.

We are indebted to the real estate professionals who shared their hard-won knowledge with us, helping pave the path for the agents of tomorrow. Thank you for taking the time away from your lead generation to answer our questions. We are grateful to Keller Williams Greater Springfield, McKenzie Anderson, Sheila Bailey, Jenn Baniak-Hollands, Tim Bilbo, Mimi Bond, Julianne Carney, Mary Cheatham King, Nancy Chu, Kate Conroy, Rebecca Cullen, Jen Davis, Joe Delia, Allan Domb, Margaux Drake, Sarita Dua, Liz Edgecomb, Sandy Edry, Danny Emmett, Stacy Esser, Joseph Eterno, Alisha Fickert, Maureen Forys, Letrissa Frieson, Tiffany Fykes, Lauren Garner, Jeff Glover, Denny Grimes, Heather Groom, Deb Jolly, Chris Hall, Ashley Harwood, Kelly Henderson, Misti Herring, Erin Holloway, Rob Howard, David Huffaker, Caroline Huo, Ryan Hvizda, Keith James, Josh Keck, Jennifer Kelly, Omar Kiki, Heather Kobs, Dave Knight, Han Li, Susan Lombardo, Jenni MacLean, Christine Marchesiello, Flor de Maria McNally, Amy Smith-Magur, Aubrey Martin, Josue Martin, Ashley Miller,

Pam O'Bryant, Sarah Reynolds Oji, Jason Otts, Papasan Properties, Andy Peters, Lesley Peters, Vanessa Pollock, Joy Powell, Sandra Rathe, Laurie Reader, Kathrin Rein, Jeff Reitzel, Monica Reynolds, Gene Rivers, Jim Roche, Kristin Scanlon, Richard Schulman, Steve Schlueter, Kendra Scott, Tesha Shannon, Tyler Shields, Alison Simon, Klarissa Skinner, Jimmy Smith, Laurel Starks, Andy Sweat, Brett Tanner, Kent Temple, Carol Thompson, Danielle Turner, Heather Upton, David Voorhees, Ty Voyles, Will Van Wickler, Troy Williams, Alex Young, David Zarghami, and Toni Zarghami.

Thank you to our publishing partners at Bard Press, Todd Sattersten and Anne Ugarte, for helping us get this book out into the world.

I love that you're still hanging in here for these acknowledgments! I saved the most important for last. The final sprint to complete this book was intense. The person who was there for me every step of the way was Wendy. She made sure I ate, exercised, and slept. She buoyed my spirits when I began to doubt. And she patiently answered endless questions, read the early revisions of the book, and suggested numerous improvements. How lucky am I to be married to an agent who has sold over 2,300 homes! Thanks, my love!

Finally, I'll give an honorable mention to Taco, who you met in the introduction. Most of these pages were written on my living room couch, with Taco nuzzled by my side.

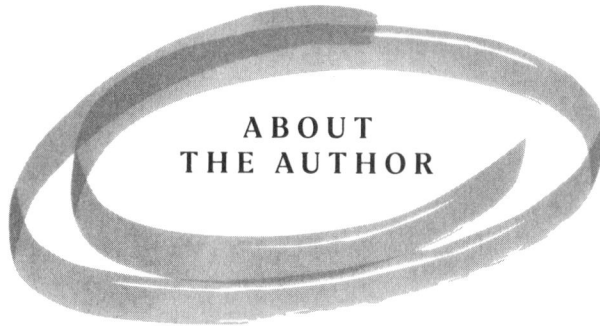

ABOUT THE AUTHOR

Jay Papasan

Jay Papasan [Pap-uh-zan] is a bestselling author who serves as the Vice President of Strategic Content for Keller Williams Realty International, the world's largest real estate company. He is also CEO of *The ONE Thing* training company ProduKtive, and co-owner, alongside his wife Wendy Papasan, of Papasan Properties Group with Keller Williams Realty in Austin, Texas.

Papasan Properties Group is one of the most successful residential and commercial real estate teams and consistently ranks in the top 1 percent in the United States. Under the co-leadership of Jay and Wendy, Papasan Properties has sold more than 2,300 homes—a remarkable feat in one of the most competitive markets in the country.

In 2003, Jay co-authored *The Millionaire Real Estate Agent*, a multi-million-copy bestseller, alongside Gary Keller and Dave Jenks.

His most recent work with Gary Keller, *The ONE Thing*, has sold over 3 million copies worldwide. He is recognized internationally as a leader, innovator, and expert on real estate, wealth building, and productivity. Every Friday, Jay shares concise, actionable insights for growing your business, optimizing your time, and expanding your mindset in *The TwentyPercenter*.